DO YOU HAVE A SPECIAL TALENT...
A FABULOUS CRAFT...
A SUREFIRE IDEA FOR A MAIL-ORDER BUSINESS...
OR WORK IN A BUSINESS THAT YOU COULD RUN
(AND RUN IT BETTER)?
THE ENTERPRISING WOMAN CAN HELP YOU
SUCCEED AT A BUSINESS OF YOUR OWN.

❑

"With women starting new businesses at twice the rate of men,
THE ENTERPRISING WOMAN is a critical tool for them to 'hit the
deck running'—in the right direction."
> **—D.A. Benton, author of *How to Think Like a CEO***

❑

"Gives women the courage, inspiration, and practical advice
needed to run a successful business. An invaluable tool for women
entrepreneurs. Don't leave home without it!"
> **—Connie Glaser, coauthor of *Swim with the Dolphins:
> How Women Can Succeed in Corporate America on
> Their Own Terms***

❑

"This book is chock-full of practical knowledge for the woman
interested in starting her own business."
> **—Kate Cheney Chappell, cofounder and vice
> president of Tom's of Maine**

❑

more...

A portion of the proceeds from this book will be donated to the American Woman's Economic Development (AWED) Corporation and An Income of Her Own (AIOHO).

THE ENTERPRISING WOMAN

Mari Florence

WARNER BOOKS

A Time Warner Company

Author's Note: Each woman profiled in this book has given consent to the use of her story. The information contained in these profiles is based on personal interviews and materials provided by these enterprising women.

Copyright © 1997 by Mari Florence
Foreword copyright © 1997 by Mari Florence and Debbi Fields
All rights reserved.

Warner Books, Inc., 1271 Avenue of the Americas, New York, NY 10020

Visit our Web site at
http://warnerbooks.com

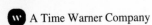 A Time Warner Company

Printed in the United States of America
First Printing: October 1997
10 9 8 7 6 5 4 3 2 1

Library of Congress Cataloging-in-Publication Data

Florence, Mari.
     The enterprising woman / Mari Florence.
          p.   cm.
     ISBN 0-446-67275-0
     1. New business enterprises—Management.   2. Women-owned business
enterprises. 3. Entrepreneurship.   I. Title.
     HD62.5.F577   1997
     658.02'2'082—dc21   97-8649
                                                                                  CIP

Cover photography by: Nancy Palubniak
Cover design by: Elaine Groh
Interior design by: Charles Sutherland

To my father, who inspired me with courage, independence, and compassion.

Acknowledgements

While many dedicated friends and colleagues contributed to this book, none were as committed or as supportive as Amy Inouye. Without Amy's insightful and tireless contributions, this book simply would not have been completed. Single-handedly, Amy brought the featured women into the project, juggled interview schedules, visited the library too many times to count, and offered many insightful suggestions for making this book the best it could be—all while running her own small business. She has been a knowledgeable adviser, an enterprising co-conspirator, and a valued friend.

Other contributors who helped bring this project to fruition include Melinda Gordon, who brought her high standard of friendship and commitment to this book. Thanks again to Lea Russo and Leigh Fortson—without whose help I would still be mired in marketing plans, franchise figures, and Web sites. Heartfelt thanks also to Stephanie Hubbard, who jumped in several weeks before the presidential elections to pin down interviews with harried political consultants who didn't necessarily want to be pinned down. A special thanks to Skye Van Raalte-Herzog, who contributed more information and advice than I can ever thank her for.

Thank you to researcher Dan Rafael, who helped with the library and Internet research, and to Stevie Stewart, who aided in the compilation and fact checking of the resources.

Thanks also go to my agent, Carol Mann, who believed in my work, and contributed solid advice when the writing process became overwhelming. I also give thanks to my editor, Colleen Kapklein, who not only shared my vision, but offered encouragement and helpful suggestions throughout the creation of this book. Thanks also to assistant editor Diana Baroni, who listened patiently to the ramblings of a frenzied writer on format, cover design, and all the particulars you never think about before writing a book.

On a separate—and very special—note, I'd especially like to

thank Kathleen A. Allen, entrepreneur and associate professor of entrepreneurship at the University of Southern California. Kathy's input reeled me back when I became too immersed in the minutiae and steered this book in the right direction of good information and the newest trends.

Several other consultants to this project also contributed to making a better handbook. Former AWED president Rosalind Paaswell was generous with both her time and advice and helped me to see all sides of the very complex picture of women's financial soundness. Joline Godfrey, founder of An Income of Her Own, introduced me to the concept of teen entrepreneurship and the importance of educating and nuturing young women to become strong and self-sufficient adults. And Vivian Shimoyama, from National Association of Women Business Owners, connected me with all the people and organizations I needed to liaise with in order to have the latest, best information. I'd also like to pay special tribute to Jonathan Kirsch, whose legal guidance and sage advice helped me to fully realize this book, and to Danny Feingold, who motivated me and helped me keep my priorities in check.

Last, but with as much enthusiasm at the rest, I'd like to thank each and every enterprising woman who gave her time, energy, story, and advice to make this book a useful text for many other women.

Table of Contents

FOREWORD

by Debbi Fields

When I picked up *The Enterprising Woman,* I discovered that this book is truly in a class by itself. It is a business book that addresses the unique challenges and opportunities that women entrepreneurs face. It's the kind of book *I* could have used twenty years ago, when I was embarking on my own business venture.

There has never been a more exciting time for women entrepreneurs than right now. In the two decades since I built my own business on little more than a recipe and a dream, the climate for entrepreneurs has changed dramatically. Back then it was uncommon for a woman to walk into a bank and seek financing for her business venture without collateral. While many entrepreneurs today still face obstacles in obtaining financing, more and more are successfully starting and running the businesses of their dreams.

I was barely into my twenties when I decided I wanted to sell my cookies to the public. I had no formal business background, no track record, and no start-up money, but I had conviction, drive, and a dream. I knew that I made the best cookie out there—and I believed that the worst failure would be not to try. Everyone—my family, my friends, the bankers, even my husband—thought that the idea of starting a store to sell chocolate chip cookies was ridiculous. But I'm not very good when someone tells me "No" or "You can't." Just hearing those words gives me enough encouragement to believe in possibilities. Eventually I found a financial institution that was willing to give me a chance, and Mrs. Fields Cookies was born.

From there, it was hardly a smooth ride to my company's success. I encountered many hurdles, and for the most part, the three most significant challenges women face in the marketplace today are much the same as the ones I had to tackle.

Although financing represents the biggest challenge for *anyone* in business, financial institutions know the importance of investing in small businesses. Banks are more receptive to loan requests from start-up entrepreneurs today, yet many people are intimidated by the process and don't know what to do to acquire the financial backing they need—and deserve—to get their fledgling ventures up and running.

The second major challenge for women in business is learning to effectively manage the responsibilities of business and family. Here too, societal attitudes continue to evolve to make women's jobs easier. Yet to be truly successful, I believe that women must set clear priorities from the outset. I've always felt that if I take care of my family, I'm in a good place to take care of my business.

One of the top hurdles facing businesswomen is self-doubt. You must cultivate the ability to shut out all of the voices of doubt, including your own, and channel the power of a positive attitude. In my work with women entrepreneurs, I'm overwhelmed by the immense talent that is out there—the combination of ideas and passion they bring to their business ventures. Where I see many women come up short, however, is in maintaining a strong belief in their goals and abilities in the face of the myriad frustrations and logistical challenges that are connected to any new (or continuing) business venture.

I have a favorite saying: "Whether you think you can or you can't, you're right." Creativity and ingenuity are critical to the success of any business. In the course of realizing a dream, everyone is going to hit the wall, so to speak. There are going to be barriers—barriers to entry, barriers to taking your business to its next level. When you hit the wall, the goal is to come up with the one thing that works, and often it's not the first (or second or third) thing you'll consider. I hit a wall on the first day my cookie store was open to the public: No one bought a single cookie! I looked around the shop and realized how much money and effort I'd put into my venture. In desperation, I got the idea to walk outside and offer free samples to people passing by. Slowly, the skeptics became believers, and that moment represents a crucial turning point for my business: It was the moment I realized I would do anything within my power to climb over any wall that stood between me and the success of my business. It's just one example of the many risks taken by entrepreneurs and the innovative strategies they employ in order to keep their businesses afloat.

When Mrs. Fields Cookies began, there were far fewer women entrepreneurs, and certainly very few visible ones. I didn't have the benefit of learning from the experiences—both positive and negative—of other women business owners. Women today are far more fortunate, and I think that many may still underestimate how much networking can enhance their lives, both personally and professionally. Women can be so busy caring for business and family that they may lose sight of the importance of taking care of their hearts, minds, and souls by connecting with others in similar positions. It's unbelievable what can be accomplished by sharing both the successes and the failings we've all experienced in building a career out of what we love.

As every entrepreneur knows, there is no magic recipe for success, but there are several key ingredients in any business. It may seem obvious, but your product or service must be the very best. If you don't take it to the top, you can be sure someone else will. Personal conviction in what your business provides is what sells. It not only gives you the power to believe in yourself; it makes other people believe in you.

When Mrs. Fields was getting off the ground, I had to talk to myself every morning. I'd get out of bed and say "I'm not giving up! 'No' is an unacceptable answer. It doesn't matter how many people are not taking me seriously—I know there's someone out there who wants to say 'Yes,' especially when it comes to financing." Sending positive messages to yourself is incredibly important, because it's too easy to put yourself down, become discouraged, and give up.

The Enterprising Woman offers dozens of positive messages in the form of profiles of women entrepreneurs across the country. It's a wonderful book for every entrepreneurial woman—from sole proprietors to Fortune 500 CEOs—because it thoughtfully presents the nuts and bolts of what it takes to run a business side by side with the personal stories of those who have done it well. The happiest entrepreneurs know that business and life can't be compartmentalized; that to find fulfillment in both takes a full-time commitment to your dream. *The Enterprising Woman* recognizes this, and in so doing it presents us with an honest, complete, and balanced business guidebook. I know you'll enjoy reading it, and I hope it will be a valuable resource for your business.

All the best to you.

INTRODUCTION

To love what you do and feel that it matters—how could anything be more fun?

—*Katharine Graham*

When browsing through the male-oriented offerings in the business section of the bookstore, I often wonder, Who buys these books? And about as frequently, I study the shelves, looking for books I wish someone had written—something I want or need to learn. It was this compulsion and this void that inspired the compilation and writing of this book.

As the owner of a small business myself, I searched for what is in this book. It's certainly easy to find books on business planning, accounting, and how to create a Web site. The shelves are full of them. Yet I—and other women in similar situations—were looking for a book that would address the obstacles women uniquely face, offer guidance, and provide mentors to get where we need to go.

Why are we women turning toward self-employment? A 1996 study by Catalyst, a nonprofit group that reports regularly on women in the workplace, indicated that while we are making gains, still only one out of every fifty of the nation's top paid executives—the Fortune 500—is a woman.

Conversely, a recent article in *The Wall Street Journal* cited a recent trend of women leaving lucrative corporate jobs to start their own businesses. The reasons many enterprising women cite for starting their own business include to expand upon an avocation, to gain financial independence, and to meet a challenge. Additionally, women entrepreneurs point to the benefits of psychological well-being and the opportunity to enrich their lives.

Today, women-owned companies currently account for one-third of all businesses in the United States and are projected to total half of all businesses by the year 2000. Women-owned enterprises also presently employ over eleven million workers—more than all the Fortune 500 companies combined worldwide. Additionally, recent studies have indicated that it is safer to work for a woman-owned business since these companies fail at smaller percentages.

Some women want to take their corporate successes and mirror them out on their own. Others want simply to cover their expenses, save for a comfortable retirement, and live a life they love. And there's nothing wrong with saying, "I just want to make a good living for myself; I don't want to be Bill Gates or Oprah." Entrepreneurship allows you the opportunity to decide the what, when, where, why, and how of your life. Rosalind Paaswell, former president of American Woman's Economic Development (AWED) Corporation, a nonprofit agency that advocates for women's financial empowerment, suggests, "Don't accept limits from other people, but don't be afraid to set limits for yourself."

The Changing Face of American Entrepreneurship

Joline Godfrey, founder of the nonprofit group An Income of Her Own (AIOHO), has made a commitment to speaking up for the young women who, without education and opportunities, face a bleak future. Why make this statement if women-owned businesses are on the rise? Despite these encouraging statistics, of the 75 percent of all women who work outside the home, 40 percent work within the poverty level.

The facts are simple, says Godfrey: "If you don't own a piece of the system, you'll be owned by it." Through AIOHO, young women learn the language of business and learn to claim ownership of their ideas and their future. Once these girls learn that they have options, it affects their planning and their educational decisions. "I advocate ownership, not only of a business, but of stocks, real estate, ideas, patents, anything that will help you gain control," says Godfrey.

While women still dominate the retail and service industries, these areas no longer command start-up in the record numbers they did a decade ago. In short, women are diversifying: branching out into uncharted territory. As such, new opportunities in areas such as health care, finance, politics, and the arts are inspiring women to reconsider their goals and dreams.

Women who are entering nontraditional industries for women, such as manufacturing and technology, face great challenges. Not only are we handicapped by our girlhood conditioning toward avoiding these areas, but we also find resistance from men who are either threatened by or undereducated about women entering into their realm. Again, strides are being made, but there is work still left to be done.

What's in This Book?

This book aims to address the challenges we face in the marketplace, while also celebrating the many opportunities available for the tenacious entrepreneurial spirit. While obstacles you'll face are less oppressive than even a few years ago, they do still exist and they will impact your success. For example, a married woman thinking of taking her home-based business to the next level today may not have considered applying for credit in her own name a decade prior—a consideration that could affect her ability to get funding for her burgeoning company.

Yet history books are full of pioneering women who brought creative minds into formidable situations. This book is no different. Through real-life examples, the women featured in *The Enterprising Woman* showcase their successes and illustrate how they have hurdled the obstacles. The chapters in this book have been organized by industry and are listed alphabetically. Also, the basic tenets of running a business have been sprinkled throughout the book.

Having the courage to break out of the mold does not come without sacrifice. It is increasingly harder to balance work, family, and personal obligations in today's world without giving up a measurable amount of sanity. Combined with that, today's entrepreneurs have few visible role models.

Positive role models do exist: women who are forming corporations, opening restaurants, and developing software are showing other women that applying creativity and innovation to business is not only probable, it's an integral part of doing business in the 1990s.

The Enterprising Woman celebrates successful businesses and the women who run them, and helps you develop your own blueprint for success. By reading some of these entrepreneurs' stories, you may find one or more women whose journey you can identify with. Many of the women in this book have traditional business backgrounds and simply made a lateral move into self-employment. Others have little or no work experience at all and jumped, feet first, into entrepreneurship.

These women, the majority of whom started their businesses from scratch, introduce you to a wide network of women-owned organizations. The profiles in each chapters, "Woman on the Way" and "Tricks of the Trade," offer opportunities to "see inside" the workings of these women's businesses—and minds—and pick up some sound business advice from those who have preceded you. In these pages you'll see, again and again, how successful women reengineered their careers by turning their passions into viable businesses.

In each of the ten chapters, you can explore the trends of that particular industry while picking up important business concepts that will help you to start up and run your business.

Arts and Entertainment faces down the difficult question of how to be taken seriously as an artistic businessperson. It also showcases the basic needs you'll face in starting up your business, such as how much money you will need and where you will find that money.

The Environment introduces you to one of the most popular entrepreneurial avenues today and examines why environmental companies are around to stay. It also shows you, step by step, how to create a winning business plan.

Finance and Consulting takes you into a world that women are beginning to conquer. Also discussed are the tenets of bank financing.

Health Care discusses why women are being drawn to this field and the special opportunities that entrepreneurs are taking advantage of. It also discusses the importance of preparing for retirement and how to create benefits packages for yourself and your employees.

Labor and Manufacturing delves into the little-discussed world of nontraditional industries and their vast opportunities for women. This chapter also discusses basic manufacturing concerns, such as how to get your product made, and touches on the importance of ethics in business.

Media and Public Opinion explores the vast and powerful world of the media. In this chapter you will learn how to navigate through various fields of public persuasion, including the dynamic world of politics.

Nonprofit and Socially Responsible Business considers new models for doing business and looks at ways to organize and raise money.

Retail talks about the radical changes occurring in the retail arena. It also deals with the very important subject of hiring and retaining quality employees.

Science and Technology discusses the difficulties women face in these fields and offers tips for combating prejudice. Also covered are issues such as computerizing your office, setting up Web sites, and protecting your intellectual property.

Service investigates why the service industry tends to be dominated by women. This chapter also discusses the pros and cons of buying an existing business, such as a franchise, and how to prepare your business for sale.

For any woman considering entering the exciting world of entrepreneurialism, there are many questions to address—both on a personal and a professional level. This book will give you a great start, and a lot to think about, before you take the plunge. And if you are already in the midst of running a business, this book gives you the information you need to support or grow your business—and lets you know that as an enterprising woman, you are in very good company.

1

Arts and Entertainment

Ever since the first settlers landed on Plymouth Rock, women have played a vital role in shaping the American arts scene. From Little Deer to Louisa May Alcott, from Mary Cassatt to Anne Rice, women have expressed themselves through literature, sculpture, painting, pottery, music, performance, and craft work. And while self-expression may have been the driving force behind women's art, few were able to consider it a livelihood. Yet they forged ahead. World-renowned potter Beatrice Wood, who has taken her second century of life by storm, adds, "I think the great painters were never thinking of an exhibition; they painted because they couldn't not paint."

The women in this chapter represent a broad diversity within the arts. For some, their artistic passions were the springboard for yet another career path. Within this group are musicians, performance artists, choreographers, designers, and sculptors—but most of all, women who have learned to color outside the lines in order to create a viable extension of their passion. Many of these women have found celebrity and success, but, as in past societies and generations, their work is often underappreciated and relegated to "hobby" status. By no small expenditure of energy on the part of these tenacious individuals, those times are changing rapidly.

While history may not pay proper tribute to the women behind the scenes, in today's art world women have attained distinction as painters, composers, choreographers, and directors. By bringing a feminine mind-set to a field friendly to new thinking, the visionaries of this new art age find few boundaries and are creating a network that will carry them to greater successes. Many twentieth-century women have been able to move confidently back and forth between high and popular art—singing opera and the blues, playing Greek tragedy and Hollywood comedy, dancing classical ballet and modern jazz, writing novels and poetry and philosophical treatises. Their own creative flexibility, combined with the burgeoning opportunities opened to them by the popular media and the interest many communities and large cities show in supporting art galleries, museums, dance performances, and concert series, have made the past few decades exciting ones for women in the arts.

Today's women are building their own business ventures in pursuit of greater flexibility and freedom. Armed with the desire for autonomy and control, coupled with creativity, increasing numbers of women are looking to the arts to fulfill emotional as well as financial needs. Not only are these women creating art, but they advocate for themselves and other women as gallery directors, producers, and publishers. As in other fields, these women fight daily battles to defy stereotypes and to be taken seriously in a male-dominated workplace.

Nowhere is this more evident than in the United States, which has given an enthusiastic welcome to all art forms and to women artists from all over the world. Artists who work in this country and are struggling to establish themselves as rightful members of a serious profession at this particular time in history have enjoyed a level of audience interest and support never before afforded them in modern history.

As the women profiled in this chapter exemplify, talent, mixed with a passion for work and the tenacity to see it through, makes for a heady combination. And with the right woman behind it, a successful business is one that is not only personally fulfilling, but profitable as well.

Marketing Your Passion:
Taking Creativity to the Bank

Glamorous success stories abound about women whose passion drove them to Broadway careers and *The New York Times* best-seller list. These fictional-sounding accounts are certainly appealing to the creative personality but are not always realistic. In today's world, where women are often the second, if not the first, breadwinner in the household, passion seems to be a luxury few can afford.

Passion alone may not be enough to start a business or keep it going. But for the entrepreneurial art lover who can bank on working up to ninety hours a week, it certainly helps. Passion is also a quality in work that appears to appeal to women more than men, according to author Marsha Sinetar (*Do What You Love, the Money Will Follow*), which is why a large percentage of women elect to work in careers that they love or are passionate about.

Webster's Dictionary defines passion as an "intense, driving, or overmastering feeling . . . the state or capacity of being acted on by external agents or forces." Others define it as overwhelming emotions that sweep the breath away, of surrender rather than control, reactivity rather than passivity. Ironically, all these definitions are in direct opposition to what society tells us is proper business practice—logic and control.

Although passion can be the driving element in a business, it's not enough to keep it running efficiently. According to Jane Applegate, *Working Woman*'s "Small Business Solutions" columnist, "If a creative vision is only anchored in blind passion, that is not a strong enough foundation; the anchor is sand. It's like relationships based on lust alone; they probably won't last." This is why many businesses, based on great ideas and limitless potential, ultimately fail.

Creating a Purpose for Your Passion

If mixing passion with business is problematic, there is a solution: create a purpose for your work. Purpose implies forethought and reason and, unlike passion, is a framework that extends beyond one person. For example, if you love sculpture and have studied extensively, your passion for the art form meets your own personal needs. If you add purpose to your passion—by forming an educational center for children or becoming a curator of sculpture—your purpose then is to share your knowledge and passion and infect others with the love that makes your heart beat. If you can clearly define a purpose, the framework of a business can then fall into place.

A purpose is simply a goal or set of goals that takes you from point A, your love for what you do, to point B, the creation of a business that utilizes your passion. For example, if you are a classically trained pianist, goals you may explore might be opening a musical academy for talented youngsters. Or you may be interested in setting up a Web site that offers to locate hard-to-find musical scores.

Judith Anne Timmons took her talent for making elegant wreaths and teamed up with a local florist to create a floral and gift store that specializes in hand-crafted items made from nature. Timmons had been making wreaths for her local garden club for many years, using the natural foliage around her Missoula, Montana–area home—and giving them away to family and friends. When some of the more upscale gardening catalogs began offering furnishings for the home, Timmons noticed the overwhelming trend toward year-round wreaths and the high prices they were charging. "In some cases, a wreath simply made of bound lavender was costing almost $50.

"I approached a local florist who had been looking for ways to expand her business into gifts and home decor and offered her an idea: helping her add a floral gift section to her store. I would display my wreaths and we would hunt down other nature-oriented products and display them as well." With this clever solution, Timmons found an outlet for her product and, by acting as the buyer for this section of the shop, received a commission on all gift sales—all without investing any start-up costs outside of the materials for her wreaths.

As she continued to expand the shop's gift offerings by soliciting new and unique craftspeople, Timmons's contacts, in both the floral and the gift arenas, grew as well. Quickly she was placing her wreaths outside the Missoula area and then outside Montana. The network of people Timmons has met by being a retailer has widened the market for her handiwork, which is now sold in over fifty stores in the western states.

Whatever your purpose, it is imperative to determine who will buy your product or hire your service. And for those artists who are shy of jumping in with both feet forward, a part-time approach such as Timmons's can be a good way to test the waters.

Is Your Purpose Viable?

What if the elements are in place—you have the passion and the purpose? Does this mean your business will be a success? Not necessarily. For many artists exploring the business waters, there are few places to get your feet wet and truly see how your work will be received. In spite of all your passion, purpose, and best intentions, there are still many variables to running a successful business over which you may not have ultimate control.

For graphic designer Amy Inouye, her labor of love has become a cottage industry, but not necessarily a financial boon. Her products, based on a twenty-two-foot-tall fiberglass figure she affectionately named "Chicken Boy," began as a labor of love. The quirky, 1950s-style mascot for a fried chicken restaurant was about to be destroyed when the building was set for demolition, and Inouye saved the statue of a boy with a chicken's head "as more of an attempt to save a piece of postwar Los Angeles history than as the motivation for a new business.

"These are the images that made L.A. famous, so when it seemed we would lose another one, I felt that I really needed to do what I could. So I saved the statue of Chicken Boy. He became a mascot of sorts," she muses, "a surrogate for the pressure I was feeling running my own typesetting and graphic design studio. . . . I started the business unknowingly by creating Chicken Boy lapel pins for my friends one Christmas and then giving away a Chicken Boy T-shirt occasionally at birthday parties or client events.

"Any time someone saw the shirt," she says, "they would ask where to buy one. On a lark, I began selling silk-screened T-shirts of him at arts and crafts festivals and would literally sell out by noon." After some success, Inouye attempted to catch the wave of momentum by opening up a small storefront off her design studio and branching out into a small mail-order company. "I planted Chicken Boy's head right smack in the middle of my studio, and sold my original artwork, T-shirts, mugs, anything to take advantage of his popularity. I was able very easily to start a mail-order catalog because, as a graphic designer, I could create it myself. Then I bartered with a printer friend to print the catalog. The money to cover the postage for the first mailing came from my savings account."

The Chicken Boy catalog now reaches twenty-five thousand potential customers once a year. The oversize chicken connected Inouye with the Los Angeles Conservancy, a local preservation society, and many people are now looking to her for guidance on 1950s-era preservation. "Ultimately, I only wanted to find Chicken Boy a home," she says, "and didn't realize that he'd become an industry and his spin-off potential for involving me in other areas was so great. There is definitely an audience and an appreciation for Chicken Boy as sculpture, pop art, and a postwar artifact. Actually, this whole venture has been an uncategorizable mixture of the commercial (my mail-order catalog), the artistic (seeking a permanent home for Chicken Boy in a public space), and the conceptual (Chicken Boy as a metaphor for people's ideas of themselves and as a symbol for the city, even)."

The Chicken Boy catalog, however popular, does not generate enough income to warrant a full-time commitment of Inouye's time.

Although the image has certainly opened her up to other options, she continues to run her graphic design studio as her main income generator. "Although I would like to run the Chicken Boy business full-time," says Inouye, "I understand that his appeal is mostly as a cult figure, and that he has limitations within the market. I've learned how to recognize a product's limitations as well as potential and try to keep a balanced eye on the validity of how much time I can devote to his success."

For many others like Inouye, moderate off-the-cuff success doesn't come easily, and many would-be entrepreneurs can relate to her experience of bumping up against a plateau. As in any business, the key to success in the arts is planning. Find out what your market will bear. What is your competition? How do you plan to support yourself during start-up? By asking yourself these and other basic questions, you can test the waters and see if your passion and purpose can team together to equal profits (see "Starting Up," page 21).

First Steps for Putting Your Passion to Work

Certainly you can't dream to paint a freeway mural and then just go out and do it. You need to plan. The following steps provide a framework for coupling your passion with a viable, creative career:

Write Down a Creative Strategy

What do you love, and how can you make a living doing it? If you're a collage artist trying to get gallery representation, try supplementing your income with craft or gift ideas such as greeting cards.

An enterprising art dealer can set up a gallery without big-money backers and great connections. Look into the vast public and private financial support provided through grants and low-interest loans to women entrepreneurs. Create a name for yourself and your space by promoting shows with a topical theme or politically active cause. The media loves these types of shows and promotes them regularly.

Amy Inouye opens her studio space to up-and-coming artists once a month. She provides the outlet, the artists provide the work, and together they work to promote the opening. "At the last show, a major gallery owner responded to our invitation and was very interested in representing the artist," she says.

Find Professional Support

Seek out women's associations or groups in your field. These women can provide valuable tips on upcoming shows, literary publications, open houses, and workshops. Many of these women have converted their passions into viable careers and provide not only moral support, but invaluable guidance for your business and a sounding board for your projects.

A host of women's organizations exist—from the Coalition of Women's Art Organizations to entrepreneurial support groups such as Women Inc.—and they provide a variety of services. Often, you will find, these types of associations offer support in many areas, such as education, networking, finance, databases, and resources. A good way to start getting active in an arts organization is to speak with other women colleagues and find out which women's organizations they are affiliated with and find helpful. *The Whole Arts Directory* lists supply houses, alternative spaces, cooperative galleries, and special exhibits for women in the arts. This publication also includes financial information and data about artists' colonies, retreats, and study centers.

Think of Your Passion as Your Life's Work, Not Only Your Hobby

Establish working hours for yourself. If you're a composer, you must sit behind the piano during your "office hours" and try to play, whether or not you feel inspired. By doing so, you condition yourself to be creative within the confines of your established workday. This doesn't mean, however, that you must work a typical nine-to-five workday. If your hours are ten to four, make the most of them. If you thrive on a night owl's schedule, work during those times.

Michele Lanci-Altomare, creator of imagik Design Studio, a full-service graphic design/photography company that services the book and entertainment industries, believes there's no such thing as standard work hours or missing deadlines. "I take my work very seriously," says Lanci-Altomare, "and the commitment to bring projects in on time and in excellent condition are traits my clients continue to hire me for. I learned early on that there's a certain level of professionalism you need to bring to your work, and it starts with your word. Clients catch on quickly if you promise one thing and deliver another," she says. Another important asset for working artists, Lanci-Altomare considers, is your portfolio: presentation examples of your work that you are proud to have your name attached to. "In addition to expressing our creativity and uniqueness, it's essential for artists to cultivate professionalism—especially since the market is so competitive." Lanci-Altomare's philosophy has brought her many rewards—personal freedom, independence to pursue other artistic endeavors, and a strong sense of accomplishment. In fact, last year imagik Design Studio expanded its services by 60 percent and added several new clients to the roster.

Set Short-Term Goals and Meet Them

The advantages of making lists have been long lauded by organizational experts, and for good reason: accomplishing tasks boosts self-esteem. For the creative mind, achievements may be more difficult to track. By setting short-term goals, such as "I will contact four gallery owners by the end of the month," you can make progress toward your goal without immersing yourself in the less exciting aspects of doing business. By creating and achieving simple goals, you put yourself, step by step, closer to achieving personal and financial success.

Putting Your Passion to Work

1. Write down a creative strategy.
2. Find professional support.
3. Think of your passion as your life's work, not only your hobby.
4. Set short-term goals and meet them.

Letting Go of Perceived Notions on Money and Watching Your Passion Prosper

The subject of money has a powerful emotional charge and brings up different emotions in different women. Yet it's usually talked about like the weather—in general economic terms. Artists often say they feel funny charging for something that comes naturally or attaching a price tag to the work they would do anyway.

Many entrepreneurial women don't want to talk about money—even though it's their livelihood. They feel squeamish about asking for money due to them and about establishing a fair price for work or services. But they're not alone—many people are uneasy when they must receive, ask for, and speak of money.

As a songwriter and lead singer for the band Blue by Nature, Karen Lawrence finds that the negotiation of money is the most difficult part of doing business. "Although I know my worth, sometimes it's hard for me to blend the creative and business sides of myself. I can sell myself, and my music, but how do you stick to a price with a club booker who's thinking only of his overhead?

"You always have to give something away at the beginning, to show your value—so they'll take a chance on you. You don't have a name. You don't have a reputation." But she finds it hard to give away her experience and the energy she brings to a situation for a small amount. "If I do some background vocals for a band, I know what my bottom price has got to be. That's it. But I know plenty of singers who will do it for a third of that amount. But they don't bring my history and focus to the gig."

Today Lawrence's success allows her to defer the talk of money to her manager. "I found that it helped to bring along a friend or band member who was good at the biz side to play the 'tough guy.' And I mean 'guy.' It's amazing how many men don't want to negotiate with women over money, or think it's 'cute' that you're doing your own deals." While part of her rebels over not being taken seriously as a negotiator, a larger part welcomes input from a respected friend or colleague who can lock in the price she believes she's worth.

Another issue that can arise is the perceived dichotomy between the "creative" and the "business" sides of the entrepreneur. In some circumstances a woman may feel completely at ease negotiating her own deals. In others, it's a distraction. "Performers are treated like objects—like a talking dog or a cute little Shirley Temple," says Lawrence. "I don't think it works if Shirley Temple's cute one moment and then sucking a cigar the next, saying, 'It's $75,000 or we walk.'"

The concept of having money usually rides in tandem with opportunities for independence, leisure, privacy, and freedom from responsibilities and time constraints. A lack of money translates into the negative backside of this. As a result, the average woman ends up both desiring and fearing money—a vicious cycle that can sabotage a business and undermine self-esteem.

The self-esteem and money issue is further confused by the rather shaky image of what having that green stuff means. Although everyone wants more money, the idea of having wealth is tainted. On one side of the coin, money is thought to be highly desirable; on the other side, it is considered bad and almost dirty.

The basis for understanding and being comfortable with money is essential for the entrepreneur. Studies of women in business have shown that one of the factors by which they judge themselves and others is money—how much is made, how it is made, and how it is spent. Unconsciously, this constitutes part of our market value. To many of us, then, speaking of income is really speaking of our value in society.

For this reason, women in artistic fields have to battle with the internal demons that put a price tag on their work and continue to harass them about what their art is worth in relation to how much money they're making. Letting go of the preconceived notions of money and value can allow you the emotional and intellectual freedom to explore possibilities for expressing your art and turning your passion into a profitable venture.

The Element of Luck

Elmer Letterman once said, "Luck is what happens when preparation meets opportunity." Indeed, some entrepreneurs seem to springboard from relative obscurity one moment into legendary success the next. For many struggling on their own paths, these people illustrate what can materialize if luck facilitates being seen by just the right person or by being at the right place at the right time.

Luck is not just having the perfect opportunity arise, it is seizing the moment and turning the situation into something you can benefit from. In this regard, women experience luck on many levels. It is the availability to open up to it that sets the successful entrepreneur apart from the rest.

Photographer Beth Herzhaft's career took an unexpected turn when she photographed a friend's wedding as a gift. Herzhaft, whose photographs are shot in a black-and-white documentary style, had already created a fulfilling career doing album covers and work for magazines. Soon after, the bride began showing others the album from her wedding.

Before Herzhaft realized that she had fallen into a niche, the word of mouth on her photography was giving her more work than she could handle alone. "Within months, I was actually turning down jobs," she said. Recognizing a good thing, Herzhaft set aside her negative preconceptions about being "a cheesy wedding photographer in a bad tuxedo" and realized that weddings could be an element of her art, in addition to photography of celebrities and musicians.

When the opportunity originally arose for Herzhaft to photograph a wedding, she could have felt that it was beneath her and turned down the job. But because she came to view the opportunity as more than merely a day's work, she was able to transform "a medium that is usually visually banal into an artistic, meaningful narrative." In Beth Herzhaft's case, the marriage of luck and vision became a vehicle for greater career possibilities.

Woman on the Way

✳

Ruth Price

President and Artistic Director: The Jazz Bakery, Los Angeles, California

Business Philosophy: Tailor the environment to enhance the artist *first*

Greatest Achievement: Growing a successful business from the ground up

Jazz chanteuse Ruth Price may not appear to be the stereotypical entrepreneur. She wasn't looking for a way to improve her career, she was living her life in a full world. With an impressive vocal career that placed her alongside Carmen McRae, Dizzy Gillespie, and Miles Davis, Price could have written her own ticket, a truth few singers could boast. In fact, her gutsy, straight-ahead vocal approach found her an abundance of bookings, even during the 1970s and 1980s, when the jazz beat began to flounder. With this legacy under her belt, Price would have seemed an unlikely candidate to open up her own place, the state-of-the-art jazz theater known as the Jazz Bakery.

Price modestly attempts to make the success of her venture sound like luck, a circumstance of being at the right place at the right time. Yet it was her passion for aural stimulation, coupled with the innovative concept—to take jazz out of the smoky dens of night-clubs and bars—that made her say yes to the impressive warehouse space that was formerly home to Los Angeles' historic Helms Bakery. This courage, along with the knack for booking exceptional talent, has made Price a two-time legend within the musical community and quite a successful entrepreneur.

Fellow artists have a heady respect for what Price set out to do. Jazz bandleader Cecelia Coleman cites the Jazz Bakery as her ideal venue—to both perform at and attend. "With the Bakery, Ruth has reelevated jazz to an art form. It's not background music or a dimly lit dive full of guys trying to impress their dates," she says. "The Bakery is for real jazz *lovers,* people who appreciate the artistry of the music and its performance. And the space is definitely the most impressive I've ever worked in."

Price laughs this aside. "Really, it's less about the space than the music. I love this music, and it's enveloped my life. I just wanted to share that love with others, even kids. The one rule is 'no age restriction, but if you interrupt the artist or cry too loudly, you have to leave (that goes for adults too).' " Price has even tailored Saturday and Sunday afternoon jazz workshops just for youth with a musical yen. And in addition to its being a very successful club, the Jazz Bakery is a nonprofit organization that benefits local artists and youth.

This humanitarian love for helping others sometimes gets in the way of Price's business priorities. "There are two ways to run a club if you're a singer. One is to have what every singer dreams about—a little place where you can sing a few songs every night. The other way is to do what I'm doing—to book major talent and discover you don't know where to put yourself. You keep getting the opportunity to book these wonderful people, so you put yourself off. Sometimes I'll go for months and forget to book myself. Or I'll book myself and then move myself out of the date because there is somebody else I can get. Somebody coming through town who's great."

Although Price is constantly struggling to keep her stellar space full—in a town where patrons are fickle and driving crosstown after a two-hour commute just doesn't cut it—she's found success by forging her own territory. "The key is to do what you love, and then put 200 percent of yourself into it," says Price. "You may get frustrated, and tired, but if you're doing what you enjoy, the scales will tip in your favor."

✳ ✳ ✳

Taking Your Right Brain to Work: Balancing Business with Ingenuity

Whether your art is performance or graphic, keep in mind that balance is the key element of success. By taking your work seriously and invoking some simple, proven concepts, you can turn your artistic talent into a thriving business. These tenets, of course, hold true for all businesses.

Not every woman has the talent—or desire—to grow her art into a multimillion-dollar business. But for those who do, perseverance is the key to success. The ability to maintain consistently good work, even in the face of adversity, is what separates the women from the girls. An up-and-coming entrepreneur needs to sustain her efforts, while never letting go of her dreams.

Even with all the start-up elements safely in place, it may take a long time to get going. Dedication is a close relative of perseverance, and the two are never far apart. While an employee working at a large company is able to enjoy a guilt-free long weekend at the beach, the dedicated entrepreneur may work all weekend to satisfy a deadline. The willingness to put in the extra three hours a day or a few nights a week will ultimately help you succeed where others would have failed. An informal poll revealed that the women profiled in this book work between fifty and eighty hours a week.

"You have to make your own niche," says Judith Jamison, artistic director of the Alvin Ailey American Dance Theater, who stepped in for Ailey after his death. No stranger to perseverance and dedication, Jamison herself had worked with the Ailey troupe since 1965, when Ailey singled her out for stardom. Their relationship together enabled her to give remarkable performances in *Cry,* Ailey's homage to black women, and in *Revelations,* a brilliant series of dances set to spirituals, both of which are considered landmarks of twentieth-century dance.

Jamison says, "If the door isn't open, you have to make your own door. You can have doors slammed in your face only so many times and then you get tired of having doors slammed in your face and it's up to you—as a vital, unique human being—to find another way of doing what you have to do."

Tricks of the Trade
Katy Meyer of Distinct Designs, on roads to success:

1. *The saying "Do what you love, the money will follow" is true* if you add a bit of common sense to the mix.
2. *Remember that half the work is in selling yourself.* Regardless of your product or service, people like to work with people they like. Get along.
3. *Don't be discouraged.* Not everyone will be enthusiastic about what you're doing.
4. *Learn to accept rejection.* The good comes right along with the bad.
5. *Be polite and courteous.* Send thank-you notes when people do things for you. Respect is never out of style.
6. *Stay focused.* No one else can help you keep your dreams in sight.
7. *Find a mentor and use her.* "My mom is mine."

✻　✻　✻

Teen entrepreneur Katy Meyer, owner of Distinct Designs, which specializes in handmade silk scarves and paintings, has faced her obstacles head-on—with kindness and calm professionalism. While Meyer found her niche somewhat unwittingly by selling the work she was already creating, she also found that not everyone is receptive of her work. For an adult entrepreneur, who may already be used to rejection in the marketplace, this is difficult enough. But Meyer's much publicized career, which started at age fourteen, made the grim reality of occasional failure even harder to handle. "It's been fun to be the only 'kid' at some of the craft shows, and in a lot of ways it's helped my business," says Meyer. "Yet it's sometimes hard for people to see beyond the fact that I'm a teenager. So I keep moving forward and hope that my work becomes just as important to others as it is to me."

The Artist versus the Businesswoman: Combining the Best of Both Worlds

To be successful as an artist in business, you must liberate your more thoughtful, organized, and logical-minded abilities. In this competitive time there is little room for the finicky artist who doesn't return phone calls, misses appointments, or forgets to return contracts. Not unless she is independently wealthy, that is. Self-discipline is mandatory to successful entrepreneurship. And while your creative juices might constantly be flowing, you must also give time to the day-to-day realities of running your business.

Finding balance is not easy. It requires identifying weaknesses and giving more attention to those areas. It means knowing your strengths and using them to your advantage—and understanding that artists often perceive the world differently from their executive counterparts.

Generally, entrepreneurs should be driven, optimistic visionaries who are highly motivated, well-organized, independent thinkers, strong leaders, able to handle pressure, and blessed with both a good sense of timing and luck—not to mention a good sense of humor.

Not every successful entrepreneur meets all these criteria. In most cases it's hard to separate the natural personality from the learned characteristics. Women add a sensitivity, passion, and nurturing touch to their styles that allows them to combine creativity with compassion and approach business from a different perspective from that of men.

Smashing Stereotypes: Creating Your Business Persona

One of the greatest obstacles artists have to face is the image problem—not the problem of the image on canvas, but the creator's image. For Sue Scott, president and founder of Primal Lite, Inc., the $5 million novelty light company that has placed strings of chili pepper and Holstein cow lights into the consciousness of the American public, it was an uphill battle not only to realize her potential, but to be taken seriously as a businessperson.

With a fine-art and sculpture background that gave her a clear, concise vision of the type of product she wanted to produce, Scott set forth to make it happen. "First, I couldn't get funding," she says. "Perhaps if I'd had an MBA from Stanford, the banks would have had some faith in me." After maxing out her credit cards to the tune of $25,000, she was up and running. But there was still the nuts-and-bolts issue of making the lights.

"Women learn, from childhood, that they're operating at a disadvantage," she offers. "You can either be angry about it or learn to maneuver around it." Scott realized that in order to level the playing field in the male-dominated plastics and manufacturing world, she needed to learn as much as she could about the production process. Her research paid off.

"From the start, I spoke their language. I used the right terminology and asked the appropriate questions. If they didn't respect me as a woman, they sure learned to as a client. Once, I was working with a plastics guy who said, 'We can't make that color.' I told him, 'Of course you can, I'll show you,' and proceeded to mix it myself." It was that measure of tenacity and research that enabled Scott to keep her highly successful lights in production, with rapid growth annually.

Scott believes that the image problem does not belong to women just in the arts. "Not just women with an art background, but women from a variety of fields get cubbyholed into having 'hobbies' and not taken seriously. Most women are coming from a cottage industry. If they get caught into that hobby environment, it's very hard to break out of it."

So how does the savvy entrepreneur break those barriers? "You just keep on going. There is no magic formula. You just keep moving forward and hopefully become more successful. Finally people start to pay attention, when you have the successes—whether that be financial or simply an acquired respect from the industry. And always take yourself and your business seriously. Never think of it as anything less than a business," says Scott.

Saving Your Sanity: The Appeal of a Flexible Work Environment, Writers' Groups, and Support Networks

The real truth of being in business as an artist is that creating is often relegated to the back burner while inventory and ledger sheets take precedence. But setting aside time to be creative—whether an hour, evening, or week—will revive the weary entrepreneur and can breathe new life into the business.

The idea of a "sponsored" artist didn't go out of style with bustles and parasols. Many private foundations and wealthy individuals regularly donate money to artists' retreats worldwide, in ongoing support of a wide range of artistic disciplines. Although entrance requirements vary, one constant remains: the artist can escape to an idyllic locale and write, paint, sculpt, or imagine the days away in a worry-free, subsidized environment.

The advantages are obvious. Without the day-to-day concerns of making money and paying bills, the artist can be free to create. For you the artist working as entrepreneur, this may save your sanity. After the grind of ninety-hour workweeks and deadlines on top of deadlines, you may feel your passion begin to wane. Since maintaining sanity is one of the undermentioned factors in running a successful business, you may need a vacation. It doesn't excuse you for the remainder of the year, but for a glorious week or two no phones will ring and no demanding clients will show up. After you've done your own art for a period, you'll be better equipped to return to your successful business.

Flexible workdays aren't the only way to go. A writer can benefit greatly from joining—or forming—a writers' group. The group can contain as few as five and as many as fifteen writers to meet on a regular basis. By sharing their work at each meeting, members benefit from the others' feedback and expertise. It's also a good way to see how other writers are structuring stories, developing characters, and creating plots.

"My writers' group is kind of a reality check for me," offers Karin Elstad, an aspiring screenwriter with some recent successes under her belt. "Sitting behind my computer, I begin to lose perspective. My group brings me back on track and validates all the hard work I put into my writing."

You can bounce your ideas off other people in venues other than a writers' group. For many, stepping back to regroup can be accomplished by organizing a guilt-free day of dining and shopping, taking an afternoon trip to the desert for inspiration, or joining a structured support group for artists. Many women find it necessary—both intellectually and emotionally—to occasionally rejuvenate from the high pressure of running a business. "Every three months or so, my core of friends from college get together for a day at the spa," adds Elstad. "It's a time to catch up, regroup, and gather the emotional and spiritual support we each need to go back into our own worlds and keep moving forward."

While artists—both visual and dramatic—need to strike a balance between their work and their creative lives, they shouldn't forget one basic element: the passion that got them there in the first place. For many, love of the arts was the deciding factor in choosing a career.

Therefore it's important to respect your personal boundaries and not burn out.

Starting Up: How to Start an Innovative Business Driven by Your Art or Craft

The time-tested truism that there is no "right" way to start a business is never more real than in a field as unpredictable as the arts. No particular sequence of steps will ensure success—what successful start-ups do, and when and how they do it, is not all predictable. While no particular time period is "normal" to get a company off the ground, most entrepreneurs who get a business going do so in about a year of concentrated effort. Although the steps along the way vary, here is what to expect during that critical first year.

The wide range of activities that usually take place within the first three months include investing personal funds in the business, writing a business plan, seeking and receiving financial support, organizing a start-up team, and getting a separate phone directory listing. Those items occurring midway through the process of establishing a business include initiating savings to invest in the business; looking for, leasing, or buying equipment and facilities; applying for licenses, patents, or permits; developing a creative model or prototype; and creating a legal entity. Activities occurring relatively late in the sequence, at least nine months after the "start" date, include developing a marketing program, installing a separate phone line, hiring employees, acquiring a federal employer identification number, and filing state unemployment insurance taxes, federal Social Security tax payments, and federal income tax returns.

This timeline is an overall picture, with lots of other factors coming into play. But among these factors, another maxim exists: Successful launches—regardless of the field—reflect an intense concentration of work, usually somewhere between fifty and eighty hours a week.

Plan and Be Motivated

The importance of serious thought to the nature, size, and scope of the business cannot be underestimated. While it's optimal to have a clear sense of direction before beginning, it's important to remain flexible enough to know that it's healthy for a vision to change, as a lot of arts-related businesses do when new market information is obtained and the cultural milieu is defined. Many times, a start-up is a part-time effort until it seems to be successful, often with more than one person at the helm. So given these factors, it can be hard to stick exactly to a specified game plan. However, it's equally important to recognize that flexibility, along with careful planning, is key to living your dream.

Careful planning goes hand in hand with motivation. But being motivated does not mean having doubts. Rather, it means confronting and conquering your fears before turning to the fulfillment of your dreams. The same motivation that keeps you passionate about your art form is the same motivation that must exist before, during, and after you start your business.

Vivian L. Shimoyama is the first to admit that she does not consider herself "a woman in the arts" as much as she does a businessperson. "I see my art as a metaphor for change. I want to get a message across to women, and it just so happens that the vehicle of my message is my artwork." In her business, Breakthru Unlimited, she creates jewelry from glass and found objects.

By utilizing the key business techniques that have made women successful—smartly manufacturing a unique product to the right market base, maintaining professionalism in all her relationships, and forever pursuing a low-key management style—Shimoyama has turned her beautiful designs into a burgeoning, lucrative business that employs several part-time artists. Last year Breakthru Unlimited doubled its revenues and now manufactures and sells close to three thousand unique jewelry designs through boutiques and direct mail and to select clients who commission pieces.

Shimoyama insists that the key to her success is that she designs something that meets her "distribution network"—and she conducted substantial research to identify exactly who would carry her art pieces. She doesn't really cater to galleries, for example, because the majority of her work is produced on consignment. And she can't churn out the number of pieces a large-scale retail outlet would require.

"Early on in my business I met with an accessories consultant and asked her questions about distributing to retail. She handed me a list of jewelry reps and I began interviewing. My meetings with them uncovered that my pieces were perfect for smaller specialty and gift shops because they're all handmade. They forced me to realize that I wasn't made for retail—I couldn't commit to the mass manufacturing I would need to churn out a new line every season."

Tricks of the Trade

Vivian L. Shimoyama of Breakthru Unlimited, on getting galleries and specialty shops to take your work seriously:

1. *Be professional.* The image of the "creative personality" may be entertaining in the movies, but it doesn't fly with businesspeople. Also, never underestimate how far word of mouth goes. If you begin to build a solid reputation as an artist, that reputation will begin to precede you and you will get sales.

2. *Treat your work like a business.* Have business cards made up, indulge in some preprinted stationery, and subscribe to a phone service that allows you to leave a professional, personal message. In my case, I invested time in a database that holds all my key contacts. If I am creating a limited-edition piece, I can easily do a select mailing off my database to make the announcement.

3. *Have a professional photographer make slides of your work.* If you've shown in a gallery or been featured in a store, create an extended résumé or portfolio.

4. *Visit the stores or outlets you would like to place in* to see if they are suitable for your work. Make sure to get the name and business card of the owner, buyer, or curator. Ask what their policy is for reviewing artwork.

5. *Make a list of several outlets you would like to solicit.* Put together a package consisting of slides, samples of the work (if small enough and you can part with them), a résumé, cover letter, and business card. Send or drop off to the appropriate people. (If sending out of the area, make sure to send a self-addressed, stamped package for return.)

6. *Allow two weeks for your package to be reviewed.* Call your contact to see if there's any interest. If he or she hasn't had a chance to look at your work, find out when you should check again. Once a week is usually appropriate.

7. *Expect rejection.* Certainly not everyone you're interested in will be interested in you. But the perfect match will happen.

8. *If accepted, work out the details in advance* before agreeing to anything. If a contract is involved, have an attorney review it to verify that the terms are in your best interest, the commission is fair, or the consignment clause protects you. (This is very important. Many artists are so excited to make a sale that they'll sign anything. Don't fall into this trap.)

9. *If rejected, ask to have your package returned.* If the venue doesn't have space now but is interested in reviewing work for the long term, you may decide to let them hold on to your package.

10. *Begin again.* Go to the next tier on your list and resend packages. It's a constant cycle, so approaching your soliciting as though it is part of the natural marketing and showcasing process will help the sometimes tedious days go a bit smoother.

✳ ✳ ✳

Take a Risk

It might seem like a juxtaposition in philosophy to say that all careful planning contains an element of risk. But every successful artist will tell you that she was willing to take a risk when starting her new venture. While the degree and type of risk vary among individuals and companies, not one woman innovator will tell you she fell into successful business without putting something on the line: finances, personal failure, the loss of a "secure" job to start up the business, even her marriage.

Many people will find that their support system begins to erode once the idea of starting a business is discussed. But an open mind to face these obstacles and the tenacity to jump in with both feet are two survival mechanisms that will take you far. Rosalind Paaswell, former president of the American Woman's Economic Development Corporation, concurs: "One of the things that hold many women back from being truly successful is that they are overly conservative and risk-averse. Whether a woman is seeking a bank loan and has to prove to the bank that she's willing to incur more risk than the institution, or simply making a day-to-day decision in her business, her tenacity and willingness to take risks is fundamental to her business's survival—and indeed, prosperity."

Define Your Purpose

A vital first step is to sit down and write out your purpose and first-year goals. Be clear and concise, and be sure to answer several all-important questions: How much capital will I need? How much do I presently have? Do I want to be a full-time or a part-time business? Do I need any employees at the present time?

For instance, if you need a lot of capital, chances are you won't be a part-time business. Similarly, if you are part-time, will you have enough time between your job, family, and friends to run the company successfully? Are you willing to make the sacrifices necessary to be successful?

Artist Sue Scott, founder of the decorative light company Primal Lite, knew she was tapping into an unmet need when she began developing her off-the-wall strings of lights such as Roast 'n' Toast (cups of coffee and slices of toast), Loads o' Laundry (boxer shorts, socks, and a woman's slip), and her infamous red Chili Peppers. Her mission statement? "To reach beyond Christmastime as being the only time people hang lights, and to awaken America's curiosity in flirting with fun home decorating ideas." Once Scott's company received increased exposure in the industry and media, it wasn't long before retailers, decorators, and customers learned to appreciate her whimsical stringed lights year-round.

Your plans, goals, and answers to basic start-up questions will evolve into your business plan, which is the beginning vision for your company. For a first-year, original business plan, the amount of detail required will vary with the nature and size of business, whether or not you need capital from a bank or lender, and how precise you personally think it needs to be. The original business plan is just as important to your business success as choosing the right business entity, the right lawyer, and the right accountant. Be careful, concise, and as detailed as possible. Consult the "Environment" chapter on how to write a business plan, and contact the National Association of Women Artists, 41 Union Square West, New York, N.Y. 10003, (212) 675-1616, for additional information on how to get started in business as a woman of the arts.

Estimate Your Start-up Costs

The steeper your start-up costs, the harder it may be to raise enough money to begin your business. Obviously the simpler the undertaking, the easier it is to get off the ground. Whatever you project your start-up costs to be, expect them to be substantially more. Lanie Kagan, Modernist-inspired lamp designer and manufacturer of New York's Luz Lampcraft, admits that she underestimated her start-up costs in every category. It cost more per square foot than she figured to build shop space, for instance. She also underestimated the specifics, such as air-conditioning systems, phone systems, and lighting. Although her total cost overruns were not excessive, she was fortunate to have a personal savings cushion and a friendly banker to make up the difference between what she projected and what she actually had to pay. Yet many women in Kagan's situation are often forced to sell out or go bankrupt—right at the start.

To avoid underestimating, you should add 20–25 percent to all your projected costs. Generally, experienced entrepreneurs say that is a satisfactory safety net, and it's much better to be left with extra cash than to be caught short.

An additional cost factor that many new entrepreneurs underestimate are expenses such as insurance and office equipment, and these hidden costs are more carefully disguised. Many women artisans discuss the wear and tear on themselves as they go the extra mile to launch a business and how they underestimate the difficulty of getting clients. Be sensitive to your own personal shortcomings and the business areas that seem a bit gray to you, and discuss with a financial adviser how these come into play in your overall start-up profile.

How Much Money Do You Really Need to Start Your Business?

The U.S. Small Business Administration provides some basic guidelines for estimating how many months' worth of funds you should have in reserve to sustain your business. Keep in mind that despite positive receipts and your best intentions, your business may not show a profit for some time.

1. **Estimate what you need to spend on certain onetime start-up costs:**

   - Equipment, machinery, tools, and so on
   - Installation of fixtures and equipment
   - Decorating, repair work, or remodeling
   - Starting inventory for your goods

- Utility deposits

- Telephone, fax, and modem installation

- Computer hookup

- Legal, accounting, or other professional fees

- Licenses and permits

- Insurance

- Advertising and promotions to announce opening day

- Reserve dollars for unexpected emergencies

2. **Next, estimate your normal monthly expenses. A good rule of thumb is that, at the very least, you should have enough cash in reserve to pay for six months' expenses (a year's is optimal), after which time your incoming cash should pay for them:**

- Salaries

- Rent

- Advertising and promotions

- Messenger and overnight delivery service expenses

- Supplies

- Telephone and fax bills

- Miscellaneous utilities

- Insurance

- Taxes, including Social Security

- Interest

- Maintenance and repair

- Legal and professional fees

- Miscellaneous

3. **Add your onetime costs and your monthly estimates for a total sum of how much you will need to get started. Many business experts suggest inflating that figure by 25 percent to allow for unforeseen circumstances.**

Secure Creative Start-up Capital

Most people start a business either with a portion (or all!) of their savings, credit card advances, and/or a bank loan. If you need a loan, you can try a lending institution, but if you don't have a steady line of income or employment history (as many artists report is a prejudice when dealing with savings and loan banks), you may consider the Small Business Administration. Banks have short- to long-term loans, such as installment loans, balloon notes, lines of credit, and floor planning. The SBA offers three loans: guaranteed loans, the direct loan program, and the 504 loan program. You may also consider going through a financing agency, but the interest rates are very high, and often sufficient business experience and a prior good credit rating are necessary to secure a loan.

The current regulatory system does make it difficult for banks to provide small loans to businesses, in part because bankers must provide the same documentation on a $50,000 loan as they do on a $2 million loan. Many bankers, according to Barbara Davis Blum, president, chair, and CEO of the woman-owned Adams National Bank in Washington State, decide that it is just not worth granting loans to small businesses with smaller financing needs. Experts agree it's difficult to determine if women are denied loans because of gender discrimination or other factors such as insufficient business experience or good credit. Due to privacy and antidiscrimination considerations, most banks do not collect and retain, much less disclose, information on successful and unsuccessful business loan applications for men and women. However, data collected by the U.S. Census Bureau reveals that women business owners start their businesses with less money, borrow much less of the start-up funds, and are less likely to rely on commercial bank loans than businesses owned by men.

Would-be businesswomen who can't qualify for regular loans are increasingly finding funding from a new, fast-growing group of "microlenders"—comprising government agencies, nonprofit organizations, and a few adventurous commercial banks. The SBA classifies anything under $25,000 as a microloan, but $1,600 is often cited as the U.S. mean. Organizations who are joining the bandwagon include the Coalition for Women's Economic Development (CWED), which provides small loans, business training, and technical assistance to previously "unbankable" female entrepreneurs in Los Angeles; the Women's Self-Employment Project (WSEP) in Chicago, which boasts a 93 percent repayment rate and is dedicated to helping women build assets; and Women's World Banking, a New York–based international lender that has made over one hundred thousand loans to entrepreneurial women and racked up a competitive 95 percent repayment rate.

Rosalind Paaswell maintains a slightly different viewpoint on the loan process as a vehicle for getting started. She states: "Banks are not a bad place to start, although most people just starting out—particularly women—are terrified of them. Go apply for a loan. If you're turned down—and you're likely to be—ask why. The loan officer will tell you where you're lacking and you can begin working toward building the resources you need to eventually get bank financing. Also, ask if there are public lending programs and the like. These people know what's out there. If you don't find a bank you're comfortable with, keep looking. Not that you'll get a loan, but you may find a loan officer who will help you work toward qualification."

In addition to standard and innovative loan arrangements, there are other "traditional" ways of raising money for your business, such as soliciting partners, attracting venture capitalists, or issuing stock certificates. However, many women, especially those in the arts, have found truly creative ways to finance their businesses. Sue Scott started Primal Lite with $25,000 in credit card advances, a tactic most business consultants would shun. Diane Jones, a choreographer, remortgaged her home to offer it as a collateral for her bank loan to open her Seattle-based arts and performance space. Bernice Reagon, vocal director of Sweet Honey in the Rock, took up several combined tactics to organize her a cappella music troupe and create money for touring: she merged her $5,000 in savings with a home-equity loan and leased some of her office equipment instead of buying it.

Many entrepreneurs suggest fresh methods for raising capital. They maintain that all it takes is a little creativity and the ability to stretch your mind beyond the information provided in basic business seminars. The first of these guerrilla financing techniques involves selling your assets for cash. For example, if you sell your luxury car for $15,000 and lease an economy car for $189 a month with no money down, you've just obtained some cheap capital. Antiques, pool tables, fine jewelry, boats, and time-share rentals all make great "For Sale" items.

To follow Sue Scott's lead, what about setting up your business with a cash advance from your credit card or several cards combined? According to recent statistics, 70 percent of women business owners are financing their businesses this way. Rosalind Paaswell believes, "In general it's not a great idea, but if it's your only way, then you need to do it. If it puts you in business, it's a good thing. If you have little or no credit, it'll help you build credit—as long as you don't incur any longtime, overwhelming debt."

Your credit card might be the perfect answer. The credit line's ceiling floats according to your financial position and payment history. And as with all revolving credit lines, you can borrow from your credit lines as the funds are needed by your business, repaying all or a part of the principal and then tapping into the line again as more capital is required. Interest is due on the outstanding balance. If, for example, you borrow $25,000 to buy starting inventory, and then repay part of the loan, such as $12,000, three months later when your business begins to generate revenues, although your credit line remains the same ($25,000), you can reborrow on the $12,000 you paid back.

Another overlooked source of capital is borrowing against the cash value of your life insurance. According to Debbie Chase at the American Council of Life Insurance in Washington, D.C., there is more than $11 trillion worth of life insurance in force in the United States. Chase says you can borrow only against whole life policies, not against term, and that most whole policies have some cash value after three to five years. "It's very easy," she says. "Simply write the agent or insurance company and tell them you want a policy loan." Chase says most companies will lend up to 90 percent of your policy's cash value and that your policy stays intact as long as you keep paying the premiums. And loans against the cash value of your insurance policy are reasonable. Unlike the 18 to 21 percent norms from credit cards, rates from insurance companies are tied to other key market rates.

San Diego–based Business Opportunities Online Inc. is one of the many on-line services that offers entrepreneurs the chance to search a database of available capital to find investors or leave a posting on the database of capital needed in the hopes an investor will call. If you're a subscriber to America Online, CompuServe, or Prodigy on-line services, you can investigate their small business or entrepreneur forums. There are forums devoted to just about every topic, including arts and business, not to mention access to more than thirty-five million subscribers.

Set Up Shop

Organizational chores are often time-consuming and tedious. They are nonetheless essential. A tip for making your organizational life easier: Do these tasks at the very beginning of your business. Setting up a bookkeeping system before you make any expenditure or take in any revenue will make your life easier at tax time, when you might tend to scramble for receipts or try to reconstruct your business transactions. Being faithful to your system will support your position in the event of disputes with partners, suppliers, employees, or the Internal Revenue Service. As you grow, it will provide you with essential information about your business performance that's not available from any other source.

If you despise record keeping, decide as soon as you launch your business how you will compensate for this aversion. If you are well disciplined, you may eventually overcome your distaste for the routine tasks entailed in running a business and learn to regard them as the price of self-employment. Some entrepreneurs who don't enjoy bookkeeping are lucky enough to have a partner who likes the sense of control and accomplishment of bookkeeping entries; others employ an outside firm as quickly as possible to help keep records straight.

Getting organized also involves setting up the legal status of your business: as a sole proprietor, partnership, corporation, or nonprofit. In some states, like Wyoming, there are also "limited liability" companies, which are hybrids of limited partnerships and corporations. In addition, the S-Corp is a form of the corporation. There are advantages and disadvantages to each business entity, and in some states, certain business entities have rules or unique requirements that must be met. To find out about your state, write the secretary of state or the Department of Revenue in your state for information. A legal adviser can also help you decide which option is best for you. The IRS defines a small business as a firm with annual gross receipts of $5 million or less for the past three years. With this is mind, the entity should be chosen carefully, in order to take advantage of tax, regulatory, legal, time, and financial considerations.

Even if you have one employee other than yourself, you must become aware of employment regulations, both state and federal. Most regulations regarding hiring practices don't apply until you have a minimum of fifteen employees. Some regulations apply to firms with twenty-five employees and some to those with fifty and more. When you reach one hundred employees, you may be forced to report to many governmental agencies. These regulations are complex and variable, so it's important to seek specialized help when your work-force begins to approach fifteen employees. Meanwhile you must be aware of minimum age requirements and various state "payday laws," which stipulate rigid rules for the regularity of employee pay periods. The best source for these issues is your local state employment office, the agency that administers unemployment insurance.

Avoid the Stress of Moving Too Quickly

Your move from artisan to entrepreneur need not be abrupt and trau-matic. It's not necessary for your business to rush into the start-up process, because the "unknowns" of starting and operating your own business can soon become overwhelming. Ideally you should ease your-self into your business slowly, viewing it as a natural progression of the craft you already participate in. The better planned your venture and the better prepared you are to run it, the more likely your chances of success.

To avoid the sudden stress of starting up, remember that you have options: you can learn about a business by working for someone else before you forge ahead on your own; you can start a venture on the side while continuing to draw a salary from the job you hold; you can go into business with partners who have more experience with the business fundamentals than you do. Starting up is not a stress-free endeavor, but the impact can be cushioned with good preparation.

Woman on the Way

✳

Nicole Hollander
Syndicated Columnist: *Sylvia*
Business Philosophy: Don't let your work be influenced by skeptics
Greatest Accomplishment: Watching *Sylvia* become a household word through syndication in over seventy daily and weekly newspapers

As the wit behind the sardonic *Sylvia* cartoon strip, Nicole Hollander couldn't appear more unassuming. A petite, soft-spoken woman who seems the complete antithesis of her trademark character, Hollander nonetheless infuses her dark-haired, cynically musing alter ego with enough political commentary and social satire to launch a thousand strips.

Trademark scenarios such as "The woman who does everything more beautifully than you," and "The woman who is easily irritated," have created a zealous following that consists of soccer moms, jaded Gen-Xers, and working women, among others—all who can relate to her very smart, very funny, and very woman-centered sensibility.

For the character Sylvia, there are no taboos. With gusto she regularly takes on topics as diverse and controversial as menopause, the new age movement, large corporations, men, and the obsessive/compulsiveness that draws women to someone like Martha Stewart.

But Hollander's creation hasn't always had a mass appeal. For several years Hollander tried, unsuccessfully, to get her strip syndicated. "People (read: the newspapermen who made the decisions) just didn't get *Sylvia*," says Hollander, who nonetheless continued to shop her strip around to papers. With the cartoon market saturated with newcomers and the daily newspapers entrenched in classic, and often dated, strips, there was little room for a cynical, middle-aged character who found humor in societal ironies.

Determined that *Sylvia* would find a home, Hollander paired up with an agent who, although semi-retired, believed in *Sylvia* and agreed to shop her. Slowly, she got through—largely due to carefully directed fan mail and clever promotions—and Hollander began gaining the exposure she deserved.

Today, with her strip in top papers and thirteen collections of her cartoons published, Hollander has a line of calendars, greeting cards, postcards, Post-it notes, refrigerator magnets, T-shirts, and myriad other merchandising offshoots of the now infamous *Sylvia*. Pursuing her passion has also enabled Hollander to write a play, *Sylvia's Real Good Advice,* that has been produced on the Chicago stage. What does the future hold? "For now, I'm into *Sylvia*," says Hollander, "because she's the perfect foil for the changing times." And as the times change, there's no doubt that *Sylvia,* cat in tow, will be there to offer her observations.

✳ ✳ ✳

2

Environment

With slogans like "Think Green," "Earth First," and "Reduce; Reuse; Recycle" numbering among the top catch phrases of this decade, there's never been a better climate for establishing an "ecobusiness," or a business providing a product or service that is in some way beneficial to the environment. The "me" decade of the eighties, embodied by a booming economy that rewarded conspicuous consumption and triggered reckless spending of both financial and earth resources, segued into the "we" decade of the nineties. On the cusp of a new century, many people are replacing yesterday's decadence with renewed passion and concern for tomorrow's social and environmental legacy, part of a shifting societal standard in which an increasing number of consumers evaluate a business's "responsibility" and mission alongside the product or service the business offers. Concern for the earth and its natural resources is at an all-time high, and consumer awareness of environmental issues has fueled the demand for products and services that generate less waste and eradicate or significantly diminish the use of hazardous materials. Companies like the Body Shop, which packages its bath and beauty products in streamlined, recyclable plastic bottles emblazoned with the words "Against Animal Testing," have made names for themselves on the basis of their strong involvement in social and environmental issues, establishing in-store recycling programs, using natural product ingredients, and even donating a portion of profits to environmental causes such as the preservation of the rain forest.

But the environmental industry isn't driven just by consumer concern or even simple economics. Tougher U.S. Environmental Protection Agency (EPA) regulations (namely, the revised Clean Air and Clean Water Acts), coupled with increasing public awareness of environmental hazards, have pushed even old-guard corporations into implementing reforms such as redesigning product packaging and creating in-house recycling programs. Not surprisingly, this climate has led to the proliferation of businesses whose offerings directly address environmental concerns. Each year the United States spends between $180 and $200 billion on environmental products and services, with a majority spent on removal and cleanup. In fact, businesses that supply hazardous waste removal and cleanup are growing at a rate of over 10 percent annually.

In 1992 Diane Weiser, her cousin, a tenant from her neighborhood, and several silent partners invested $150,000 in an environmentally friendly dry cleaners as an alternative to using perchloroethylene, or "perc," which the EPA terms a hazardous substance. Because response to their endeavor was so overwhelmingly positive, they were able to sell the dry cleaner's in just over a year for more than 100 percent profit.

While environmental safety is not a gender-specific issue, many women find themselves particularly suited to running ecobusinesses because of their preexisting concerns for their family's general health and well-being and the safety of their home, office, and school environments. In addition, women are often most conscious of energy and environmental issues within the home, such as wasteful product packaging and excessive water or electricity bills. The "ecopreneur," in choosing to start a company that addresses her existing needs and concerns, creates a more viable business by creating an extension of her value system and personal identity. This group of modern entrepreneurs recognizes that personal values can inform and strengthen rather than inhibit the growth of a successful business and that the demand is increasing rapidly for businesses with a social and environmental conscious.

One example is Tom's of Maine, the natural ingredient–based personal care product company cofounded by Tom and Kate Cheney Chappell that, in 1974, was the first to market a toothpaste made from all natural ingredients. Part of the Chappells' impetus for creating the toothpaste was concern for themselves and their family about what went into one of the common household products they purchased. The Chappells wanted a saccharin-free toothpaste for their children, and when they discovered that no such product was available, they created it, tapping into an as yet unmined vast market of people just like themselves who wanted safe, natural products. Tom's of Maine's continued success is owed to the fact that the Chappells realized "doing good"—by creating healthy products and implementing programs that contribute to the environment and general society—could coincide perfectly with the other more traditional goals of a successful business.

The term "ecopreneur" embodies the philosophy of a growing number of environmentally conscious entrepreneurs whose ideas are driven by a sense of community and global responsibility as much as they are driven by a desire for profit. The newest trend in "ecobusiness" effectively links social responsibility and profitability, not only in a business's long-range mission, but in its daily operations. Truly forward-thinking ecobusinesses are acknowledging their responsibility to the environment from the inside out, examining internal operations, product and package design, marketing approach, and other business concerns from an environmental perspective. These companies cater to the sensibilities of increasingly informed and demanding consumers while addressing long-standing issues that continue to impact the earth's finite resources. Successful ecopreneurs are lending their abilities to a variety of areas in this expanding field, including the redesign of products and services to eliminate hazardous or toxic waste; the implementation of recycling and refuse removal programs; and the creation of environmental construction programs to remove hazardous materials like lead and asbestos from existing structures.

Woman on the Way

✳

Kate Cheney Chappell
Cofounder and Vice President: Tom's of Maine
Business Philosophy: Building our business on a long-standing commitment to the needs of families
Greatest Achievement: Developing a saccharin-free toothpaste for children that they actually like!

Together with her husband, Tom, Kate Cheney Chappell founded Tom's of Maine over twenty-five years ago with the simple goal of introducing a natural, healthy toothpaste that would eschew artificial sweeteners. Today, Tom's of Maine is a staple in many medicine cabinets and the Chappells' product now captures significant market share in over thirty thousand stores around the country. It is also the first natural toothpaste to receive the American Dental Association's seal of acceptance.

Kate Cheney Chappell believes that innovations in America's work arena have stemmed largely from small businesses. "As entrepreneurs, it's our burden—and our responsibility—to look at the world through different eyes." These eyes, she believes, are what allow entrepreneurs to break new ground in business. "It's not a lack of fear, really, but a lifting of imaginary constraints" that lets upstart entrepreneurs realize their vision.

"Our personal values match our business accomplishments, and we're challenged to continually reflect on that." The Chappells promote their product persona as socially aware and don't try to scrape by behind the scenes. Walking the talk, employees at Tom's of Maine are offered flextime benefits, parenting leave ("for all parents"), and four-day work-weeks for production members and are encouraged to *donate* 5 percent of their paid work time to volunteer in the community.

Additionally, the Chappells try to create a work environment that is empowering and conducive to good communication. "What's the point of having dedicated employees if they're not leading a balanced life and aren't happy at home?"

While Kate's involvement is less hands-on than when they were just starting out, she continues to develop new products, heading up one of several small interdisciplinary creative teams called "Acorns." She also brings her watchful artist's eye to all advertising, packaging, and media for the company. A fine artist of some regard, Chappell considers her studio time "rejuvenation" from the trials of continuously growing a business.

To propel their socially conscious mission forward, Kate Cheney Chappell also puts in exceptional hours of workshops and speaking. "Our mission may drive our company, but we never forget that we're running a business. And a business can be an all-consuming endeavor, even when you love it the way we do."

✳ ✳ ✳

Ecothink: How to Develop Winning Ideas for Environmental Products and Services

Entrepreneurs with ideas for a green business will find that the current market is responsive to products and services that help preserve the environment. It is estimated that there are over fifty million green or environmentally concerned households in the United States today, and numerous polls indicate that, given a choice between a nongreen product and its green alternative, the majority of consumers would choose the latter. The current popularity of green alternatives such as nontoxic household cleaners, recycled paper products, "natural" cosmetics, and food products with organic ingredients demonstrates that there is a demand for environmentally safe options. In providing those options, successful ecobusinesses share a unifying goal—they accurately assess a current threat to the environment and create cost- and resource-conscious, realistic solutions. Examples run the gamut from a company that makes garden hoses from worn-out tires, to a small-business environmental consulting firm, to a reusable cloth diaper service, to a clothing company that uses a material made from recycled plastic soft-drink bottles. For Wendy Sardinsky, fourteen years of experience in product development allowed her to recognize an opportunity in the marketplace. In 1992, as the term "recycling" was beginning to infiltrate our conscious vocabulary, Sardinsky introduced Rewrap, a company that produces and markets fine-quality recycled gift wraps and papers. While other producers were entertaining small-scale boutiques and flower shops, Sardinsky aggressively went after the market, quickly introducing her products into supermarkets, chain drugstores, and other mass merchandisers.

The cost of manufacturing and developing environmental products and services can be beyond the means of entrepreneurs with limited financial resources. However, within the realm of ecobusiness there is a wide range of alternatives and start-up costs. New regulations continue to drive the demand for environmental business practices—for example, many of the engineers who had the prescience to start environmental consulting firms around the time of the implementation of the revised Clean Air and Clean Water Acts are enjoying considerable returns on their initial investment. While finding the money to fund your business can be difficult, an increasing number of venture capital groups are investing solely in environmental businesses, and other groups actively seek out environmental businesses. If your idea for an environmental business is backed by sound technology and research, and you can readily demonstrate that there is a market for it, investors may be drawn to your company and its potential for growth. Some entrepreneurs who lack the funds to "go it alone" are forming joint ventures and partnerships to better equip themselves to compete with established businesses. Others find that it's more feasible financially to contract out part or all of the manufacturing (or recycling) process rather than invest in costly equipment and facilities.

A great idea for a new ecobusiness may fuel your excitement for entrepreneurialism, but successful women entrepreneurs realize that it's vital to lay a solid foundation to support the launch of a new business. Whether you plan to start a consulting firm or want to sell a new, environmentally friendly invention of your own design, you'll need to conduct research that can help in determining whether your idea for a business is a viable one. In the course of your product or service research and development, you'll want to estimate production and initial investment costs, define your existing and potential customer base, carefully pinpoint and evaluate your direct and indirect competition, and determine how you will conduct your marketing campaign. If your business is product oriented, you'll need to address manufacturing and distribution variables during your initial research; if your business is service oriented, you'll need to determine where to locate it to best serve your customer base. The list of considerations extends into related areas as well, such as choosing employees and making a budget and finance projection. Experts generally agree that the road to entrepreneurial success is paved with a formal business plan. By writing a plan, you'll be better equipped to anticipate and address all the complex, interrelated factors involved in business start-up, and once it's completed, you'll have a living blueprint that diagrams how best to keep your young business running.

How to Jump-Start an Ecobusiness/Writing a Profitable Business Plan

According to the most current research, the task of writing a formal business plan is not one often practiced by small-business owners—especially women business owners. Typically, female business owners are less likely to formalize a business plan because they don't seek outside financing, which often mandates a plan. According to the Small Business Administration's latest statistics, because two-thirds of companies started by women are capitalized with less than $5,000, the cash risk is low, and the projected return for the first two years is not a large figure, the benefits from the hours it takes to research and compose a business plan may not drastically increase the bottom line.

While some women business owners recognize this fact, they also recognize that planning is essential to the success of all businesses. Without it, you run the risk of repeating the same mistakes other entrepreneurs in your field have made, mistakes that could have easily been avoided through the process of planning. And it is essential that small-business owners recognize one fundamental difference: business planning is a fluid process, one that is meant to be changed and revised; writing a formal business plan, while also meant to be revised semiannually, is less of a formal process and more of a hands-on tool. The end results will vary, but every business needs to go through the process. Indeed, the U.S. Small Business Administration suggests that a detailed business plan offers a path to follow; may help in securing loans; can provide useful information for suppliers, personnel, and others; and helps you develop your management capabilities. Women ecopreneurs, who in the course of forming their businesses will most likely need to evaluate a host of specific factors (for example, unique manufacturing issues or government regulations) that other small businesses may not need to consider in depth, will find the process of creating a business plan invaluable.

According to Rosalind Paaswell, former president of AWED, "Everyone should have a business plan. You especially have to have it if you're trying to obtain any formal source of capital. But most people are put off by the idea of creating a formal business plan. In fact, most protest, saying they're too busy running their business to write the plan. And for some, this may be a valid response. But every business should have at least an abbreviated business plan. All business owners have the answers to all the questions somewhere in their minds."

By definition, a written business plan is a written blueprint that details how an organization—or project—will be operated. Ranging from a few to hundreds of pages, a business plan can either be a cursory glance at an organization's intended operations or it can provide specific financial details on costs, salaries, actual and projected sales, and other factors, right down to projected profits. The most successful business plans, however, usually take you through the process of researching and drawing conclusions about some very *key* information, including your mission statement, a description of the industry in which you do business, an assessment of the market, a marketing plan, an operational system, a financial plan, a management plan, and a list of whom you will consult for legal and accounting advice.

The amount of detail in each plan varies among individual businesses, as well as within industries. While developing a plan, keep in mind the underlying reason for creating a business plan: your goal is to learn more about your business, your industry, and the competition. As you prepare your plan, remember that it will clarify in your mind the exact who, what, where, when, why, and how of the business you are proposing to operate. Second, the plan serves as a basis by which people outside your organization—top-level employees, investors, lenders, and vendors—can begin to determine the likelihood of success for your operation and make important decisions about their participation in the venture.

If all of this seems overwhelming to you, remember that you already have the makings of the business plan in your head: how you want your business to grow, how you see it being perceived in the marketplace; whether it is for personal fulfillment, the benefit of others, or a combination of both. A business plan can be implemented at any time. The sooner you develop your plan, the sooner you will see results. For example, when Wendy Sardinsky was considering starting her recycled paper products company and wanted to determine if it was available, she evaluated its risks and rewards through business planning research. April Smith, on the other hand, never "woke up one day and decided to start a business." Instead she "borrowed" some existing clients from her previous job and took up with a partner already experienced in business planning; between the two of them they funded their environmental consulting business, ReThink.

The Six Basic Steps to Forming Your Business Plan

Creating a business plan involves defining the problem and asking questions. It involves doing research, gathering information, and assessing the research and data you uncover. Before your pen hits the paper, you will have already done a substantial amount of investigative reporting.

Ask Questions

Remember the five W's? They apply here. Ask yourself the simple who, what, when, where, why, and how of all aspects of your business operations. Begin the questioning process by identifying your product, defining your target market, and identifying your competition. Remember to ask yourself very specific, targeted questions: **How** will my product or service fill an existing need? **Who** are the people who make up my target market? **What** kinds of start-up costs should I anticipate and estimate? **How** many employees will I need? **What** competitive products or services currently exist in my market? **Where** will my business be located?

Gather Research

Once you have formed a detailed list of questions you hope to answer, you can begin your research to uncover those answers.

Observe Your Competition

Observe your competition, ask questions of them, and take notes.

Evaluate the Data You Have Uncovered

The next step in this process involves analyzing, evaluating, and interpreting the results of your investigative work. It is a fine balance of assessing your results and listening to your intuition.

For example, if you wanted to open a children's art center that uses "found" or recycled objects, possible questions might include the following: How many young children live in the neighborhood? How many mothers take their children to classes? Are the moms currently involved in a "Mommy and Me" program? Who are these women? What are their interests, income levels, and philosophies of parenting? What other recycling programs exist in my neighborhood? What are other similar-sized communities doing? What programs have a high failure rate? What licenses are required to open a recreational program for the children?

From these questions you would research statistical data on your market through the local library, the local Chamber of Commerce, the Small Business Administration, or government agencies that may have such information readily available. Of course, you'll want to speak to many mothers in your neighborhood to get firsthand, current information about what women are looking for when enrolling their children in recreational activity programs. Licensing requirement questions may be answered through other business owners and establishing local networks. Interviewing other directors of recreational facilities may produce information regarding traffic patterns, average class size and turnover, and upcoming legislation.

As you evaluate the answers to the responses that your questions and research will generate, think about how they will affect your business's plan of operating and how you can apply those situations and facts to solutions.

Propose Solutions

After evaluating your thorough research, you will have a list of possible solutions, and you should assess those solutions on the basis of their probability. Be prepared with more than one alternative, so that if market conditions change, you will be able to implement plan B or plan C without much additional research. Choose the solution that you will feel most comfortable with—your "comfort zone" should be based on the amount of risk you are willing to undertake, given your industry's market and your financial condition.

Implement Your Findings into a Workable Plan

The objective of this step is simple: once you research and evaluate your research and have your arms around a solution that you think will work for you, you must implement that plan of action. This step should be a natural progression from the others. If you feel an overwhelming sense of frustration or caution, ask yourself why. Did you do all the necessary research? Did you explore all your options? Revisit your findings. If you cannot come to a comfort level with your plan, don't do it.

This step involves setting up goals for your business and setting realistic timetables for those goals to come to fruition. Remember, this plan is a work in progress, and it will change continually as your business redefines itself, grows, or falters and as market conditions change. Accumulate your findings, identify what trends are emerging and how your business will be shaped to ride the wave of those trends, and assess what methods of working or what products will soon be obsolete. Be open to changing your business direction as a result of these findings. Continue with the planning process. As long as you are in business for yourself, it will never end.

Forming Your Business Plan

1. Ask questions.
2. Gather research.
3. Observe your competition.
4. Evaluate the data you have uncovered.
5. Propose solutions.
6. Implement your findings into a workable plan.

The Written Plan

The written business plan is the document that emerges from this process. It outlines the most fundamental elements of business operations and projects. A sample outline for a business plan is included in the following pages. It was adapted from the Small Business Administration's model for creating a business plan. There are also software programs available that will help you create a business plan specifically targeted toward your industry. Other sources to consider: certified public accountants and business consultants frequently prepare business plans for their clients.

Although good business plans come in a variety of shapes and sizes, the best are prepared in both two- and five-year periods (although a five-year projection can often be a stretch for a fledgling business). These time windows allow you to project for the future while you operate in the present. They should be reviewed semiannually, so that you can constantly revisit how your market is changing and how to adapt to it.

If you are still debating whether or not you need to formally chronicle your business plan on paper, here are seven reasons most successful women entrepreneurs give for writing a business plan:

1. *To prove to yourself that you should go into business.* This is better known as a "reality check": you need to convince yourself that starting a business is right for you, both from a personal perspective and from an investment/financial perspective. By the time you finish

documenting on paper the myriad business issues or concerns you will be forced to think through, you'll know whether or not starting a business is right for you.

2. *To obtain financing from a bank or major lender.* The fall of the savings and loan industry of the late 1980s and early 1990s changed the face of small-business lending for the future. Banks are under greater scrutiny by federal regulators and, as a result, are requiring entrepreneurs to include a written business plan with any request for loan funds.

3. *To secure investment funds.* Whether you are seeking venture capital or informal capital from private investors, you will need a written business plan. By seeing the scope of your business plan on paper, potential investors can evaluate whether or not you have a well-thought-out and viable concept and whether the market for your product or service is large enough to be profitable. Likewise, a business plan can help investors estimate your company's potential for growth, and the scope of that growth, over the next several years.

4. *To obtain large contracts.* When small companies seek substantial orders or ongoing service contracts from major corporations, a business plan is critical to show corporate executives that you are thinking about the future. Moreover, in today's selling environment corporations are increasingly looking toward their suppliers as partners, and the entrepreneur's business plan helps convey that sense of partnership.

5. *To attract star employees.* A written business plan assures prospective employees that a new company's partners and management have thought through the key issues facing the company, have a plan for dealing with them, and have their eye on expanding for the future. The prospective employee can also help envision him- or herself in your working environment and assess whether he or she shares your philosophy for business. With a grasp on where your business sees itself in five years, the employee can envision what his or her role in the future company might be.

6. *To complete mergers and acquisitions.* Whether you want to sell

your company or buy one, the business plan serves almost as an extended company vitae.

7. *To motivate your management team.* As your company grows and deals with more critical and complex issues, a business plan can be a much needed tool for keeping your management focused on the same short-term and long-range goals.

Before you get to the "meat" of your plan, many small-business experts recommend prefacing the sections with a brief title page containing the date, the business name, the address, and the phone number, followed by a brief table of contents for the plan.

An Overview of the Business

This component addresses your business, your product, the mission statement for your business, and the industry in which you operate. In a nutshell, this section of your business plan should provide a clear and concise introduction to your business—an overview of the kind of business you are in, an explanation of how it works, and the rationale of why you are in business. The most basic information should be included here:

- The name and nature of your business

- The kind of business you are running—such as wholesale, retail, service, or manufacturing

- The industry you are in—such as textiles, garment, food

- A detailed description of the product or service you offer; the benefit of your product or service; competitive advantage or disadvantage; and any relevant design, production, or legal considerations

- How you will run your business: Will it be nonprofit, will you incorporate? Will you have a DBA (doing business as) statement? Will it be run on a full-time or part-time basis? Try to paint a picture in the reader's mind of what your business looks like.

- How you know you have a successful and marketable idea

To write your mission statement, ask yourself the following questions: Why does this business exist? Why am I in business? What is the business's purpose? What is my desired image for the business? Then develop a one- to three-line statement that straightforwardly explains why you are in business.

Market Research

Marketing research provides statistics for the entire industry you are in. Break down the data for both the total market and your specific clients or customers. In this section you identify and quantify your target market and explain the following:

- Your customer, as defined by age, sex, race, education, income, geographic location, and so forth; in other words, who will be most likely to use your service or buy your product?

- Your target market's interests

- Their spending habits in relation to their disposable income

- Why these groups would want to buy your product or service

- What, exactly, it is that they will be buying

- Whether or not your target market is growing

- Your overall predictions about the market at large, your target market, and your entry into the field

The Marketing Plan

This section of your plan should define how to reach your customers with your product or service. It looks at potential obstacles, including industry regulation, technological advancement, and other factors, as well as at the special advantages of your product or service to your target market. In this section you review how what you do is special; how what you sell is superior to or different from the competition; and how you plan on communicating that to your target market. Be sure to present the following:

- How you will sell your product

- Why the market needs your product or service

- How you will position yourself differently from the competition, with your pricing, location, packaging, or customer appeal

- The price of your product or how you will charge for your services

- Your dependence or reliability on supplies or vendors

- Who will handle your customer service

- Your objectives for advertising, marketing, and promotions

The Operational System

Operations involve the physical location of your work space, whether it be a home office or a ten-thousand-square-foot factory, and how, exactly, you will use your given space to actually produce your product or service. It also discusses, in a more overall sense, how you will make your product or service for a fee or a price that will sell.

If you are selling a **product,** you will want to broach these specific issues:

- How much your space costs to rent or lease or buy

- Your space's ability for growth

- The manufacturing process involved in producing your product

- Your needs in terms of contract or equipment purchases

- The minimum you must make or sell to avoid losing money

- How many employees are necessary to operate the business and what they will cost

- If you are planning to subcontract manufacturing and to whom, under what terms and conditions

- The suppliers you will use and their various credit and delivery terms

- How you will implement inventory control

- Shipping procedures

If you are selling a **service,** you want to broach these specific issues:

- How much your space costs to rent or lease or buy

- Your space's ability for growth

- A description of the design and development of your service

- Your needs in terms of contract or equipment purchases

- The minimum you can make or sell to avoid losing money

- How many employees are necessary to operate the business and what they will cost, including the employees responsible for supervising the quality control of your service and who will handle your business's customer service

- If you are planning to subcontract manufacturing and to whom, under what terms and conditions

- Your transportation and parking facilities for customers

The Financial Plan

From initial start-up costs to ongoing costs, this section addresses everything having to do with the financial status of your company. Ultimately the financial component of your written plan examines your quantitative projections for doing business and must include the following:

1. *A summary of your current financial situation,* which translates into how much capital you have for your business and how much additional capital you need to borrow in order to start up:

- How you will use these funds in the first year and in the years to come

- Your anticipated working capital, month by month, for eighteen months

- Additional money you need to borrow or obtain from a funding source

- How this additional money will be used

2. *A profit and loss, or operating, statement,* which looks at projected revenue over the next three years compared to the cost of doing business, in order to conclude a net profit or loss. To assist you with figuring your profit or loss, contact the SBA for an operating statement form, which follows one basic formula:

Revenues – Expenses = Profit/Loss

3. *A cash flow statement;* in other words, how much cash is expected to come in each month and what you expect monthly expenses to total. Your business plan should include a monthly cash flow chart for year one and a quarterly cash flow chart for years two and three. The charts you create will help you estimate the "money in and money out" figures for your business.

4. *A break-even analysis,* a calculation of at which point your

income for each of the three years would completely offset your costs. The break-even point is reached when your gross income equals your total expenses. You determine your break-even analysis by calculating your fixed costs (unvarying expenses), variable costs (fluctuating expenses), and contribution margin (selling price per unit minus variable expenses per unit).

Incorporating an accurate and thorough break-even analysis as a routine part of your financial planning will keep you abreast of how your business is really faring. Determining how much business is needed to keep you in business will help improve your cash flow management and, ultimately, your bottom line.

Karen G. Collier, owner of an eight-year-old dental practice, is one entrepreneur who can attest to the benefits of conducting a break-even analysis. Collier, whose Baltimore-based practice grossed $1.3 million in 1995, admits that when she started out she didn't know the difference between a debt and an expense.

When Collier wanted to purchase an additional office seven years after launching her own business, she calculated the minimum volume of business she needed to break even. In the end, she decided that it wouldn't be a wise financial move simply because the necessary volume of business wasn't there. By using break-even analysis, Collier was able to make an objective decision based on hard numbers. Without it, she asserts, "I'd be so much less aware of how to run my business."

5. *A balance sheet of your assets and liabilities,* which basically sums up your financial data and shows you where you really stand. Your total assets should equal your total liabilities plus capital—in other words, they should balance each other.

If at any point during the course of developing the financial data for your business plan you become overwhelmed or unsure of how to proceed, you might want to consider hiring an accountant.

SCORE, an acronym for the Service Corps of Retired Executives, a business management counseling service offered by the Small Business Administration, can also be invaluable for providing advice for pulling together your business plan. SCORE is a nonprofit organization made up of retired businesspeople who have acquired a wealth of experience in a wide variety of businesses. They provide objective, impartial advice as outsiders who are experts in your field of choice. SCORE provides counseling in the following areas: business planning, advertising, accounting, market and customer analysis, inventory control, and cash and credit management. According to the SBA, this free service "counsels persons who plan to go into business and those already in business—to help them deal with problems, upgrade their management skills, and improve their prospect for success."

The Management Plan

In a nutshell, you are describing the organizational structure of your business and the business and professional resources you have in-house. This section provides a look at the management team, their strengths and weaknesses, and their roles and philosophies on how to run a business. Include the following:

- Internal staffing, such as your employees and management, both quantity and quality

- Specific responsibilities and authority of key personnel. Many experts suggest attaching the résumés of key executives involved in the business

- Plans for hiring, salaries, benefits, sales training, and supervision

Consultants and Advisers

This portion of the business plan assesses what external assistance you will hire. Here you figure out whom you will consult for legal advice, who will do your accounting, how much money you will invest in advertising or marketing, and whom you will use to do your banking, including what types of accounts you want to set up. Describe the following:

- Your attorney and his or her business qualifications

- The business licenses you have acquired

- Your accountant and his or her qualifications

- Your insurance agent and his or her qualifications

- Any special insurance you have acquired

- Your banker and his or her qualifications

- Your record keeper or bookkeeper, if an outside consultant

Conclusion

To wrap it all up, write a brief summary of the company: its potential for growth, its ability to expand management, and its probability for success. Attach any documents you feel are valuable, such as building or equipment contracts, leases, personal credentials or degrees earned, and any special licenses you have as a businessperson.

Components of a Business Plan

1. Title page (business name, address and phone number, and the date).
2. Table of contents.
3. An overview of the business.
4. Market research.
5. The marketing plan.
6. The operational system.
7. The financial plan.
8. The management plan.
9. Consultants and advisers.
10. Conclusion.

Cultivating Customers:
Marketing Green Products and Services

The discovery of a hole in the ozone layer above the Antarctic, the explosion at the Chernobyl nuclear power plant, and the Exxon *Valdez* eleven-million-gallon oil spill into Prince William Sound are but a few of the events in recent years that have contributed to an increased level of environmental awareness among the general public. In addition, government regulations have made environmental issues top of mind for many corporations and consumers alike. The passage of legislation mandating the regulation of water and air pollution levels and the phasing out of ozone-depleting chemicals such as chlorofluorocarbons (CFCs) found in old aerosols and coolant systems have literally brought the environment home to many people who were formerly less aware of pollution's impact on their day-to-day lives.

The increased awareness, coupled with new pro-environment legislation, has created an exciting and vital new market for business. Consumer surveys have indicated that, price, quality, and service being equal, a staggering 90 percent of shoppers are more likely to buy products from companies that have the best reputations for social and environmental responsibility. A recent Roper poll indicated that over half the buying public identify themselves as green consumers and that they take into account product sourcing, packaging, and disposability as part of their purchase considerations. In fact, some market research has indicated that many environment- and health-conscious consumers are willing to pay a premium for natural and environmentally safe household products.

As part of the marketing plan, the successful ecopreneur needs to understand her customer. To determine why the market needs her product or service, she must carefully research the existing market and get a profile of the typical green consumer. Demographics indicate that environmental awareness increases proportionately with education and income level—in other words, the better educated and more financially well-off the consumer, the "greener" her purchase practices tend to be. Environmental consumers are more concentrated on the East and West Coasts than throughout the rest of the country, and more women than men tend to be green. Families with children make up the majority of green households, and studies have indicated that children have influenced their parents' purchase decisions by alerting them to specific environmental concerns or pointing out packaging or a specific household product that is or is not good for the environment.

Even if a consumer is environmentally aware and leans toward green purchase decisions, the ecopreneur still faces obstacles on the road to her success. The same factors other entrepreneurs take into account in marketing their businesses must be carefully evaluated by the ecopreneur. Think about the marketing plan you're drafting as part of your written business plan. How will you set your product or service apart from the competition? How will it be distributed (if you're selling a service, where will your offices be located)? Will you need to contract out manufacturing or processing, and will you need suppliers or vendors? In addition, you'll want to play close attention to how your product or service measures up in the following top three consumer purchase considerations:

Price

While surveys have indicated that most consumers are willing to spend more for green products, all but the most ardent green shoppers won't "buy green" if they can get a similar product for a much lower cost. How much of that cost is passed on to the consumer is an important consideration. Note that while the *process* of recycling materials may be more expensive than using preconsumer materials, the recycled material itself is less costly. Companies that "green" their production usually report savings a few months to a year after the initial investment.

Performance

Some early prototypes of green products, such as nontoxic detergents and household cleaners, were initially deemed less effective than their nongreen counterparts. Although research has indicated that the overwhelming majority of today's green products perform on a par with their competition, low performance is still a common misconception that marketers must overcome.

Convenience

Even the best new product will languish on the shelves if not positioned properly. If your chemical-free shampoo in a recycled plastic container is stocked only in health food stores and not side by side with the more general toiletry items at the supermarket, few consumers will be inclined to make the special trip to purchase it. Likewise, if your recycling center isn't centrally located, few customers will be inclined to make the trip. If you plan to operate your business out of a storefront, whether retail or service, ask yourself the following questions: Are my hours of operation appropriate for my clientele? Is there adequate parking? Are the methods of payment convenient?

Beyond price, performance, and convenience, the green marketer must address other, more specific concerns if she is to market her product successfully. The responsibility for educating and informing consumers about a product or service's specific environmental benefits rests squarely on the green entrepreneur's shoulders. If consumers cannot understand *why* a given product or service is beneficial to the environment, most likely they aren't going to be motivated to purchase it. In addition to informing consumers, effective marketing can communicate genuine concern and respect for the target audience. Tom's of Maine, for example, has built its considerable reputation in part by using a multitiered approach that conveys the company's philosophy and objectives through packaging, media advertising, and customer service. The following areas are among the most important to address:

Packaging

Innovative packaging can make or break a product, and because packaging is one of the most direct ways to convey company philosophy, this can be especially true for ecopreneurs. Green marketers often choose to use minimal (even recyclable or refillable) packaging accompanied by printed matter that includes not only environmental symbols, but concise text explaining the benefit of the green product. According to Deborah Churchill Luster, president of Annie's Home-grown, a company specializing in "totally natural" macaroni-and-cheese products, "Our marketing materials are our packaging. First, there's a bright color, which gets people to pick up the box. Then they read the back, which tells about Annie and may have an offer for a free bumper sticker." The box also talks about Annie's all natural philosophy and introduces its high-quality ingredients. "Generally, if they pick up the box, they buy it," says Churchill Luster. "We put a lot of thought into our packaging."

Research has indicated that many consumers still don't recognize the three arrows recycling symbol. If your customer can't immediately see and understand what sets the green product apart from the other products on the shelf, she probably won't be inclined to choose it.

Publicity Campaigns

A campaign that spotlights your company's role in benefiting the environment—for example, publicity about your company's role in implementing a recycling program at elementary schools in your area—can bring your product or service added exposure and credibility. What's more, if done right, it can be one of the least expensive and most effective ways of getting your name out to the community. One company that developed biodegradable disposable diapers was able to launch an effective offensive campaign prior to a consumer boycott of biodegradable plastics. The campaign, which included video news releases, in-depth interviews with the company's founders, and educational kits, led to balanced media coverage and deflected most of the criticism when the boycott was called. As a result, the product has been very successful.

Educational Advertising

If your customer doesn't immediately understand the benefits of your product or service, he won't be motivated to buy it. Many consumers begin "green" shopping practices as a result of self-education through news or other media. By using clear language in your advertising that includes easy-to-understand statistics and proposes solutions or aid to current environmental problems, you'll show respect for your customer and allow her to make informed, responsible decisions. Remember that the unifying goal of the majority of ecobusinesses is to define a problem (for example, tires contributing to overflowing landfills) and design a solution (shoe soles made from recycled tire rubber). You can use educational advertising to show consumers how your product or service "solves a problem" in the environment.

Customer Service

One of the main tenets of ecobusiness is the promise to "do good" for the community and the environment at large. By extension, green businesses convey a desire to "do good" for their customers on a more personal level by giving them healthier and safer options. Solid customer service can do as much for your business's reputation as a costly, sophisticated advertising campaign, often with more lasting effects. In fact, good customer service can give your business the competitive edge over others in your field. Make sure you have a comprehensive plan for customer service in writing that reflects your personal business principles. Communicate to your employees their responsibility to uphold these principles—you can even provide an incentive plan for the best customer service representative. Take your customers' own comments and questions seriously—they can be valuable tools in making your business better. Keep in touch with your customers by sending postcards or a newsletter about your business and any community or political events that may affect it. Consider installing a toll-free phone number and/or setting up an e-mail address to make it easy for your customers to contact you and get a quick response, and if at all possible, respond to written customer inquiries and comments with a nonform letter. The "extra mile" you go to show that you truly value your customers' concerns will surely be noted.

Deflecting Consumer Skepticism

The majority of customers are receptive to green products and services. However, several well-publicized cases in recent years of false "green" advertising claims on the part of marketers have contributed to a lingering climate of skepticism as to not only the quality and efficacy of green products or services, but whether these products and services stem from a "green" business sense. To overcome consumer skepticism, ecopreneurs must successfully communicate that their concern for the environment and their customers is part of a genuine philosophy and is not a marketing ploy. Notable ways established ecobusinesses have done this include donating a portion of proceeds to an environmental cause, encouraging customer inquiries and sending written responses, and forgoing glitzy and flashy advertising campaigns in favor of a more serious and educational tone. "Every customer who writes Annie's Homegrown gets a personal, handwritten response from Annie," says Deborah Churchill Luster. "It's getting harder now that the company's expanding. We used to put Annie's phone number on the box, but that's not possible anymore."

Tricks of the Trade

from April Smith, of ReThink, on getting your business, product, or service publicity:

1. *Get in print.* Ads don't work as well or as credibly as an editorial or article about you or your company. One story about your innovative recycling program—you pick up and deliver to your customer's door—will attract immediate business and has immeasurable residual value when photocopied and mailed to business prospects.
2. *Get on the broadcast media.* Get interviewed. TV or radio talk

shows, even if they're only local, can have a large impact. One evening news report on your merits can lift you from unknown to known in the community.

3. *Get published.* Write about your industry or expertise. Your best bets are local newspapers, journals, city magazines, trade publications, and newsletters related to the industry.

4. *Speak in public.* Use business and civic groups to get your message out, especially if you're an advocate. You don't necessarily have to talk about your business; you just have to have an impact. If you are a powerful presenter, your audience will assume you have a powerful business.

5. *Give a seminar at your client's business or trade association.* Offer classes that provide guidance and inside tips. A one-time, no-cost look at your skills and expertise will land business, build confidence, and earn respect.

6. *Network with the right people.* Be seen and get known by those who can have an impact on or can be customers of your business. Directed networking is the fulcrum of entrepreneurial marketing. And it's inexpensive, great one-on-one exposure, productive, time effective, and fun.

7. *Join the Chamber of Commerce.* It's the single most powerful business organization in your community, so get involved. Meet with the leaders, attend every networking event you can, exhibit at its business fair, and make a five-year plan to join their board of directors.

8. *Join the trade associations* of the businesses you most want to establish or maintain relationships with. You will be an associate member with a chance to affect your customer—and others like her. Attend meetings regularly, get involved, and speak to or lead a group. Magnify your impact by developing a reputation for helping others get business (by providing them with leads and referrals).

9. *Persist.* Dedicate time to making it happen. As most entrepreneurs know, persistence is the secret. Don't do anything once,

then sit back and wait. You must keep plugging. Soon your phone will start to ring.

✳ ✳ ✳

Creating Marketing Materials

The ecopreneur faces some tough challenges when creating her marketing materials. Besides promoting your product or service, your marketing materials should strongly project the motivating philosophy behind your environmental ideas—in other words, help to position your company in your customers' minds. If your materials seem to contradict your message (for example, you print brochures for your recycling company on heavy, glossy, nonrecyclable paper), you'll have difficulty achieving credibility in your field—and, equally important, growing your business and its customer base.

You don't need to have a huge advertising budget to come up with an effective and memorable marketing campaign. The following marketing materials can be relatively inexpensive options for small, start-up businesses:

Brochures

Brochures give your potential customers a chance to learn more about the product or service you offer. Brochures can help create an identity that sets your company apart from the competition; they can educate the consumer about the ways your product or service benefits them and the environment; they can be combined with special offers to drum up new business or with questionnaires to gauge the response of old customers. A start-up company can gain credibility through a brochure that is well written and professionally designed. Remember that your brochure will also project what author Jay Conrad Levinson calls a "metamessage"—a nonverbal statement about your company—which comes through in everything from the paper stock you choose to the design and layout of your write-up. You can create effective marketing materials on a budget but should never sacrifice professional presentation and clear, concise (and, of course, error-free) copy. There are several excellent written sources you can consult that provide detailed instruction and tips on what to include and what not to include in a brochure. Above all, remember that your brochure is a forum for your company. Clearly describe the benefits of what you offer, include eye-catching graphics or photos, provide useful information that will make your brochure a "keeper," and if possible, stimulate customer response with a special offer, a questionnaire, or an order form. You can distribute your brochure at your business, at in-store displays, or through the mail—if you choose to mail it, enlist the help of a direct-mail company to obtain targeted customer mailing lists and ensure a larger response.

Catalogs

Environmental company Seventh Generation conducts its business entirely through catalog sales, as does American Environmental Health Foundation, which sells natural home care products. According to Jay Conrad Levinson and Seth Godin in the book *Guerrilla Marketing*, the three top rules for catalog marketers are "Start small," "Target your mailings," and "Test, test, test." It's a good idea to start out with a simple flyer that's only one or two pages in length, so that you can gauge the response before investing a lot of money. Streamline your mailing list as much as possible, or you'll wind up wasting money on sending catalogs to uninterested consumers who'll just throw them away. If you have one, start with your existing customer list, and from there select carefully researched mailing lists. Several companies sell mailing lists with names that fit the profile of green consumers; some are so specific that they may even seem tailor-made for your service or product. Finally, don't be tentative about making modifications to your mailing list, your catalog layout or text, your pricing, or anything else until you feel that you've achieved the right balance. *Guerrilla Marketing* also repeatedly stresses that one of the best ways to gain the competitive edge on an entrepreneur's budget is to clearly define your market and narrow it down to a specialty group. Big corporate marketers may have the budget to produce thick, glossy catalogs and do mass mailings, but they often fall short on service. You can make a big impact through niche marketing that caters to a specific kind of customer. If you're selling only one or two products, you might want to consider "piggybacking," or marketing your product through another company's catalog. There are companies that can help you find a company whose catalog and product selection closely reflect your own philosophy. This can be a low-cost approach, especially if the company will allow you to sell your products on a commission basis.

Free Samples/Promotional

Gifts. Free samples and promotional gifts are a great way to generate positive word of mouth and demonstrate that your company stands behind the product or service it offers. They can bring first-time customers into your business and reward loyal customers for their continued patronage. These offers can be even more effective when used in conjunction with other marketing efforts. For example, your organic food catalog can offer a free grocery tote emblazoned with your company logo with orders over a designated dollar amount. Or your direct-mail piece can offer first-time customers who try a week of your diaper service a free rattle or baby bottle with your service's name printed on it.

Annie's Homegrown offers a toll-free number on its box for consumers to call and have coupons for a free box of pasta sent to their friends. "We get about 1,500 calls a month from all over the country," adds Deborah Churchill Luster.

The Internet

Many savvy marketers have discovered the benefits of promotion on the Internet. In fact, the Web could be considered the perfect "green" medium, because it doesn't create waste in the form of flyers or brochures that people can throw away. If you create a relatively simple and straightforward Web site, the initial cost can be quite affordable, and when used in combination with print advertising, Web site advertising can be highly effective and affordable. You may be able to afford only a very small ad space in a popular journal, but by placing a small ad with an eye-catching phrase or graphic and including your Internet address at the bottom, you'll greatly enlarge your ad size at no additional cost. Computer users can call up your Web site to learn more about your company, get current environmental news, see pictures of your product(s), or even order from an on-line catalog. Some companies have created thriving mail-order businesses that revolve around an Internet "superstore."

Sponsorships

"Doing good" is a fundamental credo of ecobusiness, and your business can go one step further in demonstrating its responsibility to the community by actually creating an event that revolves around community involvement and renewal. One of the least expensive ways to get your name out and create an identity for your business is through the sponsorship of a local community group or concern. If you live in an urban area, one idea is to join forces with a community youth group to sponsor a neighborhood cleanup event in which you provide paint, trash bags, brooms, and so forth, along with refreshments and commemorative T-shirts (your business name on the back, "Brooks Avenue Cleanup, December 1997" on the front). Another possibility is to sponsor a school recycling drive and donate art supplies to the class that brings in the most newspapers by the contest deadline.

Woman on the Way

*

Deborah Churchill Luster
President: Annie's Homegrown
Business Philosophy: Women have to start businesses to create the lives they want
Greatest Achievement: Putting Annie's products on the supermarket shelves

With innovative challenges such as "We'll give you $10,000 if you show us the cow that gives Day-Glo cheese," Deborah Churchill Luster has brought Annie's Homegrown to a new level. When she joined the fledgling company in 1991, Annie's had already made quite a splash in the regional gourmet and health food stores. Under Churchill Luster's tutelage, the business became profitable in 1992.

Churchill Luster is unlikely to take the credit herself. "This is Annie's vision [owner Annie Withey]: A company that is inspirational to other companies—an example to other companies." What Churchill Luster has brought to the mix is a financier's head for business. A former banker, she shares Annie's vision and also understands Annie's discomfort in the spotlight. And with Churchill Luster in the foreground, Withey can stay close to the kitchen of her Connecticut farmhouse, creating new, natural ways to feed America.

It's no secret that the natural food market is booming. "Most educated mothers are ashamed to serve food with chemicals but need something that's easy and fast to prepare. Annie's is attempting to fill that niche."

Sometimes its hard to convince consumers to switch over. "It raises the price point to have a better quality food producer, and that the boxes are recycled. But we also don't spend great volumes of money on advertising and marketing, like our competition. We put our money back into the community."

Like many environmentally concerned entrepreneurs, Withey and Churchill Luster are concerned with issues such as artificial dyes, whether boxes were truly recycled, and that the cheese comes from cows not treated with the bovine growth hormone. "It's a constant challenge to maintain your mission," says Churchill Luster, who, with Withey and other members of the company, met with ice-cream guru Ben Cohen to help define their goals, "but we wouldn't be doing this in the first place if it weren't for our values."

✳ ✳ ✳

3

Finance and Consulting

In the high-stakes world of international finance, women are emerging as a powerful presence. While the larger companies are promoting women at a snail's pace, some smaller organizations are learning that the language of money is gender blind.

Unfortunately, the stigma of women and numbers exists even as women entrepreneurs redefine the concept of the small business. Our educational inequities—boys directed toward math and science, girls directed away—still fester in an arena dominated by men. It is largely for this reason that women are electing to find specialized "niche" organizations where they can use their savvy, or create a business based on their own values and good sense.

According to Peggy Farley, managing director and CEO of AMAS Securities, very few women occupy front-office ranks within investment firms, and only a handful or so manage investment house or mutual fund portfolios.

"I've never really had any women mentors to guide me along the way," says Farley. "All of those who have recognized my abilities and promoted me have been men."

According to author and educator Kathleen A. Allen, Ph.D., associate professor in the Entrepreneur Program at the University of Southern California, "If women have a disadvantage in the financial markets, it comes principally from two sources. First is the culturally internalized perception by women that they're not good with numbers. For hundreds of years women have not been encouraged to take an interest in or improve their mathematical and analytical skills, so it's no wonder that they find finance issues difficult to master. They actually set themselves up mentally for failure. The second is the general perception of the financial community that women tend to create "hobby businesses," not serious ones.

Women can overcome these two barriers by improving their financial skills through community and college courses or with the many books on the market that make learning finance easy; and by creating companies that are the result of careful planning and research. In other words, preparing a well-documented business plan will give any woman more confidence when she approaches a potential financial source and will make that source more convinced that she knows what she's doing.

In this chapter, you'll find a variety of consultants and financial advisers who will share their formulas for success and also guide you on your journey to business financing. According to Joline Godfrey, author and founder of An Income of Her Own, an agency that empowers young women in the language of economics, "Women's issues with money are generally unresolved." While this truth may hold back some talented women, it is also a challenge to those who want to move beyond what was predetermined for women's work.

Bumping Up against the Glass Ceiling: How Women Are Taking Their Business Smarts and Hitting the Road

Despite mavericks like Peggy Farley, who advocates for the women in her field, finding a suitable match with an organization that respects you as a professional *and* a woman can be difficult. For many, the desire to excel is the main motivator that sends them out of "the system" to open a new venture.

Maria Elena Toraño arrived from Cuba in 1960 with five dollars in her pocket and a degree in education. Initially, the only work she could find was in a bakery. Then for twenty years she rose up the ranks of corporate America, flourishing in her marketing and corporate communications position with Eastern Airlines while also participating in civic affairs programs for the Little Havana district of Miami.

Her activities parlayed her into a choice economic development appointment as associate director of the U.S. Community Services under former President Jimmy Carter.

When her participation in that appointment was over, she couldn't envision herself going back to working for others—so she started her own business. Public relations was a logical field, and soon she had a client list that boasted the Miami Dolphins and Coors Brewing Co.

Over the last twenty years her business has experienced myriad transformations. She learned that a flexible approach enabled her to better respond to the constant changes of the business climate. Today Maria Elena Toraño and Associates (META) has grown to almost 250 employees in six offices across the United States and an annual revenue of $22 million. "A flexible approach is the only thing that works," she says with a smile.

The Best of Both Worlds: Enjoying Autonomy as a Consultant

Edith Weiner always knew she wanted to do her own thing. After a childhood spent shuffling between foster homes, Weiner learned to capitalize on her obstacles and plan for the future.

Her company, Weiner, Edrich, and Brown (WEB), does just that. With her trademark brashness, Weiner projects trends to some of America's leading companies. "There's a glut of information out there," she says, referring largely to our country's obsession with the information superhighway. "But what do you do if you haven't the knowledge to process it?" That's what WEB does: disseminates social, economic, political, and technological information for its clients and projects trends for the future.

Weiner started her business because she "wanted to raise her child with her husband—not a nanny," and she knew no organization would give her the space she needed to do so. "It was a challenge at first to be taken seriously, especially in the Peter Pan–collared maternity dresses we pre-nineties women were subjected to."

Like Weiner, Fran Sussner Rodgers found that the glass ceiling didn't present as much of an obstacle as did the reality of being a hands-on mother in a type-A work culture. When her infant daughter developed asthma in 1979, Rodgers found that her job at an educational consulting firm was beginning to be too much—even part-time.

She decided to quit her job and launch a consulting firm based at home. As a baby boomer herself, Rodgers had spotted several generational trends, from the stampede of women into the workplace to the growing concern over aging parents. In her new business, she set out to help companies deal with the very problems she had faced.

Rodgers has built a $65 million business that advises companies on what supports employees need to fully engage in their work and care for their families. She's long since moved out of her home and has brought in a president to help her run the firm. Her organization, Work/Family Directions, is the first major for-profit player in its field and looks ahead to greater profits in the future.

In Esther Dyson's climb to success, she grabbed a great opportunity in her path. As a go-getter in the then all-male bastion of information technology, Dyson was offered the opportunity to purchase the industry newsletter she was working on. She did, and she hasn't looked back since.

As president of EDventure Holdings, Inc., a small, diversified company focusing on emerging technology worldwide, and on the emerging computer markets of central and Eastern Europe, Dyson also manages EDventure Ventures, a venture capital fund dedicated to active investment in software and information start-ups in Eastern Europe, including Russia. She also edits *Release 1.0*, a monthly newsletter.

"By operating my own business, I have the freedom to be who I want, come and go as I please, and take on the challenges that appeal to me. How much better can it get?" Dyson says.

Woman on the Way

*

Edith Weiner
President: Weiner, Edrich, and Brown, Inc.
Business Philosophy: Showing clients and colleagues that knowledge is more valuable than simply information
Greatest Accomplishment: Breaking ground for working mothers by "flaunting" her pregnancy in the workplace and the corporate boardroom—long before it was acceptable

When you imagine a career as a futurist, what comes to mind? For many, it's a bejeweled, round lady with a box of tarot cards, not someone like Edith (or Edie, as she likes to be called). A bright, petite woman, Weiner regularly—and unabashedly—tells America's top execs where to go and what to do.

Her company, Weiner, Edrich, Brown (WEB), is a combination think tank and strategic-command planning center. While other execs may not have time to pick up a periodical, WEB reads everything it can get its hands on—and then distills the information for its clients and offers organizational perspectives for social, economic, political, and technological trends.

And because WEB is right more often than wrong, Edith Weiner has cultivated a reputation for accurate forecasting that would put Jeanne Dixon to shame.

Since the business started in 1977, WEB has advised clients that include American Express, Avon, NYNEX, Owens Corning, the New York Port Authority, and even the U.S. Congress. One of Weiner's successful predictions include warning pharmaceutical companies back in the late 1970s that there would be a backlash against animal testing. Who knew? Edie Weiner did.

"While most clients are stuck putting out fires, we try to get them thinking strategically about the future." she says. And continued success is written all over Edith Weiner's future.

✳   ✳   ✳

Beyond the Start-up: How to Finance Your Business

Despite the great gains that women entrepreneurs have made in the last twenty years, many still believe they are operating at a disadvantage in today's financial climate, primarily because they find start-up and venture capital difficult to obtain. "There are certain [woman-owned] businesses that have probably stayed small or haven't reached their potential because they didn't have the proper financing," says Annette Taylor, president of the Women's Equity Fund, a Denver-based venture capital firm that has obtained $660,000 to invest in enterprises owned by women.

So how do woman-operated and -run businesses gain financing? What are their methods of obtaining innovative start-up capital, and how do they grow their businesses? And how, exactly, have women entrepreneurs achieved tremendous success without any money of their own, relying on the strength of OPM, otherwise known as "other people's money"?

You have already started up your business, maybe from cash advances from your credit card or a loan from your friends or family, or maybe you had low enough overhead that you really didn't pursue any starting-up capital when you decided to start your business. Now that you're up and running, you might have decided that you have a viable business that needs an infusion of cash. How do you expand? Where do you obtain your capital?

Most financial experts divide the term capital into a number of classifications—such as *initial, operating* (or *working*), and *reserve.* All of these terms are variations of the same need: enough money to see the business off to a strong financial start. *Initial capital* refers to the money you will need to cover all of your start-up costs—costs such as legal fees; deposits for utilities, machinery, and fixtures; advances for the rental or leasing of your property; and modest beginning promotions. *Operating* or *working capital* refers to money needed to keep the business in operation until the profits begin coming in—costs such as raw materials or merchandise, salaries for employees, monthly rent, and insurance. *Fixed capital* refers to assets retained for a long time, such as land, buildings, machinery, and equipment, that may easily be converted to cash if necessary.

No matter what kind of capital you are seeking, go armed. This is where your business plan preparation can come in handy. Remember, you should always have this minimum information available at your fingertips when you seek financing:

- A detailed explanation of your business—if you have a written plan, which may be a requirement from some more traditional lending facilities, all the better; detailed financial statements are often necessary

- The reason you want the loan—for example, what you plan to do with the money

- The exact amount of money you are seeking to borrow

- A plan for how the loan will be repaid, the amount of time in which you wish to repay the loan, and collateral offered to guarantee the loan

---

Financing Sources for Your Business*

Equity (sell part of company)
- Family, friends, and other nonprofessional investors
- Venture capitalists
- Small Business Investment Companies (SBICs) and Minority Enterprise Small Business Investment Corporations (MESBICs)

Personal Loans
- Banks
  —Unsecured loans (rare)
  —Loans secured by
    real estate
    stocks and bonds

- Finance Companies
  —Loans secured by
    real estate
    personal assets

- Credit Unions
  —Unsecured "signature" loans
  —Loans secured by
    real estate (some credit unions)
    personal assets

- Savings and Loan Associations
  —Unsecured loans (rare)
  —Loans secured by real estate

- Mortgage Brokers and Private Investors
  —Loans secured by real estate

- Life Insurance Companies
  —Policy loans (borrow against cash value)

Business Loans
- Banks (short-term)
  —Unsecured loans (for established, financially sound companies only)
  —Loans secured by
    accounts receivable
    inventory
    equipment

- Banks (long-term)
  —Loans secured by real estate
  —Loans guaranteed by
    Small Business Administration (SBA)
    Farmers Home Administration (FMHA)

- Commercial Finance Companies
  —Loans secured by
    real estate
    equipment
    inventory
    accounts receivable

- Life Insurance Companies
  —Loans secured by commercial real estate
    (worth at least $150,000)

- Small Business Administration
  —Loans secured by
    all available business assets
    all available personal assets

- Suppliers
  —Trade credit

- Customers
  —Prepayment on orders

*Reprinted by permission from the U.S. Small Business Administration's Small Business Management Series pamphlet, No. 44.

Alternatives to Traditional Avenues for Funding

Women are starting to see that the traditional avenues for funding don't necessarily work for them—especially if they are seeking access to these conventional avenues through traditional relationships. Women in a variety of businesses are learning to seek out financial mentors, networks, and sources and develop key relationships with lending facilities who can meet their needs.

"Women and banks have a paradoxical relationship," said Sandra Maltby, senior vice president, Small Business Services, KeyCorp, as she addressed the University of Chicago Graduate School of Business in October 1995. "On the one hand, I'm a woman who heads the small-business services division for the nation's tenth largest bank, which is the country's third largest lender to small businesses, many of which presumably are headed by women. At least that suggests a bank sensitive to the capital needs of women business owners and committed to providing that capital. On the other hand, maybe it's all a cynical facade. Pick a woman. Give her a title. Make her our mouthpiece to say all the right things. And continue business as usual. And 'business as usual' doesn't seem to be very good for women. What do women business owners, in survey after survey, identify as among their top problems? Being taken seriously and having access to capital. The paradox is that there is compelling data that women-owned businesses are a large and growing force in our economy—and, more from a banker's perspective, no worse than businesses in general at repaying their loans and staying in business."

During her years as a banker, Judy Phillips, senior vice president at Harris Trust and Savings Bank in Chicago, noticed that women were uncomfortable approaching financial institutions and wanted to make it her personal credo to assist more women business owners in getting bank loans. Several years ago she formed the Women in Business banking team at Harris Bank. The team consisted of two trust officers, four bankers, and six assistants—all part of the bank's private banking department.

"It was clear to me that women-owned businesses represented a huge growth area," she says. "Women were just beginning to emerge as business owners, and there was the additional group of smart women that had hit the corporate glass ceiling. Many decided to go out on their own—forming a powerful group of business owners."

Phillips says she saw a chance to "give back" by providing some of the expertise and knowledge working in financial services had given her. During its earlier years, the Women in Business unit sponsored seminars that helped women develop business plans for obtaining financing. "If we [as women] don't bring women along, I don't know who will," Phillips maintains.

Phillips, and other bankers targeting this market, noticed a lack of networks and mentor groups. As a result, corporate sponsorships and networking with women's organizations are a big part of Harris's strategy. Harris sponsored a program that gave women business owners an intimate look at the lending process. Representatives from the bank played a banker and a customer in a skit of what to expect when applying for a loan. The bank then took it one step further and staged a mock loan review committee.

"We wanted women to understand why we ask the questions we do so they don't think that bankers are picking on them," says

Phillips. "We also wanted them to understand how and why we lend money."

Phillips maintains that education and understanding will continue to be the cornerstones of her program and believes that these two tenets are the only things that will propel women financially strong into the twenty-first century. "Women combine these traits with perseverance, patience, and openness to make their strategies work, and in our loyal, steadfast market, that will keep generating business for years to come."

Joan Helpern, co-CEO, Joan & David, agrees that education and understanding of the business of finance is critical to any businesswoman's lasting success. Joan Helpern recently applied these principles when she and her husband completely reinvented their business. They literally started a new form of taking a business forward when they chose to end a business relationship that was producing 60 percent of their volume.

In just four years, Joan & David saw through the vision they implemented when they avoided the pitfall of the dissolution of a longstanding business relationship with Ann Taylor. Tapping into their resources, they replaced their main method of distribution with forty-three stand-alone boutiques, including flagship stores in Paris, London, and Hong Kong, that carry a full range of footwear, ready-to-wear, and accessories, which Joan Helpern designs and produces in Italy. Joan Helpern has turned her company into a major worldwide fashion leader with a volume of over $100 million due to good business sense and a knowledge of who her consumer is and what he and she would like. She did this with no long-term debt and not a single person fired.

Helpern strongly attributes her success to conducting business in the many similar ways that men have. "We're not doing anything unusual or unique, we're doing it the normal way." Helpern believes that often women create obstacles for themselves by acting as though things are not possible. "I never believed, for one moment, that I couldn't run a successful business."

As a financial mentor to other women, Helpern provides tips for succeeding when you need to grow your business. "Our biggest challenge has been to reinvent new ways of doing business, ways that don't degrade the consumer, give her an inferior product, or compromise our distribution," says Helpern. According to Helpern, who had to restructure her entire company in a matter of months, traditional funding doesn't work, and she believes women have to constantly network and look at creative methods for generating money for their business.

So, if the reality is that woman-owned businesses are not very different from other businesses in their financial and business successes, why are banks generally hesitant to loan women money, and why do women entrepreneurs feel they are treated by banks as if they are less viable or less creditworthy?

Banks are usually hesitant to make small commercial loans (under $50,000) because they are not particularly cost-effective. It's unfortunate, but true, that the most obvious money source, banks, are the least receptive to female entrepreneurs. Common reasons for denial include insufficient owner equity in the business, lack of an established earnings history, a history of past-due trade or loan payments, and insufficient collateral.

There's also history. Like it or not, lenders and other vendors have tended to look at a woman's business as her hobby. Moreover, women historically don't have the networks of business contacts that, in effect, presell her to vendors.

And although it should be obvious, entrepreneurs—whether male or female—and bankers are two very different breeds. "Entrepreneurs accept, even thrive on, risk and uncertainty," says Maltby, "two words that give bankers palpitations.

"But the world is changing. These changes are coming about not because it is currently fashionable to romance small businesses, but because of deeper structural changes in the nature of banking and of small business in our society." Maltby points out three major changes in particular that are mutually beneficial, enabling small businesses to grow and helping banks to both grow and serve their communities:

1. The rise in the number and prominence of women-owned businesses
2. The emergence of small businesses as a significant force in the American economy
3. The changing structure of competition in the banking industry

Is what Maltby says true? Statistics show that women entrepreneurs often borrow short-term funds from commercial finance companies by offering inventories, receivables, and other similar holdings as collateral. Although many personal finance companies are willing to extend loans, the high interest rates these firms usually charge does not generally make them a viable source for the savvy entrepreneur.

Because these traditional lending channels often present many obstacles, more than 80 percent of new entrepreneurs start their businesses without any commercial loans or debt financing. The following sections present traditional avenues that work only for a limited number of women-owned businesses. The SBA has recognized this and has created a women's loan component, to assist women in obtaining a higher percentage of loans. In addition, as Maltby insists, banks and finance companies are beginning to realize that women-owned businesses succeed in higher numbers and are starting to capitalize on that trend by actively developing programs to assist women.

In *The Smart Woman's Guide to Starting a Business,* author Vickie L. Montgomery discusses "the five C's of Lending." She maintains that whether you seek financing from friends, family, or a commercial bank or savings and loan, your requests for financing will be based on five C's: credit, credentials, character, capacity, and collateral. Almost certainly your credit will be reviewed; lenders will expect you to be knowledgeable about both your business and your industry; your individual character will certainly be assessed; lenders must be assured that the capacity exists for you to handle the debt structure proposed; and collateral is a lender's "safety net" for loaning you money.

According to Montgomery, "Understanding and preparing for these five C's will go a long way toward achieving your goal, the funding of your dream. Preparation starts long before you are ready to open the doors. Credit takes time to establish. Credentials must be mastered. Character is a lifelong commitment. Yet, without these, financing will be difficult, if not impossible, to achieve."

Tricks of the Trade

Joan Helpern, Joan & David, on what to consider when you need to move quickly to get cash:

1. *Find female bankers!* Women need other women. Call it kindred spirit, but Helpern believes that women loan officers and managers bring a certain sensitivity to the business that their male counterparts don't.
2. *Develop relationships with other women who don't see things like a textbook.* "Innovative thinking is the only component of successful business that people don't spend enough time considering. You have to think constantly about how to push the barriers and partner with other like-minded women to achieve your business goals."
3. *Remember, no path has ever been forged that is the only path.* Be creative! Be bold! Don't dismiss an idea or concept simply because it hasn't been done before. "What makes me unique is that I took a nonexistent area and by accident was forced to become an international businesswoman who did all my manufacturing in Italy. When the U.S. factories refused to produce a little of this and a little of that, I was forced to find factories with a mind-set that could reach beyond mass manufacturing. My willingness to explore my options is the only reason I found vendors in Italy I could work with."
4. *Surround yourself with people who are more business savvy than you.* "I do all my own designs, and I play a very important strategic role in the finances and overall direction of my

company. But I'm weakest, probably, in the day-to-day operations. So I hire competent managers who learn how to run my business, and I count on their expertise to manage the stores and report on trends."

5. *If you're in a crisis, you're allowed to fall apart only for twenty-four hours before addressing the solution.* You must react only for a time and then examine your business and look at concrete, serious, and positive ways to change your situation. You must consult your network and come up with a list of action steps.

6. *Remember that running a business is not a democracy.* The truth is, someone in your company needs to be held accountable for financial decisions and be able to act assuredly when it comes time to make those decisions. "I'm all for consultation and advice, but I hate when decisions don't get made because someone—usually the head of the company—is noncommittal. I've seen a lot of missed opportunities because businesswomen, for whatever reason, don't feel empowered to make decisions."

∗   ∗   ∗

Small Business Investment Corporations (SBICs)

Private companies that were authorized by Congress in the 1950s, SBICs are funded by the Small Business Administration (SBA) and licensed to provide financial services to small businesses in the form of equity/venture financing for modernization and expansion. Interested in purchasing stock in a small corporation that shows a promise of success, the SBIC usually wants to become involved in the actual day-to-day business operations, often in the form of providing management direction. You should decide whether this is acceptable to you before seeking this type of financing. Minority Enterprise Small Business Investment Corporations (MESBICs) have been licensed by the federal government to provide the same kind of aid to small enterprises owned by minorities.

Multiple Loan Assistance and Support from the SBA

The U.S. Small Business Administration is an agency that every woman should call on. This independent federal agency's primary function is to assist and counsel the millions of American small businesses—primarily through financial assistance, management training, and counseling. The SBA's Office of Women's Business Ownership offers a host of specialized services, including financial assistance, free publications, and a counseling program.

The most common loans the SBA offers are funded through the SBA 7A program, which is structured to provide lenders with an additional tool for constructing long-term lending packages for small businesses. Contrary to popular belief, the SBA rarely lends money itself directly to individuals. Rather, its primary lending function is to act as a guarantor to financial institutions. The SBA is set up to encourage banks to accept the higher risk associated with smaller companies and to offer its lenders more favorable terms.

The SBA will guarantee a loan of up to 90 percent (to a maximum of $750,000), and the terms depend upon the type of loan requested. Working capital and inventory loans can be financed for up to seven years. Currently there is no official minimum on SBA lending programs, but in reality banks have imposed voluntary minimums (often above $50,000).

Women account for less than 10 percent of all SBA loans. The SBA is attempting to increase this percentage to a minimum 15 percent. For example, the microloan program, which is designed to assist entrepreneurs in the inner city and rural areas to form small businesses, is targeted toward women. There are also the low-paperwork loans, referred to as the Low Doc program, which reduce the amount of paperwork required on loans under $100,000. The SBA paperwork requires business owners to submit only one form, along with three years of tax returns.

The Southwest Los Angeles County Small Business Development Center is one of the many small-business development centers that have minority and women prequalification loan programs, which basically help eligible small businesses access capital through the coordinated efforts of both the public and the private sectors. Here's how it works: A prospective borrower works with the Small Business Development Center to develop a viable loan application. The application is then submitted directly to the SBA for expedited consideration of a loan prequalification. On approval, the intermediary can also assist the applicant in locating a competitive lender. All owners and guarantors need to submit a business financial statement or tax returns and personal financial statements, and applications from new businesses require the submission of a business plan. Loan funds can be used for normal business purposes, such as working capital, debt payment, equipment and inventory purchases, and the construction and purchasing of real estate; the program is for loan requests of $250,000 or less.

Many women have criticized the Small Business Administration for failing to respond to the financial needs of women who own—or are trying to start up—small businesses. "It's tough to get SBA financing, and you have to have perfect credit," says Nina Brown, president of Women's Collateral Worldwide, a Philadelphia-based venture capital firm. Brown hopes to change the SBA's lack of support by partnering with them to set up the agency's first Small Business Investment Corp. dedicated to funding women-owned businesses. Brown's firm will collect private dollars to be matched up to $40 million by the SBA for the sole benefit of women entrepreneurs.

Lines of Credit

According to a survey conducted by the National Federation of Independent Business, approximately three-quarters of business owners use lines of credit for working capital.

Unlike a regular bank term loan, which is a "onetime deal" with a set payout period of anywhere from one to five years, a "revolving" line of credit is a popular and viable option for entrepreneurs, primarily because you can borrow as little as $5,000 or as much as $1 million, drawing on, and replacing, the funds as needed. At the end of the year, the credit may be renewed. And unlike a term loan, which demands repayment of both interest and principal, a revolving line of credit requires borrowers to pay interest charges only.

A line of credit is generally used to maintain or expand a business—not to start a new one.

Issuing Stock

If your business is a corporation, your charter specifies the amount of shares your corporation is authorized to use, and you may be able to raise equity funds by selling some shares to individuals, making them shareholders and thereby granting them with part ownership of your business.

The big bucks necessary to catapult your fledgling enterprise into the public arena come from private funders who expect to make huge returns on their initial (and often very risky) investments, as well as part ownership (equity) in the company and a say in running it.

An initial public offering (IPO) of company stock is the most common way to generate the huge influx of money needed to satisfy the venture capitalists. Thus the feasibility of going public is often an overriding factor from the very beginning of their evaluation of a start-up company.

In order to go public, a company must register the IPO with the Securities and Exchange Commission (SEC) and become subject to SEC regulations for a publicly held company. The rules are detailed and stringent, aimed primarily at full and accurate disclosure of companies' financial status and protecting investors' interests.

An underwriter, usually an investment banker who also works with the IPO-issuing company to handle the SEC registration, contracts to buy the IPO. The underwriter then resells the stock either directly or through brokers and dealers and makes a profit on the underwriting spread between the stock's public offering price and the lower price paid the issuing company.

If you're not a corporation, there are other innovative ways to issue stock. Annie's Homegrown, a distributor of gourmet and organic pastas, included stock slips in their macaroni boxes and offered their loyal consumer base an opportunity to buy directly from them. "This way our customers own a part of the business, and who will better advocate for us?" offers Deborah Churchill Luster, president of Annie's.

Credit Unions

Credit unions are often viable sources of capital. Since most are member oriented, you have an advantage as an active member, especially if you have established a borrowing history with the credit union. The interest on the money you borrow is often much lower than if you were to seek a loan from a more traditional lending source, such as a bank. Because credit unions tend to be more customer service oriented and relationship based, they will work with you to help you obtain financing. And while most credit unions don't have business loans per se, you can achieve some creative financing by applying for a personal loan or a line of credit at a reduced interest rate and using that money to grow your business.

Business Incubators

The trend for the 1990s in business financing is a lender known as a "business incubator." There are thousands of business incubators in the United States, and this number is increasing every year. Intended to bring businesses together to increase their successes, the philosophy helps stimulate economic development while at the same time fostering the entrepreneurial mind-set. A business incubator provides both office space and services for entrepreneurs, along with office support services, business management, and financial assistance. The National Business Incubation Association publishes a directory of incubators; for information, write to them at One President Street,

Athens, OH 45701. Although these incubators usually make more sense for fledgling businesses, they can indeed nurture a business. Although they do not lend cash per se, they lower the cost of the office and personnel in an effort to encourage cash flow for businesses.

Once You're Up and Running:
Why Venture Capitalists Appeal to Many Women Entrepreneurs

Just like men, women business owners face a number of basic problems in raising start-up and growth capital for their businesses. Start-up ventures are very risky, so most entrepreneurs have to rely on their own resources—savings, credit cards, borrowing on a home or life insurance policy—or money from family and friends who believe in them. When it comes time to grow the business, private investors—"angels"—are the most frequent source, with professional venture capital funding less than 1 percent of all businesses for both men and women.

Yet many business owners who experience rapid growth credit venture capitalists as their means for raising capital. Marguerite Sallee, president and CEO of Corporate Childcare, says that part of what enabled her to position her company for 1,000 percent growth over the last five years was her aggressive approach to raising capital. As the founder of a Nashville-based company that develops and manages employer-sponsored child care centers, Sallee began teaming up with some influential investors and was able to secure venture capital in her second year of operation. In 1989 she sold 20 percent of the company to the Marriott Corporation—this investment supported Corporate Childcare in earning $25 million in annual revenues in 1994.

In search of $2.5 million in venture capital to expand her already established software firm, Louise Short demanded the undivided attention of one hundred potential business investors at an annual meeting of the Oklahoma Investment Forum, a program sponsored by the Tulsa Chamber of Commerce to match investors, primarily venture capitalists, with entrepreneurs. At this forum Short described her two-year-old business's capital needs and presented her long-range sales projections for her marketing multimedia soft-ware to the educational and entertainment markets. Following her presentation, eight venture capital investors spoke to Short about gaining a stake in her growing company.

Venture capital is money invested in a business in return for par-tial ownership. As such, it is usually used to fund high-risk busi-nesses that show the potential for high profit. Venture capitalists, whether they are private individuals or small investment groups, make their profits by selling shares of stock of the successful ven-tures to the general public. Although many won't become involved in new, risky businesses, others can be a good source of income once you have grown a healthy business over the course of several years and are looking for money to expand. Venture investors hope that small firms they invest in will perform so well that their initial investment will grow substantially—from three to five times in ten years or less. After a period of years, assuming the firm is suc-cessful, the investor may choose to sell out—to either the com-pany, the public, or another business that would acquire the company.

Although traditionally conservative, venture capitalists have lately begun to open their doors to women-owned businesses. Alliance Capital, of Houston, Texas, a venture capital firm aimed at women and minorities, often agrees to invest in businesses that exceed a certain amount in sales each year, in exchange for an equity stake.

As a venture capitalist, Esther Dyson, president of EDventure Holdings, believes that investing in high-tech start-ups and playing an active role in those businesses is the way to foster their growth and ultimately make money all the way around. The venture fund's goal is to foster companies that service local markets with local value added. Its investments include New World Publishing, pub-lisher of the *Budapest, Warsaw,* and *Prague Business Journals;* Poland Online, an Internet-based information services start-up; and a share in Scala ECE, with operations throughout central and Eastern Europe. "I invested $200,000 in Scala ECE several years ago, and today it is worth more than ten times that amount," says Dyson. "I believe that whatever I invest in demands strategic planning, long-term investment, and careful consideration of all the people involved. It's ultimately the people you're investing in, not just the business plan."

How do women hook up with these venture capitalists? Many venture capitalists say that they seek out compatible business owners who they feel will partner in their philosophies of growing a business. Although the major criticism of venture capitalists is that they play such an active role—sitting on your board, contributing to your marketing plans, and even participating in staff meetings— many business owners find that a strong managerial bent from an established venture capitalist can help take their business one step ahead. Therefore it's critical that as a business owner you understand who is investing in your company; likewise, if you are a venture capitalist, you want to know who the people are who make up your "investment" and whether these are the types of people you can actively work with.

Small-business owners who want to learn more about individual investment forums should pick up *Venture Capital Journal,* a monthly publication from Venture Economics, a New York research firm that specializes in the venture capital industry. Write Securities Data Publishing, 40 West 57th St., 11th floor, New York, NY 10019; or call 1-800-455-5844.

Woman on the Way

*

Esther Dyson
President: EDventure Holdings
Business Philosophy: Sit and listen and absorb from other people—you'll learn invaluable things
Greatest Accomplishment: Still having fun and learning at forty-five!

Esther Dyson was once described by a journalist as one of the "leading savants in the field of information technology." While Harvard educated and extremely well read, Dyson relies a great deal on instinct and opportunity in her business dealings.

"My key to successful investing is to develop long-term partnerships with the companies I fund," says Dyson. While most venture capitalists look primarily to paper—the business plan and extensive financial documentation—Dyson likes to get in and get dirty.

"When I invest," she says, "I'm in for the long haul." Because Dyson's not looking for a get-rich-quick scheme, it makes good sense to her that she understand the owners, the process, and even the employees of the organizations she invests in. "Whatever you invest in, problems will inevitably arise. If you work with people you like and trust, these are the same people you can tackle problems with."

For entrepreneurs seeking capital from venture funds, she offers the following advice: "Don't think of investors as faceless money. They'll want to see where their money is going." In other words, if you don't like the style of your investors, look elsewhere until you find a good match.

✳ ✳ ✳

Tricks of the Trade

Rosalind Paaswell, former president of the American Woman's Economic Development (AWED) Corporation, on the five financial stumbling blocks that women seem susceptible to:

1. *Not understanding the difference between revenue and profit—they're distinctly different.* Your business can be bringing in a ton of sales, but you're not showing a profit. Many things can factor into this, such as overhead, pricing, and distribution. If you figure out the "why," then you can come up with the "how" to fix it.
2. *Reading and understanding financial statements.* If you can't read a cash flow statement, a balance sheet, or a profit and loss document, you've already set yourself up either to be ripped off or to make a bad financial analysis decision. Ask your accountant or financial adviser how to read these three vital forms.
3. *Fear of bringing in a partner or gathering venture capital to take you to the next level.* Although a woman will stop and ask for directions when she's lost, she may be afraid to ask for additional help past her start-up. If you want growth, you have to not only plan for it, but go for it!
4. *Being afraid to try for expansion financing.* This type of financing is often the first bank loan that women aim for. Sometimes they sabotage themselves by projecting that they'll be denied before even applying.
5. *Being reluctant to take financial risks.* Women business owners are a conservative lot, prone to slow growth and limited investment. Yet you can't grow if you're not willing to invest yourself—emotionally and financially—and take the financial risks necessary to build a successful business.

✳ ✳ ✳

How to Land Your First Bank Loan: You May Be the Perfect Candidate

What do banks look for? And how do you determine if you are the "perfect" candidate for a loan? Obviously there are no easy answers. Maybe it's really about building a partnership and finding the right entity to partner with, as many lending organizations have determined. Entrepreneurs tend to think of banks solely in terms of access to capital. And banks tend to think of small business solely as a recipient of lending services. But to build a business, one needs more than just loans—women need counsel, connections, education, support, and chances to network. Believe it or not, those sorts of services are at the heart of the new relationship between small businesses and banks.

What kinds of banks are more likely to lend you money, and how can you look for that perfect lending institution to meet your needs? Many banks are finding innovative ways to stay tied to the women's community and truly stay aware of their needs—financial and otherwise. The whole theme of many of these banks is to educate women about the financial options available to them while creating a forum in which women business owners can create their own networks.

Rosalind Paaswell speaks to this new era of banking: "One source that women need to understand better are the programs that are available through economic development bodies that offer loans to people who can't qualify for conventional funding; also, programs that help you understand the different types of financing. Many women don't understand the difference between debt and equity."

The Busey Bank in Urbana, Illinois, has no formal women's banking center, yet it is committed to serving women business owners by sponsoring focus group lunchrooms and hosting seminars for women business owners. Fleet Bank in Melville, New York, on Long Island, relies on a strong community outreach program to facilitate its ties with local women business owners, one that provides space and equipment to them. The bank and the Urban Development Corporation of New York are participating in the program for minority and women-owned businesses that provides working capital financing of up to 50 percent against contracts with government entities. And targeting women business owners is so important to CoreStates/First Pennsylvania Bank, in Philadelphia, that it is part of the bank's mission statement. In May 1992 First Pennsylvania began specifically targeting women business owners and spent $35,000 in corporate sponsorships, seminars, and workshops. The bank is a corporate partner with the National Association of Women Business Owners (NAWBO), and the Entrepreneurial Edge, a not-for-profit regional group for women business owners, and has an alliance with the Women's Resource Center, an organization that helps women start companies.

In 1994 Pam Davis, vice president of Meridian Bancorp Inc. of Reading, Pennsylvania, formulated a strategy to target the women-owned business market through the Women's Banking Connection. The initiative helps women business owners by planning educational seminars, working actively with NAWBO, and supporting community activities. Meridian is also exploring the development of specialty products for women businesses, says Davis. "Financing is always a top concern for women entrepreneurs, but they're also concerned about not being taken seriously by their male counterparts," says Davis. She believes that the difficulties women face are twofold: First, financial institutions are just beginning to recognize women-owned businesses are an important part of the community; second, there is a learning curve to entrepreneurship. Women simply haven't been in the arena as long as men have. "Yet some large institutions are recognizing the importance that women entrepreneurs bring to the economy and the marketplace," says Davis.

Susan Hatchett, vice president and manager of the Women's Banking Center, says many women become familiar with her only after a traditional lending institution has turned them down for a loan. Hatchett maintains that one of her obligations at the center is educating women on how to obtain financing. Since Small Business Administration loans require a three-year profit, many start-up businesses don't qualify, she explains. "I try to look at the individual loan needs and assets of the business to help get the capital needed so the business can eventually qualify for an SBA loan."

If you are applying for a traditional bank loan or an SBA loan, you should prepare certain documents before you approach a lender. Often these items are on a lender's "most wanted" list:

- A current business balance sheet listing your company's assets, liabilities, and net worth

- Current proof of income statements for the current year, as well as statements for the most recent three fiscal years

- An up-to-date personal financial statement of the proprietor, or of each partner or shareholder owning 20 percent or more of your corporate stock

- A list of collateral to be offered as security for the loan

- A statement explaining the total amount of the financing you are trying to secure and the specific purpose of the loan

- Tax returns for the past three years—both personal or your company's, depending how long you've been in business

If you're looking for something specific from a bank, then you need to do some homework to find the right one for you. Many banks work with customers to draw up business plans and think through growth projections. Often they share all of their financial analysis and sit down with their clients to talk over what it means. Because commercial lending at large banks—historically the core of the banking business—has dropped from 65 percent of the total short-term borrowing of nonfinancial companies to 36 percent, and because banks today much compete with nonbanks such as Sears, American Express, General Electric, and even the Money Store, they are forced to develop partnerships they may have not yet considered or found necessary to survive. Over the last thirty years, as small businesses have been growing, banks have lost their dominance in certain aspects of the financial marketplace. Those shifts have also helped bring banks and businesses together—and it's a shift the woman entrepreneur can't afford to ignore.

Here's a quick preview of some traditional lending institutions that are recognizing women's financial needs in more ways than one:

Wells Fargo Bank, a $51 billion commercial bank, is placing a billion-dollar bet on women-owned businesses. With its newly created loan fund, the first of its kind in the nation, the San Francisco–based bank is allowing established female entrepreneurs to set up credit lines of $5,000 to $50,000 (and, for California-based businesses, up to $100,000). The money, with interest rates from 12.5 percent to 15.5 percent (based on financials and the prime rate), can be used for any business expense, including hiring staffers, updating equipment, buying inventory, and expanding an office. The bank has teamed up with the ten thousand-member-strong National Association of Women Business Owners to hunt for creditworthy female entrepreneurs. "Women business owners are a large segment of the small-business market, and one of the fastest growing," acknowledges Terri Dial, executive vice president of Wells Fargo's Business Banking Group.

Applicants must have clean personal and business credit records, not have filed for bankruptcy protection during the last ten years, and have owned—or, in some cases, played a responsible role in running—a related business. But they don't have to submit tax documents or financial statements, since Wells Fargo will verify information through TRW and Dun & Bradstreet reports. Entrepreneurs who own at least 50 percent of their business can apply via phone (for a forty-eight-hour turnaround). Call (800) 359-3557, ext. 120.

The Minority-owned and Women-owned Business Enterprise (MWBE) Financing Program is offered by Bank of America and is meant to meet the special financing needs of women across the country. To qualify for the MWBE Financing Program, your business must be:

- at least 51 percent owned and operated by one or more individuals who are minorities or women

- in business a minimum of two years

- profitable in its most recent year

Additionally, the business and owner must have a good credit history. With an MWBE loan you may borrow from $2,500 to $50,000, with repayment terms of one to five years.

If you want to assess whether or not you are a key candidate for a bank loan, ask yourself the following questions—and be able to answer them!—since these are the five key issues bankers address when they consider a loan application:

1. *How much money do you want?* Go in with a set figure, and never ask how much a banker is going to lend. If you need to borrow $100,000, then hold firm to that figure, and present the most precise calculations and documents you can assemble to explain why you need to borrow that amount.

2. *How will the loan help your business?* Your banker will want to know that the loan is going to result in a positive gain, whether it be higher sales, additional cash flow, or cost reductions. Be prepared to show this result in hard and fast projections based on the prior success and growth of your company.

3. *How will you repay the lender?* The primary sources of repayment are business proceeds, conversion of assets, or cash flow. You need to be able to document that your business has lasting earning power, which is reflected by a yearlong monthly cash flow statement and quarterly projections for the term of the loan.

4. *How will you repay the lender if your business does not grow as anticipated?* Although "collateral" is the most often quipped response, be sure to have a contingency plan for repaying the lender if you encounter business situations that

are beyond your control and don't survive the growth you project.

5. *What is your personal contribution to the business, and how can you demonstrate savvy business skills?* Do you have any cash that you will contribute? Have you already secured capital in an aggressive or nontraditional way? And what does your credit history look like? "Businesses don't pay the bank back, but people do," is a term that bankers can relate to. Often the only way that bankers can assess the character of a potential borrower is to look at his or her credit report and previous business history.

Regardless of the initial response from the bank, if you stick with the lending process and continue to learn more, you will eventually get a loan. Like anything, lending is a give-and-take experience from which you can gather great volumes of knowledge—information that not only will benefit your business, but will make you a more savvy entrepreneur.

4

Health Care

Whether or not you work in a health-related business, keeping abreast of the major developing issues in health care is an important task for every entrepreneur. New developments in the health care industry—legal reform, technological advances, organizational restructuring, groundbreaking research—are occurring at such a rapid pace that it's difficult to stay up-to-date and informed about the myriad options and opportunities in this vital field.

The growth of managed care organizations, the rise in popularity of alternative medicine, and the general increase in "burnout" and stress as workers log longer hours have all had an impact on the way we view our own health care as well as on the state of health care in general. And unfortunately, statistics indicate that many people continue to consider health care an afterthought. Currently, forty million Americans remain uninsured, and in spite of the recent passage of health care laws designed to aid the small-business person, studies continue to indicate that the self-employed are one of the most underinsured groups in the country.

The time is ripe for entrepreneurs who want to enter the health care industry. The changing face of modern health care has created a need for a variety of health-based businesses—from consulting agencies and databanks that provide medical professionals or consumers with timely research and information, to independent insurance brokers who help subscribers navigate the maze of HMO options. Alternative medicine, with its unique approaches to the prevention and treatment of illness, has become increasingly appealing to consumers and health care practitioners alike, creating still more business opportunities. And any woman who decides to start her own businesses must make health—her own and her employees'—a number one priority.

Woman on the Way

✳

Christiane Northrup, M.D.
Cofounder: Women to Women, Yarmouth, Maine
Business Philosophy: Envisioning health care in a new way
Greatest Accomplishment: Riding through the downside of entrepreneurship and watching the joy return to the business

Christiane Northrup is no ordinary doctor. As past president of the American Holistic Medical Association, she's respected by conventional and alternative practitioners alike. Her recent book, *Women's Bodies, Women's Wisdom,* is quickly rising to meet the respect that *Our Bodies, Our Selves* garnered over twenty years ago.

So why all the hype? Northrup was one of a group of M.D.'s to pioneer what we now understand as "complementary medicine"—that is, the interrelationship between conventional (or Western) medicine and alternative therapies.

Her own business, Women to Women, was founded

in 1985 with lots of good intentions but few sound business practices. "We wanted to be all things to all people," she says, "and ended up feeling like failures." Within two years she was burned out, overstressed, and doing too much. "The irony was that no one was pressuring us; we were doing this to ourselves."

It was difficult to talk to her peers about this, Northrup says, because of a socialization among doctors that is similar to that of alcoholics. "We just don't air our dirty laundry." Finally the situation came to a head, and a ten-day intensive for the business was planned.

"It was very necessary, as a caregiver, to give myself the permission to take care of myself," says Northrup. "I felt the need to be there for everybody, rather than understanding that people have their own inner resources."

Those ten days became a turning point in the business as Northrup learned to set parameters on her involvement in her own business. Learning that she couldn't—and didn't need to—do it all was the best possible revelation she could have had.

Over a decade later Chris Northrup is a published author, writes a monthly newsletter for women, and lectures tirelessly. "Learning to honor my own boundaries in turn made me a better physician," she says. "Now I can better understand the women who come to me with health concerns."

✻ ✻ ✻

The New Business of Health Care

With the sweeping movement toward managed care creating an upsurge in HMO and PPO enrollment, the developing issues that surround the state of medical care are growing more and more complex and, some might argue, depersonalized. It's not surprising, then, that many of the growing business opportunities in this field seek to address the complexities that can arise within an increasingly developed health care system. One of the emerging markets in medicine uses computer technology to assist health care providers in processing the vast amount of data they must use to conduct research and treat their patients. Another growing market works to simplify and personalize medical treatment by offering alternatives to conventional medical care.

Information management firms that monitor and control large electronic databases of medical information perform a much needed service by deconstructing a sometimes convoluted health care system. They work to provide doctors, hospitals, pharmacists, and insurance providers with important updates on medical research, legislation, and other health information. Often these companies also create education and support networks for the ill and their families. One such health information service is the nonprofit Direct Link for the disABLED, founded in 1985 by former microbiologist Linda Lee Harry in Solvang, California. Using a computer database that links fifteen thousand agencies throughout the country, Direct Link provides up-to-date medical information on seven thousand diagnoses, includes information from medical glossaries and journal articles, lists helpful organizations, and even describes various financial and other resources. Harry, who herself suffered severe damage to her immune system through chemical poisoning in the lab in which she worked, began Direct Link partly in response to the frustration she experienced in going through numerous doctor consultations and an eighteen-month wait before ultimately receiving her own diagnosis. Direct Link's volunteer staff fields about fifty calls a day and also takes fax and e-mail inquiries. In addition, the company trains disabled volunteers and prepares them for a return to paying work.

Another firm, HPR Inc., helmed by CEO Marcia J. Radosevich, has developed billing software called CodeReview that helps HMOs and insurers spot the anomalies in the claims process. This software, which can quickly detect if extraneous tests or doctors fees are being billed, has turned HPR into one of the fastest-growing businesses in the country.

On the other end of the spectrum, the field of alternative medicine seeks to reestablish the interpersonal link between doctor and patient and to educate patients so that they feel more in control of their well-being, equipping them with basic preventive- and self-care information. The popularity of alternative medicine is in part due to Americans' newfound interest in a more personalized approach to health. Alternative medicine's guiding philosophy of whole-body health, preventive- and self-care, and nonhierarchical involvement between patient and practitioner appeals to many of the ranks of disaffected HMO members. On average, alternative practitioners such as chiropractors, acupuncturists, homeopaths, and herbalists spend more time per office visit with their patients than do conventional medical practitioners. Alternative practitioners are often more conservative in ordering expensive tests and invasive surgical procedures and in many cases provide more information regarding self-care therapies than do many conventional medical doctors.

Woman on the Way

✳ ✳ ✳

Ana Dumois

Executive Director: Community Family Planning Council, New York City

Business Philosophy: To empower women, through health care, to take charge of their lives, their politics, and their future

Greatest Accomplishment: Spearheading a movement to get mobile health care units out on the streets to serve homeless and low-income women

In the 1950s she was a member of the underground in her native Cuba. Today the revolution Ana Dumois seeks is in health care. During her first nine months as executive director of the Community Family Planning Council (CFPC) in New York City, the chair behind her desk stayed empty. The avid motorcyclist was off and running, meeting people in the communities the council serves, listening to their needs, talking to workers, and making plans. When she finally sat in her desk chair, she discovered it was broken. Dumois hasn't sat much since. For the last decade she's been busy creating new systems, focusing the two-hundred-member staff on delivering innovative, culturally sensitive health and community services—such as same-site HIV and gynecological care, child care, financial planning, and bereavement counseling—to five specific low-income neighborhoods in New York City.

The council's eight clinics serve diverse communities in some of the city's most beleaguered areas. To expand their reach, Dumois added two mobile units. The "health centers on wheels" reach out to homeless people, sex workers, undocumented immigrants, and substance abusers. For Dumois, providing health care to homeless pregnant women is a special concern. (Since the mobile units were implemented, prenatal visits by homeless women have increased from an average of one and a half visits per pregnancy to five and a half.) Empowering women is at the heart of all she does. Dumois says: "I've spent the last decade creating the roots. I'll spend the next one creating a movement. If you raise a woman's aspirations, her expectations, you raise her power. We can begin to change the country."

Mobilizing communities to advocate on behalf of

women's health care is at the heart of what Dumois does. But she's also set on running her nonprofit seriously. "As a nonprofit, we have to fulfill our social responsibility. But we also need to run our business like a business, and look at things like bottom line and productivity. The trick is, you can never let the bottom line affect the people you are serving—never let your obsession with your business override social justice and the advancement of the people you serve." Dumois admits that it's a fine line to walk and says she's always asking herself key questions: Are we utilizing our funds correctly? Are we meeting the needs of the community appropriately? Is my overall strategy on track?

Dumois does not have a formal business plan, but rather relies on needs assessment surveys to guide her business, and she has conducted three to four over the last twelve years. "It may be a bit unorthodox, but the strategic planning is in my head. I constantly monitor the political and health care environments and make my projections. Once a year, our managers attend a retreat to review all our assumptions and strategies; we meet with our board often to stay on track; and we work with an advisory committee to come up with innovative ideas and basic grass-roots fund-raising." One example is the "Buy a Brick" program in Crown Heights Brooklyn, which allows members of the community to buy a brick from the center to help repay a loan the center took out several years ago to construct new clinics.

Her words of wisdom to women starting a business? "You have to ask yourself some very tough questions. Questions like What is my purpose in life? Who am I? What do I want to accomplish through my business? How do I want my epitaph to read? Can I create a working environment that allows me to enforce my values, beliefs, and philosophy?"

Dumois asks those questions and adds her latest personal one for health care: How can we use the tools of the business-making community in order to advance our nonprofit mission? Currently the center is exploring community-based home health care services and has started incorporating with other community-based organizations—merging resources with other centers to serve more women. "In every other business, major corporations are merging, so why shouldn't nonprofits look at starting nonprofit branches?" questions Dumois. "We cannot operate in a vacuum. I question whether we are going to survive the twenty-first century and be relevant as a community-based organization if we don't look at some long-term for-profit strategic planning."

When asked about her programs and all of their benefits to women, Dumois is very modest. "We don't have a choice but to serve. If we want to change the community, we must equip the girls of today with knowledge about birth control, their bodies, and safe sex. These young girls are the women of tomorrow."

✳ ✳ ✳

Why Women Are Drawn to Health-Related Fields

As the health care industry continues to undergo reform and modification, one thing remains a constant: women make up a large proportion of the health care industry. Women continue to outnumber men in social service professions like social work, more women than men are nurses and doctors' assistants, and by the year 2000 it is projected that at least half of all first-year medical students will be women. What is it about the health care field that draws women in such large numbers?

Ironically, although women make up to 70 to 90 percent of the health care decisions for themselves and their family, many feel alienated from the health care system when it comes to getting adequate treatment themselves. Statistics indicate that women are twice as likely as men to be talked to in a condescending manner by their physicians and to be told a condition is "all in their heads." One recent study indicated that 41 percent of women (as opposed to 27 percent of men) had changed physicians because they were dissatisfied with their care. And other studies indicate that women are much more likely than men to be misdiagnosed, have unnecessary surgery, and not get needed cancer and heart disease screenings.

Many women drawn to the health care industry seek to employ a unique model for doing business that transforms the hierarchy of classic conventional medicine into a more cooperative system. By working within the medical field themselves, women can educate and help empower their clients to regain a sense of control over their health and their bodies. Linda Lee Harry's Direct Link is one example. In a recent profile of Direct Link in the *Los Angeles Times,* Harry describes the goal of her organization: "We want to be educators, teach you how to help yourself. . . . You need to be your own best advocate, and you can't be if you don't know."

While the "nurturer" stereotype has its limitations, many women who work in the health industry capitalize on the fact that they are more comfortable in the caregiver role than many of their male counterparts. Many of the "new breed" of female medical practitioners consciously design their practices with women's health interests and issues in mind. Simultaneously, an increasing number of women are choosing female physicians, nurse practitioners, and even nurse-midwives for their own care in hopes of closing the gender/communications gap between themselves and their doctor. Certified nurse-midwives, in particular, are currently in high demand—by 2001 the number of practicing nurse-midwives is projected to triple from the current 3,500 to over 10,000. Women who choose midwives for prenatal care and childbirth often cite the more comfortable and relaxing birthing environs and the calmer and more intimate birthing experience. Unlike many conventional obstetrician-gynecologists, nurse-midwives do not "medicalize" pregnancy, but treat childbirth as a normal, natural process. The midwife's approach appeals to many women who have been conditioned to view pregnancy as a medical condition that requires a doctor's regular medical intervention and supervision. This field's resurgence in popularity is especially gratifying when viewed through the lens of history: in the nineteenth century, a financially motivated, physician-organized campaign virtually eradicated the practice of midwifery in America.

Marcia Radosevich suggests that women considering a career in the health care industries understand that it's an industry in tremendous flux. "In periods of great change come great opportunities." She highly recommends her process: "I picked an industry first, then a job within the industry."

Taking Care of Business: Providing Health Benefits

At some point, most entrepreneurs are faced with the question of whether to provide health insurance for their employees. The advantages of providing health benefits are obvious: benefits make a business a more attractive place to work, and statistics indicate that employees who have access to regular health care lose less time from work and report greater job satisfaction. However, the cost of premiums can seem prohibitive, and deciding on what type of plan to offer can be confusing if you're not prepared to ask the right questions. What are your employees' specific needs? How much can you afford to spend on a plan—do you want to split the cost of premiums with your employees? What are the tax advantages to you and to your employees?

Thanks to recent legislation, the small-business owner who wants to provide health insurance for her employees is better off now than she was a few years ago. Self-employed people can also get a bigger tax break on policies they buy for themselves. Insurance companies, under pressure from elected officials and small-business lobbying groups, are beginning to provide more affordable coverage for small companies. However, it's still important to do a fair amount of research before choosing a health plan, as you'll find a wide range of cost and coverage.

Health Insurance—Options, Alternatives, What's Available Now

Providing an HMO (health maintenance organization) or PPO (preferred provider organization) plan is often the most affordable option for the small-business person, but it's a good idea to carefully examine all of your options before deciding on what suits your company's needs. HMO and PPO plans offer medical services to a group of employees from a network of hospitals and doctors. Subscribers choose a primary physician and must get the primary doctor's authorization before seeing a specialist or undergoing medical or surgical procedures. Subscribers pay a nominal "copayment" for doctor's visits and prescriptions and, depending on the employer's plan, may pay a monthly portion of the insurance premium. PPO members, in addition to these services, may choose from a larger group of doctors. Members can also elect to see doctors outside of their group, with their insurance covering a percentage of the cost.

A currently less common (and usually less affordable) form of employee health benefits is the traditional indemnity/reimbursement insurance plan. Subscribers to this type of plan have the freedom to pick the doctor(s) and hospital of their choice, but instead of copayments, they must pay a percentage of medical fees as well as a monthly premium. Indemnity plan subscribers pay their percentage of the medical costs at the time of the doctor's visit, and their insurer pays the balance. Reimbursement plan subscribers pay their entire bill and then submit a claim to their insurance provider for reimbursement.

Other—and more radical—forms of health insurance include high-deductible catastrophic health care policies, which are less expensive. Christiane Northrup, M.D., recommends that you encourage your employees to take responsibility for their health care by offering them a monthly stipend equivalent to the standard health insurance premium. "This way, the employees can bank the money, invest it, or spend it on something else," she explains. "If they want to go to a chiropractor or an osteopath, it's their money. If they want to get plastic surgery or join a health club, it's up to them. If they choose to spend it on Fritos and beer, that's their decision as well."

Tricks of the Trade

Marcia Radosevich of HPR Inc., on determining what type of insurance plan is most appropriate for you and your employees using a "benefits checklist":

1. *Cost.* How much does the insurance policy cost? Is the rate guaranteed for a given length of time? Will everyone's premiums go up if one employee makes a major insurance claim? How is the billing schedule structured?

2. *Coverage.* What is the maximum coverage? What medical services are covered? How (if at all) do preexisting conditions affect coverage? Do my employees have specific needs that can be met by this plan? How does the plan cover prescription drugs? Can employee family members be covered under the same plan?

3. *Service.* Does the plan have a satisfactory level of customer service? How long does it take to get a claim processed? Does the plan offer a good selection of physicians? How easy is it to change physicians? Is there an adequate number of doctor and hospital locations within the service area? Does the plan offer special health programs, such as prenatal care classes or smoking cessation? Are published reports on the plan's performance available?

✳ ✳ ✳

Entrepreneurs who operate small start-up companies may consider the cost of an insurance plan beyond their initial needs. With many plans, coverage is more expensive for smaller groups. There are other options for small-business owners who are currently unable to provide the coverage of a group plan but want to take steps to help protect their employees' health.

One option for employers who can't afford to pay the premium for group coverage is to offer a deductible plan in which employees pay an annual deductible (between several hundred to one thousand dollars) before their coverage is activated. At the very least, employers can offer "catastrophic" coverage with a higher deductible that would enable employees to receive hospital care in the case of accident or serious illness. A pilot program being tested by 750,000 small businesses may soon become another option. The "medical savings accounts" program allows employers with less than fifty workers or the self-employed to make tax-deductible contributions to a medical account to pay for expenses not covered in a medical plan with high deductibles. Money that is not used can earn interest tax-free, similar to an IRA. Account funds not used for medical expenses are considered income. If money is withdrawn from the account, other than for medical expenses, before age sixty-five, there is a 15 percent additional tax penalty.

Entrepreneurs may also want to consider purchasing life insurance and disability insurance plans for their employees. Group term life insurance is the most common kind of life insurance used by small businesses, and the premium payments are tax-deductible for employer and employees. Often the plan is set up so that employees can contribute to the initial coverage at no additional cost to their employer. Disability insurance is more costly than life insurance, but for many entrepreneurs it's an important consideration. Disability insurance ensures that policy holders do not lose their entire source of income if they are unable to work because of illness or injury. Costs of disability benefits can vary—employers can take a tax deduction on the benefits, and some policies allow businesses to split the cost of premiums between employer and employee, the type of occupation or business can determine the level of premiums, and so on. Entrepreneurs with no employees may be especially interested in purchasing disability insurance—their personal livelihood may be the only thing that keeps their businesses afloat.

Managing Anxiety, Stress, and Burnout

With the sometimes seemingly irreconcilable demands of work and family, the long work hours, and the unique responsibilities of running a small business, women entrepreneurs are especially susceptible to the destructive forces of stress. It can be easy to forget to incorporate the most basic building blocks of good health—adequate exercise, sleep, and nutrition—into your life plan at the same time that you're implementing a new business plan. But finding time for personal health care is vital for the entrepreneur. In her book *Inc. Your Dreams,* Rebecca Maddox acknowledges the entrepreneur's tendency to neglect her health, then cautions, "As a business owner, how well you take care of yourself has a direct influence on your success. . . . On the most basic level, all you have is your body, mind, and soul." Maddox emphasizes the importance of creating a contract with yourself to keep scheduled doctor's appointments, eat healthy meals at regular intervals, sleep a minimum number of hours per night, and incorporate physical exercise into your weekly (or even daily) routine.

According to Dr. Alice Domar, Ph.D., chief of the women's health programs at Harvard Medical School's Division of Behavioral Medicine and Mind/Body Medical Institute, stress is the number one health problem facing women today. Recent studies indicate that job-related stress costs American businesses $60 million annually and that 70 to 80 percent of people who visit a physician each year suffer from a stress-related disorder. The physical effects of chronic stress take an especially heavy toll on women, and women entrepreneurs are even more vulnerable.

For Laura Gasparis-Vonfrolio, entrepreneurship was the solution to stress and burnout. As a critical care nurse in Staten Island, New York, she was increasingly frustrated by what she perceived as a lack of respect. "When you're working in a hospital, the biggest challenge is to your self-esteem," she remarks. "If you have suggestions or voice your opinion, you get knocked down."

It was this understanding that motivated Gasparis-Vonfrolio to break free of the corporate hospital environment and establish herself as the publisher of *REVOLUTION: The Journal of Nurse Empowerment.* Sick of the bureaucracy that silenced nurses' voices, she raised $250,000 to start up the new venture.

"We do not accept any advertising dollars whatsoever from anyone who may want to dictate our editorial content—hospitals, pharmaceutical companies, and so on." Vonfrolio strives to publish information here that nurses wouldn't be able to find anywhere else. "Some of the best nurses get fired simply for providing good nursing care," she says. *REVOLUTION* helps them better understand their rights and how they can prevent this patriarchal backlash from doctors.

The stress of attending to the variety of responsibilities business owners face in the day-to-day operation of their businesses is compounded by the pressure of maintaining family relationships and preserving an adequate amount of personal time. The entrepreneurial "I can do it all" attitude may ultimately be what makes small-business owners so prone to stress-related disorders. Many counselors and psychologists recommend that the burned-out entrepreneur complete a careful self-evaluation that itemizes each of the major factors in her life that triggers stress, then note the physical and emotional impact stress has on her mind and body. Does your stress cause insomnia? Headaches? Back and neck pain? Does it make you feel depressed, irritable, isolated, demoralized? Once you understand the main causes of stress in your life, you should be able to take steps to minimize or eliminate the problems. Entrepreneurs need to recognize their limitations and set boundaries so that they can preserve a modest amount of their time and energy for things outside their work. The business can't run itself, but it shouldn't end up running you. Support from family and friends, adequate physical activity, and unstructured leisure time all help to mediate the effects of stress.

When the inevitable stress does hit, relaxation exercises can help entrepreneurs increase their coping mechanism. A stress management workshop, a yoga class, or a book on mind-body techniques can provide instruction on meditation, deep breathing exercises, or stretches that can relieve tension and bring a sense of calm to home and work environments. It may also be helpful to talk to your regular doctor about stress support—he or she may have special nutritional and other medical recommendations.

Marcia Radosevich, CEO of HPR Inc., advocates taking personal time for stress management. "It's important to take the time necessary to care for yourself. I exercise regularly and do yoga. Sometimes I have to force myself to go on vacation—but I understand the benefits."

Healthy Employees Make a Healthy Company

Why we fall victim to chronic conditions such as heart disease, cancer, and stress, and how we can alter patterns in our lives to prevent these illnesses, are among the key subjects of modern medical research. According to the National Centers for Disease Control, more than 60 percent of all disease is caused by lifestyle factors such as smoking, poor diet and nutrition, and lack of exercise. The shift from a curative to a preventive focus on chronic illnesses such as cancer and heart disease has not only changed our national conception of health, but has forced business to reevaluate its stance on this important issue. Whereas business owners once viewed employee health and job performance as two distinct issues, more and more employers are beginning to incorporate wellness programs into the workplace environment, with positive results. It comes as no surprise that research indicates healthy employees perform better on the job and report higher job satisfaction.

While few small-business owners can afford to offer programs such as on-site workout facilities, there are steps even new entrepreneurs can take to increase employee job satisfaction and help the workplace at large remain a healthy environment. Smoking cessation classes, nutrition bulletins, and workshops on stress management are low-cost programs entrepreneurs can offer to educate employees on healthier lifestyle choices. Company-sponsored recreational activities like "Bowling Night" or a company softball team can boost morale and physical activity. You can set up a "Health Account" pool into which employees can contribute money for monthly or quarterly health-related office activities (such as a visit to a spa, a hiking trip, a sailing expedition). Some companies designate a private "relaxation room" where employees can escape to "destress" on a coffee or lunch break. Others offer an extended lunch hour and a slightly longer workday so that employees can use their midday break to work out. Measures as simple as designating the office area "nonsmoking" and substituting bagels for doughnuts at the morning coffee break can project a healthier company philosophy. Marcia Radosevich says, "I empower my employees to take care of themselves, mentally and spiritually."

Creating a healthy company extends beyond providing insurance benefits, education, and fitness programs. Many entrepreneurs strive to create a company philosophy built on respect, communication, and empowerment. The company Tom's of Maine calls this effort "doing good" and drafted a "statement of beliefs" that, in part, illustrates their commitment to cultivating good relationships interdepartmentally as well as within the greater community. Tom's of Maine's mission statement adds on to the statement of beliefs, pledging a healthy work environment that "encourages openness, creativity, self-discipline, and growth" and stressing the importance of respect, teamwork, fair compensation, and the acknowledgment of each individual's contribution to company goals. The company also made a concerted and ultimately successful effort to bring more women into management positions, not only promoting company diversity, but, according to Tom Chappell in his book, *The Soul of a Business,* providing "a new perspective that has quickly enhanced our company objectives. . . . [As] a result, Tom's of Maine has become more attentive and responsive to the needs of our customers."

The entrepreneur faces many difficult tasks on the road to creating a successful and vital business. She must understand the complex interrelationship between the health of her business and her employees and find the time to ensure her own physical and emotional well-being. Additionally, many women entrepreneurs must carve a place for family time into their already hectic schedules.

Preparing for a Healthy Future

While doubts about government entitlements such as Medicare and Social Security are cyclically perpetuated, no matter what happens, preparing wisely today for the years you *won't* be working means a better future for yourself and your family.

Choosing Healthy Investments for Yourself and Your Employees

Corporate downsizing and the specter of diminishing Social Security and Medicare benefits have dramatically altered the old concept of job security. The archetype of the "corporate worker" who puts in a faithful fifty years of service at one company is becoming rare, as the demands of a global economy and an electronic marketplace shift to accommodate a growing number of smaller, more flexible businesses. Indeed, financial security and independence is one of the leading factors that draws many small-business owners to entrepreneurship. Keeping a small business "in the black" is a huge accomplishment in itself. But once the business is up and running, what is the best way for entrepreneurs to create plans to help ensure a healthier financial future for themselves as well as for their employees? From companies with one employee to those with one hundred, there are many retirement plan options that may not only help in the building of a nest egg, but can provide a business with valuable tax benefits as well. It's a good idea to talk to an accountant about what type of plan best suits the needs of your particular business, but it doesn't hurt to do some preliminary research before the consultation. The following are some of the most common retirement fund plans for the small-business owner:

401(k) Plan

A 401(k) plan is a salary reduction plan that allows employees to put a percentage of their salary determined by their employer (between 2 and 15 percent and not to exceed approximately $9,000) into a tax-deferred investment account. The portion of the employee's salary put into the 401(k) account is subtracted from the employee's gross income. Many employers match their employees' contributions to the 401(k) plan up to a certain percentage—typically, fifty cents on every dollar. The maximum contribution to a 401(k) plan (or any company savings plan) per year is $30,000 or 25 percent of the employee's income (whichever is less). Depending on what a particular company offers, employees can invest their 401(k) money in options such as company stock, money-market funds, and/or mutual funds. Contributions, including employer's matching funds, and return on 401(k) investments accumulate tax-free. However, if you withdraw the funds before age 59½, there is a 10 percent tax penalty in addition to the regular taxes owed.

Individual Retirement Account (IRA)

Like a 401(k) plan, an IRA is a tax-deferred retirement savings plan. Both the self-employed and those employed by a company can set up one (or more) IRA account(s). Where you set up your IRA depends on what type of investment you plan to put into it. An IRA can be set up through a variety of institutions, including a bank, credit union, mutual fund company, insurance company, savings and loan, or brokerage firm. You can contribute up to $2,000 a year to your IRA, but the entire amount isn't necessarily tax-deductible. If you are self-employed, or your company does not offer a retirement plan (or you are ineligible for it), you can deduct IRA contributions up to $2,000, regardless of your income. If you use a company retirement plan or another qualified retirement plan, the lower your income, the higher your deduction on your IRA. Whether or not your contributions to the IRA are tax-deductible, any capital gains, dividends, or profits from IRA investments are sheltered from taxes as long as they remain in the IRA account. Again, like the 401(k) plan, funds withdrawn before age 59½ are subject to a 10 percent tax penalty.

Keogh Plan

A Keogh plan can be an especially attractive retirement plan option for self-employed people, entrepreneurs who run a small company, or anyone with income from freelance business—the plan typically offers higher deductibles and better tax benefits than an IRA. There are two types of Keoghs: money-purchase and profit-sharing. The main difference is that with the money-purchase Keogh, you must contribute the same fixed percentage of your income every year. The profit-sharing Keogh allows you to vary the percentage you pay into the plan. Both have a cap of $30,000 for yearly contributions, but the money-purchase Keogh allows you to contribute a higher percentage of net earnings. Keoghs are offered through the same financial institutions as IRAs. Entrepreneurs with employees have special considerations when setting up a Keogh. Employers who have Keoghs for themselves must set up Keogh accounts for their employees, and they must contribute an equal percentage to their own and their employees' accounts.

Simplified Employee Pension (SEP) Plan

Simply put, an SEP is an individual retirement account (IRA) that a small business owner can fund for each employee. SEPs, IRAs, and Keoghs have similar rules regarding contributions, withdrawal, and range of investment choices. As with Keoghs, entrepreneurs with employees must set up SEPs for each worker and must contribute the same percentage of income into their employees' accounts that they put into their own. The level of contributions can vary each year, but the maximum is 13.043 percent of income or

$30,000, whichever is less. SEPs are also similar to Keoghs and IRAs in the respect that those who set up SEP accounts are free to place the money into a wide range of investment options, including stocks and bonds, mutual funds, CDs, options, and futures funds.

In addition to the above-mentioned retirement plans, entrepreneurs can set up several other investment options and benefits plans for their employees, including programs that offer profit sharing and/or shares in company stock.

Retirement Fund Plans for Small Businesses

1. 401(k) plan.
2. Individual retirement account (IRA).
3. Keogh plan.
4. Simplified Employee Pension (SEP) plan.

5

Labor and Manufacturing

In the 1970s and '80s, women entrepreneurs who succeeded were thought of as the exceptions. But the 1990s are proving that women are making it big in all kinds of businesses, including those traditionally dominated by men.

It's hard to gauge where it's all going, though, since the government tracks only women who have sole proprietorships, the smallest type of business. However, of those, one-third are women owned, and analysts figure that by the year 2000 women will be at the helm of half of those businesses. Furthermore, a study conducted by the Business Women Leadership Media, Inc., suggests that 48 percent of women-owned businesses are not sole proprietorships. Rather, they are partnerships, corporations, or S Corporations. Even though this study isn't fully comprehensive, it does suggest that a much larger percentage of businesses are run by women in America than ever before.

Most women-owned businesses were started in the 1980s, and as is true of most start-up operations, they were small. But nearly twenty years later, many of those women have thriving businesses pulling in profits of nearly $100 million or more. And a significant percentage of these are nontraditional businesses.

The social climate is certainly contributing to the success of these bold women: fifty years ago it was difficult, if not impossible, for a woman to get a credit card, much less a bank loan, without a male cosigner. These days there are plenty of female bankers, many in high places.

Other resources are also available that help women bypass the obstacles of yesterday. Technology is available to everyone, as are classes, seminars, and an array of business books that educate women on the ways of savvy business practices. Women venturing into the lonely world of male-dominant fields will find those resources especially helpful.

Being a woman can work against you if you take on a nontraditional role, but if you persevere and are good at what you do, eventually you will most likely earn well-deserved respect and realize a good profit. Prejudice may flank you throughout your career, as it has many women who own nontraditional businesses. New investors may avoid handshakes and eye contact with you in the first meeting, focusing instead on your male colleagues. But once the "good old boys" realize who signs the contract and pays the bills, you'll probably be greeted with great reverence.

Christine Thompson, vice president and co-owner—with her six sisters—of Seven Sisters construction in Sedro Wooley, Washington, recalls one such incident. "Our first project was in 1982 when we wired a bus garage for the municipality of metropolitan Seattle (METRO). The project nearly ended our life as Seven Sisters, Inc. Our estimate was wrong in some critical areas, and we were one and one-half times over budget.

"As has happened so many times in the life of our business, a near disaster turned out to be a benefit in the long run. We had messed up, but we didn't make excuses. We completed the job and we made sure that, however slowly, everyone got paid. Not only did we manage to survive our losses, but we also established a long working relationship with METRO and a reputation for hanging tough and making sure we lived up to our commitments."

One empowering quality that carries women through the harsh currents of male-oriented fields is the pleasure they get from their work. In fact, some believe that women measure their success differently from men; while men rely on the dollar signs to gauge their accomplishments, many women regard their success as much in the rapport and satisfaction of their clients, as well as in having a fulfilling personal life, as they do in profits.

Another surefire resource to "make it" outside the lines of convention is to mentor, network, and subcontract with as many other women as possible. The more you utilize women as resources in your business, the more confidence you may gain in your own efforts to succeed. Also, since women have markedly differing managerial styles from those of men (women tend to use open-door policies more, be less autocratic, and encourage a team effort throughout the company), other women will have tips for you that could contribute greatly to the building of your business.

Rising Up through the Ranks: Paying Your Dues in Nontraditional Fields

If you want to, say, sell diesel engine parts to distributors, be prepared for crass comments ("Will you lube our parts upon delivery?"), easy dismissal ("Does your husband know you do this?"), or simple mistrust. But that doesn't mean you shouldn't do it. In fact, once you brave these petty comments and prove yourself to small-minded people, you just may find that your unusual position can actually attract business. After all, if you do what you do better than others, you'll stick out and be in demand, says Christine Thompson.

Every story is slightly different, but many tales reveal a similar message about how women rise to the top in a nontraditional field—namely, open-minded bosses who let a woman function to her greatest capacity, and a woman driven by a desire to be excellent at what she does, willing to educate herself and persevere under often difficult circumstances.

Linda Alvarado owns Alvarado Construction, a multimillion-dollar construction business that has built high-rise office buildings, transportation facilities, and the largest naval reserve training center in the United States. How did she do it?

Like many others with similar accomplishments, she started out as an office worker. She was only a part-time employee in a commercial development company, but she liked it, so she pursued her knowledge of it. Her boss trusted her and delegated work to her, which she completed successfully and promptly. She took classes to learn more about the industry and focused on the technological end of things, which gave her a substantial edge over her male competitors.

After years of hands-on experience and education, Alvarado started her own business with an engineer. About a year later she was completely on her own—and turned down by six banks for a loan she sorely needed. Finally the Small Business Administration approved a $20,000 loan that started her on her way. Even so, being young, Hispanic, and a woman in the construction trade threw her against unyielding resistance, and she found it nearly impossible to get clients. At long last she applied for a women-preferred government contract through the Department of Transportation and got her first big break. That was the beginning of her success and what paved the way for attracting private clients. Now her company is one of the largest, fastest-growing Hispanic businesses in the country.

Paying your dues may mean borrowing money off of credit cards, weeding out business partners who don't have what it takes, and fighting off archaic beliefs from both friends and business professionals. But like Alvarado, you can find ways to conquer, and conquer big.

Many successful women started out by identifying their strengths and weaknesses and acting on those. For instance, if you are a brilliant mechanic but know nothing about business, find another woman who is a master businessperson who knows nothing about mechanics. Pool your resources, start a business, and watch it grow!

One way to speed your success is to leapfrog unnecessary middlemen. If, for example, you manufacture a product that women will eventually buy, consider going directly to the outlets in which the product will be sold—such as department stores, boutiques, and so on. By speaking directly to the people who sell the product, rather than using trade shows, megadistributors, or other middlemen, you'll have vastly more information about what the public wants, what they think of your product, and how well sales are going.

Also, as you're getting started, be sure to investigate the pros and cons of trademarks, copyrights, and patents. Some women have found them invaluable in protecting their products from being ripped off by copycats. Others claim that the expensive legal steps necessary to recoup their losses is prohibitive. Many agree that there is a great deal of piracy on the market, and the best way to ensure that you get your rightful piece of the pie is to produce a superior-quality product sold only through certain venues. That way, even if someone steals your name, your product will outrank the competition, and word of mouth and effective advertising will inform buyers where to get "the real McCoy."

Such is the case with Laurie Snyder, owner and founder of Flap Happy, a company that specializes in headgear and clothing for children. "The majority of my competitors make their product overseas and are serving the mass merchandisers and discounters," says Snyder. "That's not the market I'm going after.

"The big thing I have going for me is my quality and my name. A lot of people will go into stores and say, 'I'm looking for a Flap Happy hat.' And if they are shown the competitor's cheap version, the majority of them know the difference and won't buy it. For me, it's worked very well doing domestic manufacturing for lots of different reasons. Someday we may do something imported, but for now, this is working."

Hire an attorney to help make the best decisions about how to protect your product. Talk to other businesspeople about what they did to ensure their rights, as well as to those who chose legal action to defend their name. What did it cost? Was it worth it? Would they do it differently a second time around?

Tricks of the Trade

Sara Ramsdell of Concrete Quality Consulting, Inc., on making a career work in a nontraditional industry:

1. *Success is doing what you like to do and getting recognition for doing it well.*
2. *Service to the customer has to be more important than the convenience of the employees.* We do whatever they need, whenever they need us.
3. *Expense control is at the heart of it.* Let revenues support purchases. I'd rather go without something I don't absolutely need than go into debt to get it. It seemed silly to get a business loan for a start-up just to pay my own salary.
4. *I think of how I want to be treated when thinking about employees and clients.*
5. *Let your employees know what's going on.* A lot of people keep their employees in the dark about finances. Then their employees think that the money just rolls in and the employer cleans up all the profits. It's essential that they know that we pay payroll taxes, insurance, and other overhead. I invest a lot in on-the-job training and send my employees to seminars. They have a vested interest in the company.

✳   ✳   ✳

Is It Really a Man's World?
Making It in Nontraditional Industries

The nineties are turning out to be a good era for women in nontraditional jobs. According to the *Business Women's Network Directory,* women in nontraditional occupations grew by more than 75 percent between 1994 and 1995. Likewise, organizations that support and train women in these fields have also increased by 75 percent during the same time. Networking with other women in jobs usually held by men also increases information and boosts self-esteem. And there's a lot of networking available to those who pursue it.

Take Claudette Weber. She was a high school dropout, divorced, and a mother of three children all by the age of twenty-one. She got a job as a secretary in a construction office and stuck with it, working her way up the ladder until, in 1980, she started her own company, Brero Construction. Fourteen years later she grossed $23 million and Brero had become the largest women-owned general contracting firm in the United States. One formula for her success: working seventy hours a week and loving it.

With a nod of approval from her male boss, Julie M. Stasch, CEO of Stein & Company, started the Female Employment Initiative Program. She takes a portion of the profits from the $2-billion-a-year construction business and offers seminars, open to the public, to teach women about the construction field. The objective: to increase the number of construction tradeswomen and help them succeed. That includes establishing close working relationships with women in every angle of the construction business from the laborers to the building trade unions to the contractors. Her emphasis is to promote an atmosphere of cooperation instead of the demand for compliance.

Like many other powerful women in these positions, Stasch believes that by employing more women in traditional male jobs, you will alter negative attitudes toward them and, most especially, increase their confidence and skills by dissolving feelings of isolation. Once she has more female comrades, then, believes Stasch, the woman can succeed or fail according to her own merits.

Once a secretary herself, Stasch believes in empowering women through education, seminars, and a voice in how things can improve. Her efforts to assist women in nontraditional roles are exemplary of what women can do to change what used to be considered intractable mind-sets and discrimination.

Another key to ensuring success: Don't take no for an answer. If you don't get what you want, ask why. Then look closely at your proposal or work and see if you can change it to meet the needs of the buyer. Flexibility can take you a long way in a world where the disadvantages may feel much heavier than the advantages.

Things are changing for the better, but the numbers are still terribly imbalanced. There are, for example, only seven thousand female mechanics, accounting for a mere 1 percent of the grease monkeys in this country. But the innovative women among them use their gender as an advantage: smaller hands can find their way deeper into an engine, thus tracking a problem to its source. And for those who believe you have to pump iron and come from the Amazon to be a successful mechanic, take note: as in most every other business, technology offers superior information, service, and products, so the only strength you really need in the garage is the ability to push buttons on a keyboard.

Just ask Karen Valenti, who owns North Hollywood Discount Auto Center. Communication is often the key to her success, as her customers tell her that her "nontechnical speak" is part of her charm. "The use of jargon in car repair intimidates and frustrate customers," notes Valenti, who states that about 75 percent of her customers are women.

"Women are treated like imbeciles when they bring cars in to a mechanic, when it's the mechanic who is the one with the problem—he doesn't know how to communicate," says Valenti. For Valenti's customers, the experience is quite different. "Not only do I fix their car to the best of my abilities," she offers, "I also try to demystify the process for them. It's not the space shuttle."

Tricks of the Trade

Barbara Bissett of Bissett Steel, on staying competitive with bigger companies:

1. *Become an extension of your customers.* Listen to what they are saying as if it will make the difference between your success and failure. It will.
2. *Don't rush to judgment.* Your first instinct is usually to say, "This is going to cost me a half million dollars and it doesn't make any sense." But if you have enough customers telling you the same thing, you've already found a way to pay for it.
3. *Compete on service and quality, not on price.* "Small businesses don't do well in pure price competition."

✳ ✳ ✳

Establishing Credibility for Ultimate Entrepreneurial Growth

Credibility isn't an asset already assumed, like an education or experience—it must be earned. And women who already find themselves facing overwhelming obstacles in nontraditional industries can't take the risk of being labeled "shady" or "dishonest." As your business grows, be aware that your practices will be scrutinized more carefully by clients and competitors trying to gain an advantage in the marketplace.

For Barbara Bissett, owner and president of Bissett Steel, stepping into her father's boots was a lesson in true courage. Taking over after her dad's unexpected death, Bissett had had the experience of working alongside her father and knew the business. But that didn't make the transition smooth. "I've changed just about everything in this company since my dad died. Initially, the employees didn't want to take it from the 'kid.' But I still feel my dad coaching me through this. I was successful because my father saw me as successful.

"People are afraid of change," she says, "and you can't force change down people's throats. So I call this a 'new' old company. I challenged that status quo on just about everything—from computer systems to hiring, managing, motivating, human resources, sales— and have empowered some people in the process." Yet Bissett believes that despite her successes, change comes slowly, and she's prepared to wait it out. "I'm in this for the long haul," she says. "My dad would have it no other way."

Woman on the Way

✳

Laurie Snyder
Owner and Founder: Flap Happy, Santa Monica, California
Business Philosophy: Take a bit and give back more
Greatest Accomplishment: Turning one great product into an entire apparel line

Snyder's innovative company stemmed from a need to keep her fair-skinned baby boy safe from the sun. "I was frustrated because every time I went to go get him hats, they were cute but not protective." So she began to put her husband's baseball cap backward on her son to try to protect him.

One day a friend from New Zealand showed her the perfect hat. "I thought it was really good idea but couldn't find a quality one like it anywhere." She decided to make the hats, having absolutely no idea how to go about it. Snyder put her son in a backpack and went to downtown Los Angeles and started asking around at the sewing shops. "I had to learn really quickly how to get something manufactured. I figured it out."

Simultaneously she received an order from a mail-order catalog. At the time, it was a big order. "It was for twenty dozen hats for their first order, and they gave me a down payment for half of the order, which helped to finance my first production. During that time I had met with a pattern maker, had a pattern made, and found out where to purchase fabric. The first production run ended up taking three months when it should have taken only two weeks."

She didn't take any money out of the business for the first four to four and one-half years. At first people didn't take her seriously, "partly because I was a woman and partly because the product looked so funny, people didn't understand it." She started going to baby shows—going directly to the public to intro-duce her product. "Those mothers and fathers then went to the stores and said, 'Don't you carry this product?'" This created a demand for her product and then, when she'd visit the stores, they were open to it because their consumer was already asking for it.

"Pretty soon I had stores calling me, saying, 'I understand you have a product. I'm interested in it.'

"At these baby shows, I got immediate feedback from both customers who had previously bought the hat and those who knew customers who had. 'Oh, do you have it in this color or print?' or 'Do you make anything to go with it?' This was great, because other-wise they'd be saying that at the retail stores and I would never have heard it."

Today, other mothers and upstart entrepreneurs call

her for advice on their ideas. "I always try to make time for these women, but it gets harder the busier I get," says Snyder. "If it weren't for all the people who helped me, I wouldn't be here today."

✳ ✳ ✳

Ethics: Do You Pass the Test?

Though it's considered a large issue for both big business and small, ethics in the workplace almost always takes a backseat to profit. The reality of America is that behaving ethically costs money, and sometimes a lot of money. Most leaders and employees strive to do what's right for humanity, but when it comes down to closing the business or losing their job, people have a tough choice to make. Is behaving ethically worth losing everything they've worked for?

Usually leaders don't have to make such radically extreme choices, but they do have to be prepared for them. Ethics and credibility go hand in hand in the eye of the consumer, and business owners know that profit and public perception go hand in hand. If the company has a bad reputation, women leaders have found, their market shrinks, their stocks go down in value, and they eventually lose money.

Business owners lament their tough choices. If they act ethically, say, by buying a million-dollar treatment plant for toxic waste, they may become financially unstable. Yet if they act unethically and dump their refuse in the local swimming pond, they are liable to be sued, have profits driven down by public outrage, and decrease employee morale, not to mention that innocent people or the environment will likely be harmed. Many companies pay lip service to ethics while they highly publicize their do-gooder deeds, but more often than not, they are acting unethically in one way or another. To many businesses, having ethics apparently means not getting caught.

According to Faye Becker, owner of Bubbles and Bleach, "The

most important thing in business is credibility. If you don't have credibility, you have nothing. If you lose it, you can never get it back." She strongly believes that your word must mean something. "People have to know that when you say something, it holds water. If it doesn't, soon it will get around to bankers, customers, and vendors—all of whom expect to be treated fairly and honestly."

There are no easy answers to ethical dilemmas, yet there are ways to nip problems in the bud. They sometimes cost money but in the long run will result in a stronger, more effective, and honest company.

Stand by Your Word

Many women business owners have found that if they keep their word on any issue, their employees are more likely to follow the example. It's not easy, leaders recognize, and requires foresight. Knowing when to promise and when not to promise is the mark of the profound leader. Women leaders have found that good behavior must come from the top if it's to be taken seriously.

Have a Written Code of Ethics for Your Business

It should be easy to understand, well written, and designed to help employees make better decisions. While many businesses today do have written ethics codes, often employees don't even know they exist. Effective leaders make their employees aware of the importance of ethics and train them to handle dilemmas well. They also have written consequences for the offenders. These leaders continuously upgrade their ethics code and inform their employees of changes, so the employee learns to act out the company's goals. They also have seminars, workshops, and meetings on ethics to keep the employees abreast of proper behavior. Entrepreneurs know that if they prove to their employees that ethics is a serious matter, their employees will be more apt to perform more ethically.

Enforce the Ethics Code

Women leaders have found that having an ethics code and enforcing an ethics code are two separate issues. Most companies have ethics codes, yet rarely do they enforce them. Larger companies sometimes hire people whose sole jobs are to carry out the company's ethics policy. They are company watchdogs and continuously check on product quality, employee behavior, and public complaints. Corporations sometimes hire ethics experts, auditors, and consultants to ensure that the overall company, from finances to product, is working at its ethical best. In small companies, women leaders sometimes have an ethics hot line, through which employees, management, or customers can anonymously report wrongdoings. Women leaders find that theory is no good without practice.

Reward Ethical Behavior

While many business owners punish employees who behave ethically and jeopardize the bottom line, women leaders are choosing instead to reward those who make ethical decisions. Promotions, raises, and bonuses, they find, will encourage employees to think before they act, respond bravely to tough situations, and find solutions that are ethical and cost-efficient. Not only will the employees behave better, they will have more confidence and feel better about themselves, which results in higher productivity.

Running an Ethical Business

1. Stand by your word.
2. Have a written code of ethics for your business.
3. Enforce the ethics code.
4. Reward ethical behavior.

Workplace Safety: A Legal and Ethical Concern

Women entrepreneurs believe safety in the workplace is a necessity for building credibility with employees and the public. Though accidents happen, many women leaders choose to take preventive measures to avoid as many job-related injuries or deaths as possible. Some companies need better equipment and training but offer employees more money for high-risk jobs, rather than spending the money on preventive measures. But businesswomen caution against this approach—even though many workers would rather have the high salaries. Regardless of the worker's wishes, the government or citizens may see highly publicized accidents as a reflection of the company's poor standards. Moreover, companies may be liable to damaging lawsuits for work-related deaths. Women leaders also suggest that companies will have to shell out large quantities of workmen's compensation in addition to covering the medical bills of injured employees. Further, these companies will have to worry more about absenteeism than businesses that have taken preventive measures. Entrepreneurs also point out that companies that aren't safety conscious fall under the scrutiny of the Occupational Safety and Health Administration (OSHA).

At the same time, women managers recognize that a risk-free environment is almost impossible. There are ways, they believe, to cut down on the number of accidents in relation to job-related activities. They also believe that cost can't be above the preservation of human life.

Personal Protective Equipment

Demanding that employees wear safety protection equipment, such as goggles, work gloves, hard hats, and dust masks, business owners and managers cut down the chance of injuries. In addition to providing the protective equipment, managers should ensure that employees are well trained in its use and upkeep.

Educating Your Workers

Every worker should know all of the equipment inside out, especially heavy machinery, rather than relying on a single safety expert. If employees understand the workings of a machine, they may be able to spot small defects before they become big accidents. A safety specialist servicing an entire operation is likely to miss some potentially hazardous situations, whereas a team of workers will catch many problems. Competent and informed workers will cut down human error–related accidents.

Thorough Safety Evaluations

A piece of equipment that is old, faltering, or poorly designed can wreak havoc on a workforce, unless managers and employees set up daily monitoring of all dangerous equipment. Likewise, when new equipment is purchased, it should be thoroughly reviewed for potential hazards by a group of highly trained experts. Any faulty equipment should be repaired immediately; this increases maintenance costs but will cut down on human injury or death.

Safety Meetings

Gathering together machine operators, managers, and safety specialists can help reduce potential disasters. Discussions at these meetings should include reviewing a course of action in event of a disaster, bringing up new ways to increase safety, and examining any problems that may be occurring. Women leaders know that by stressing the importance of safety, employees will feel valued and operate equipment with knowledge and expertise.

Key Issues in Workplace Safety

1. Personal protective equipment.
2. Educating your workers.
3. Thorough safety evaluations.
4. Safety meetings.

Tricks of the Trade

Dran May-Reese of Trevco on steps to successful product development:

1. *Ask lots of questions.* Continuous research helped Dran May-Reese find a chemist to produce the original adhesive putty.
2. *Don't be afraid of testing.* Laboratory and consumer testing can save money in the long run.
3. *Steer clear of preconceived ideas about production.* Yes, it might be cheaper to manufacture offshore, but it can sometimes be more complicated with fewer assurances at quality control and deliveries. Producing a "Made in America" product can be easier to supervise. Either way, this does not guarantee that products will fly off retail shelves.
4. *Have nothing to prove.* Just because it's your business doesn't mean you know it all. Many beginning entrepreneurs stumble because they simply can't take criticism and advice.
5. *Stay organized.* For many business owners, keeping organized helps them create order in their heads.
6. *Give up power.* Hire people you can and will trust and give them the power to do their jobs well. They'll make mistakes and learn from them, and your company will be better for the investment.

✳   ✳   ✳

Getting the Job Done: How to Get Your Product Made

Many women entrepreneurs start their business at home or in their garage. The tendency of these women is to focus more on the quality of the product than on the promotion of it. Then, through word of mouth and smart business decisions, the business grows.

Once your business outgrows your garage, you must strategize how you want to develop things. Do you want outside investors to get involved, enabling you to quickly grow much bigger but also releasing you from some of the decision-making powers? Or do you want to grow slowly, more methodically, and keep the decisions in your court? What about quality control? How can you maintain that? Will taking on a larger business create more stress than you can handle? Can you be content with a thriving small business? Will you remain more profitable by blasting into a whole new arena, or is a smaller enterprise actually going to bring in the amount of money you need to prosper?

Whether you elect to stay small or reach for the corporate stars, you'll need to move yourself out of the garage and into a place where you can keep up with the demand.

Some people believe that manufacturing items out of the country is the only way to go, since it tends to be less expensive. Others argue that the quality of products made outside the United States is considerably lower than that of those made within the borders. Then there's the time element: if you go overseas, you won't necessarily have your product as soon as you want it. If it's made here, you're more likely to be able to depend on the time frame you were promised.

Woman on the Way

∗

Kathleen A. Allen
Cofounder: Gentech
Business Philosophy: Put the customer on the team
**Greatest Accomplishment: Using her expertise and experi-
ence to help hundreds of college students realize their
dreams of becoming entrepreneurs**

Kathleen Allen, cofounder of Gentech, launched her fledgling company with an innovative new product. The PowerSource is a combination air compressor/generator that allows the user to run air and power tools off the same unit. The unit, which offers power to remote sites, is the product of over four years of development and loads of hands-on research.

By bringing their customer base into the development of the product, the Allens were able to design their prototype to reflect real needs in the marketplace. Even so, launching a product of this size to the trade means taking your chances. "You have to make a commitment if you believe in your product," says Allen, "and take a risk."

Allen maintains a long-standing business partnership with her husband, John. "His role is largely product development, while mine is in the financials, market research, and contacts for distribution."

This is not their first venture together. "At first we weren't mature about work and our marriage. We were bringing our problems home."

While progress had positive effects on their partnership, progress also enabled them to get the jump on their competition and patent the PowerSource. "The construction industry isn't very technical," she says, "but we're hoping to change that." She's excited about the new company and product, but Allen knows best that you can't rest on your laurels. "We're constantly looking for gaps in technology," she says.

* * *

Overseas Distribution

Most foreign markets are growing much faster than domestic ones. So even though finding a good overseas distributor can be a lengthy process, your efforts should pay off nicely. Your main objective must be to find reliable people who have a high level of expertise in the field of the product you are selling.

While investigating distributors, find out what kinds of products they already handle. Whom do they sell to? Why do they think your particular product will do well in that market? Who else from the United States have they represented? Talk to those companies and make sure they've been happy with the distributor.

Once you choose a distributor who suits your needs, be sure to get a written budget of how much it will cost to do business in the country of your choice. Prod the distributor for as much data as possible that will enlighten you as to the length of the process and how well your product will do there. Obtain all legal requirements and restrictions of the country in which you will distribute before committing to anything. What will it take to get your product shipped? How do you transfer moneys?

Sometimes the easiest, most efficient way to distribute your product overseas is to merge with a business that has already established itself in that market. Create a win-win situation where you can take advantage of the structure in which they operate and distribute their goods, while they can profit from your services or a percentage of your sales.

Cooperative business practices can work on many different levels, and new, innovative ways to pool resources are created every day.

Women and minority businesses are ripe for this type of marriage, since they tend to be smaller and can be more flexible with how they fit into the bigger, more corporate infrastructure. If you're a minority woman, check the "Resources" section for specific organizations that will guide you to a big business that could help launch you to your next level of success.

Be sure your distributor is a creative thinker. If you want to sell books about dinosaurs overseas, ask the distributor where he will place them. If his answer is simply, "In bookstores," keep shopping for someone who might answer, "In bookstores, curio shops at the entrances of parks, and at historical sites where people will want to know how the vegetation or wildlife of the area developed and thrived."

The Hot Overseas Market: Is Your Business Right for Import/Export?

It's an exciting time for business because so many foreign markets are open now that weren't even ten years ago. Russia, Germany, even China, have all opened their doors to American products and services with an eye toward making money. That's good news for the entrepreneurs who furnish the goods.

Exporting your goods isn't quite as simple as selling door to door, however. A considerable amount of research is necessary to ensure that your decision to deal overseas is an intelligent one.

Some basic questions to answer: Does your product have a place overseas? If so, where? Look for those areas where competition has not yet set in. Be sure your product fits in nicely with the culture you're considering. If, for example, you manufacture bicycle gears, look carefully at places like Scandinavia or China, where bicycles are the primary mode of transportation. These are the proper markets for you, not ones where people either walk or drive or use boats to get around.

Before shoveling out thousands of dollars on airfare to visit the places you think you might want to do business, call the Department of Commerce and get their mailing list of representatives who live in other countries. If you contact them first, they can alert you to the pros and cons of the place and help you know whether you're on the right track. Also, the Export Small Business Development Center, a nonprofit organization that's both state and federally funded, offers free advice from consultants who know the ropes and can prevent you from tying yourself up in knots before taking the big plunge.

The U.S. Export Assistance Center, One World Trade Center Drive, Suite 1670, Long Beach, CA 90831, (310) 980-4550, provided the following information and can send you a detailed brochure about these and other valuable resources.

U.S. Export Assistance Centers (USEAC)

This organization works with state, local, public, and private organizations as well as with federal agencies such as the U.S. Department of Commerce (USDC), the Export-Import Bank of the U.S., the U.S. Agency for International Development, and the U.S. Small Business Administration. The USEAC coordinates and leverages all available resources to help businesses increase exports and compete in the global marketplace. Counseling is available for businesspeople as well. Marketing specialists can assist in identifying and penetrating new international markets.

U.S. Department of Commerce

In addition to the mailing list just mentioned, the USDC has a worldwide network of commercial officers in international markets, providing market research, counseling, on-site assistance both in America and abroad, and assistance with organizing trade shows and missions.

Eximbank

Can help qualified companies finance the export of U.S. goods and services with working capital guarantees, insurance for foreign receivables, and medium- and long-term loan and guarantee programs.

The Small Business Administration

This versatile government agency assists with financial and business development to boost small business's ability to export. Counseling services are also available to small businesses or new-to-export businesses.

USAID

Supports long-term sustainable economic development in eighty developing countries. Nonprofits should contact this organization for further information.

The National Trade Data Bank

This is a CD-ROM system containing international market information compiled from twenty federal government agencies and is accessible at all Federal Depository Libraries (202-482-1986). Online services are also available for trade leads and the latest overseas commercial information, which is announced through the Economic Bulletin Board through the National Technical Information Service (703-487-4630).

Flash Facts

A free, automated fax service providing timely market research and data for the various international markets. Call the U.S. Export Assistance Center in Long Beach, California, for fax numbers related to the country you're interested in (310-980-4550).

The Agent Distributor Services, Gold Key Service, and Customized Sales Survey

They provide customized services designed to locate viable overseas representatives or partners or market research with specific information such as sales potential, market competitors, sales channels, and pricing of comparable products.

Commercial News USA

A magazine advertising U.S. products and services that is distributed overseas, reaching 650,000 subscribers in 155 countries.

Matchmaker Trade Missions and Catalog Shows

Targets specific industries and is an excellent and cost-effective method of promoting U.S. products and services overseas.

In 1994 the federal government named the top emerging markets for U.S. exports and investment: China, Hong Kong and Taiwan, India, Indonesia, South Korea, Argentina, Brazil, Mexico, Poland, Turkey, and South Africa.

These countries make up more than half of the world's population and contribute more than $2 trillion, or about one-fourth, of the gross domestic product (GDP) of the industrialized world. Many believe that in about fifteen years the GDP of these countries will rise to about half of that of the industrial world.

Meanwhile the Department of Commerce has reported that exporting will increase dramatically as the big emerging markets (BEMs) become more technologically advanced. And with Americans exporting a wide range of technology to these markets, the advances are happening very quickly.

If you're not certain what you might want to export, be reassured: just about anything American is in demand. Indeed, the taste for American goods goes way beyond our technology. Everything from electrical appliances to entertainment systems sells well. Basic food items like sugar is still a rarity in some foreign lands, as are tires, insurance, natural gas, even pollution control devices. It's endless.

Each country has its own needs, and the interested entrepreneur should investigate what the needs are and how she can satisfy them. Check with the State International Trade Offices or private firms like Dun & Bradstreet and ask about *Global Scope,* a tailor-made report on the largest, fastest-growing overseas markets (800-999-3867 ext. 6514).

Keeping the Money Rolling In: Debt Collection

Although some people say that going into debt is inevitable to start a business, most others agree that getting out of debt, and staying out, is one of the wisest financial commitments you can keep. Fortunately there are hundreds of books on money management and debt reduction. Consultants also help balance the books. Whatever approach you take, do it sooner rather than later so the pain of cutting the fat doesn't sting quite so badly.

It's a sad fact that 60 to 90 percent of small businesses fail in five years. Before you even start your business, you might want to implement cost controls. Once your business is up and running, you can take routine debt-preventive measures like closing outlets, reducing staff, and considering, at least temporarily, making your product in a country where you'll save money.

Regardless of how long you've been in business, be sure that your business and marketing plans include aggressively seeking new customers. One of the oldest pitfalls in business is that of sitting comfortably in the lap of an old client who pays well who, for no reason at all, and without warning, may suddenly be gone, along with those cushy revenues. Hence, never let a day go by that doesn't include at least brainstorming about how to attract new business.

The following tips of what to avoid help you steer clear of debt collectors:

1. *Bad customers.* Fully 232 million accounts were passed off to collection agencies in 1991. Bad debt costs the economy $250 each year per person, according to the American Collectors Association in Minneapolis. A thirty-day cycle for receivables helps. Solve collection problems before they start.
2. *Bad employees.* They account for nearly 90 percent of the theft that occurs in businesses. Increase security measures. Be clear with employees of the consequences of theft.
3. *Don't put all your eggs in one basket.* If you rely on one

client and they go belly up, or if they suddenly decide to try someone new, you're left with a mountain of unpaid bills. If you get any messages at all from your biggest client to round things out—such as to hunt for new customers—take it as a gracious tip that they're considering backing out of the relationship.

4. *Ineffective money management.* You need to stay on top of what's going on. Put at least a share of the money you make from your business back into it. Avoid spending it on personal pleasures. Be sure to have a good credit line, but don't come to depend on that. If you pull more money from your credit line than you can repay, you'll end up paying way too much interest. Use bankers, accountants, and a business plan as both reference and a map. If you stray too far, reconsider your direction. Print reports each month so you can know what you're bringing in, what you're spending, what you budgeted, and what you expect to get in next month.

5. *Denial about the money facts.* Use your profit and loss (P&L) statement and balance sheet, which shows what you have and when. Develop a relationship with an accountant you can trust, and use the most basic tools available to keep track of your money; then respond to them according to the information you're getting.

6. *Expensive, ill-fated insurance.* Be sure to shop around for the right insurance. It's expensive, and if it doesn't pay off, you're throwing your money away. Negotiate any kind of price break possible, and be sure to work with your accountant about what portion of your insurance, if any, you can write off.

7. *Ignoring government regulations.* It won't work, and the fines you end up paying may be far more costly than the fees, permits, or regulatory measures you must satisfy. Your business could even be closed down. Look to experts in your industry to help manage it all, including finding a few legal ways around the bureaucratic end of things.

8. *Bad tax management.* It's complicated, because payroll taxes aren't the only consideration . . . benefits, retirement, profit sharing, and so on all enter in. Again, use a qualified accountant to help stave off any grave errors that could catch you off guard and put you deep in the hole. Cash management and taxes are closely related, too. Use your statements to help see clearly what's been done and what needs to be done.

9. *Poorly managed employees.* It's a simple fact—if your employees are happy, believe they're appreciated, and feel as though they play a vital role in the company, they'll be more loyal and less inclined to steal from you. Do what you can to make sure they get what they want and won't take their resentments out on you.

6

Media and Public Opinion

As the number of women business owners increases each year, so do the channels through which they can sell their products or services. The ever-expanding media provides the best possible opportunities for exposing a woman's goods to the marketplace while at the same time creating a powerful venue for her unique talents to shine both in front of and behind the camera.

Women working in the media are becoming more common, although it's clear that men still dominate the airwaves. A 1992 survey conducted by Women, Men, and Media found that 86 percent of the network story interviews aired were conducted by men. At the same time, 79 percent of the sources used to develop those stories were also men, with only one in five of the interviewees women. Only one-quarter to one-third of the total number of correspondents were female. This could be due to the fact that there aren't many women in positions of power to delegate the stories to other women. This is changing slowly.

Meanwhile women are emerging as a behind-the-scenes force in the area of public opinion making. The same needs that drove our foremothers in the suffrage movement to fight for fair representation today motivates women who aspire to become political entrepreneurs. Regardless of what branch of public opinion you seek out, be it advertising, filmmaking, or politics, influencing the way people think, act, vote, or buy is a heady experience.

Combating the Fierce Competition: Making Money among the Industry Giants

A 1992 *Fortune* magazine poll revealed that less than 5 percent of women hold positions within three levels of the CEO in American corporations. The flip side, however, is that according to the United States Small Business Administration, women are opening businesses at twice the rate of men. And for fiscal year 1996, the federal government committed 5 percent of its contracts to women-owned firms. It's estimated that by the year 2000 women-owned businesses will exceed ten million.

These are all good reasons why every woman—from home-based one-person public relations agents to career-minded women determined to break the television networks' glass ceilings—should know what it takes to compete.

Regardless of the size of your business or what channels you choose to promote it, your number one objective must be to satisfy customer needs.

The most effective means of knowing your customers is through surveys or market research. Let's say you produce, direct, and videotape commercials for your local television stations. With such a regional market, you can send out surveys to both existing and potential clients to find out

- how they feel about your overall product or service

- if they think the price is fair

- if they are satisfied with the end result

- what needs your product doesn't meet

- what more they'd like that they think you could offer

If your business reaches a broader market, consider hiring a market research firm to conduct focus groups to gather samples of the same kinds of data. Asking people what they want is the absolute best way to know their needs, meet them effectively, and, hence, prosper in the otherwise mysterious jungle of a dog-eat-dog business world.

This strategy worked for Teresa Iglesias, who pioneered the catalog *Niños,* which caters to a largely juvenile Hispanic market through parents and educators. "Finding an audience for our niche offerings took a lot of planning," says Iglesias. "We not only had to build up a mailing list—a hit-and-miss venture—but we had to carefully select the best products. All this took time."

Customer service is another important factor that helps match the competition. If, for example, you improve your delivery time after discovering your clients have been dissatisfied with it, be sure to promote that change. In advertising, brochures, slogans, or any other public communication, mention that your new improved time schedule will meet their current needs. Use guarantees if necessary, but only if you can back them up. It's essential to be consistent with your messages so the market knows you've done a thorough job correcting the problem.

Woman on the Way

✳

Teresa Iglesias
Creator: *Niños* catalog, Ann Arbor, Michigan
**Business Philosophy: Really "believe" in the mission of
    your business**
**Greatest Achievement: Finding and making a worthwhile
    business from an underserved niche**

While juggling her full-time job in 1990, Teresa Iglesias began working on her business plan for a catalog that would feature products either teaching Spanish or having Hispanic themes. The following year she launched her catalog, *Niños,* from her home, selling books, videos, musical cassettes, videos, software programs, and electronic games in Spanish-only, Spanish/English, and English. Actively seeking out quality media that reflect the Latino spirit, Iglesias "doesn't include anything with negative stereotypes or poor Spanish language."

The catalog targets children from preschool through high school and largely solicits teachers and parents. Teachers have responded to her catalog overwhelmingly, in many instances paying for *Niños* products out of their own pockets. With a mailing list of over twenty thousand customers nationwide, the catalog is projecting sales of over $2 million next year.

Iglesias prides herself on her well-trained telemarketers, who must be fluently bilingual in Spanish and English—no small feat in Ann Arbor, Michigan. "We have a great group of people who read, watch, and understand all the merchandise. In fact, we keep all the merchandise handy for our telemarketers, so if a customer has a question, our salesperson can pick up the product and immediately address the issue." Iglesias further empowers her employees by including them in decisions about not only the catalog, but the operations and warehousing of the products. "Ultimately, I have the final say," says Iglesias, "but everyone has valuable input."

People have begun to turn to Iglesias and *Niños* when looking for smart, entertaining educational products. "It's been tough," says Iglesias, who found herself in the position of trying to set her catalog apart from the glut that debuted in the late 1980s. "But when you have something of value and can find your market, that's when you know you have a business."

✳ ✳ ✳

Dealing with Big Egos: Don't Let It Get You Down!

Whether you work at a high-powered newspaper or you're just trying to find the right public relations agency to help you launch a product, big egos run amok in the world of media.

In a *New York Times* interview, motion picture executive Dawn Steel conceded that as she rose in the corporate world, she decided that if only one woman was going to make it, it would be she. And she is not proud of some of the behavior she demonstrated to get there.

Now perched at the top rung of the ladder, Steel says, "The best thing women can do to help each other in fields run mostly by big egos is to find support from other women." She didn't do that at the time of her climb, but now understands the value of it.

There is a great reservoir of resources to choose from when you are in need of support by other women. Start by turning to the "Resources" section at the end of this book.

Support Yourself

To survive in a world of big egos, discover ways to compose yourself when your blood pressure rises.

Marie Reiko Miyashiro, owner and president of MRM Public Relations, recognizes that her own frame of mind is often what determines a good or bad day. If she slept well the night before, got exercise yesterday, and meditated in the morning, she finds herself in a good frame of mind today. If she was unable to follow the steps necessary to maintain her emotional well-being, she relies on a proven system to elevate her from the low spots.

For Marie, this can be as simple as going for a walk on a mildly bad day or retiring to the beach (when possible) on a truly miserable day. Marie admits that a poor attitude can sour any attempts at producing good work; but if she can't leave the office on one of those miserable days, she "goes to her heart" to find out what kinds of feelings she's trying to avoid and to identify what's making life hard, and discover what she needs to do to change it so she can give herself fully to her work.

By setting herself up as her greatest support system, Marie doesn't allow the egos or outside forces that surround her to dictate her mood or the successes of the day. She's accomplished what everyone could benefit from: taking responsibility for her moods and emotions—a critical skill in a world where big egos are experts at playing the game, and not necessarily with fair rules.

Asking for Help: When to Hire an Independent Contractor

There are countless times in the ups and downs of business when we need help. That's what independent contractors are good for. You may need a marketing expert to help you devise an effective marketing plan. Maybe you're ready to take a leap from selling your products locally to selling them nationally, and you're in need of a good public relations agency. It may be simpler: you know your product and marketing strategy, but you need a good copywriter to put together a brochure. Or you may need tailor-made software that only a specialist in the computer software industry could design.

Independent contractors are available for practically any angle of your business. When you hire them is completely dependent on when you need them . . . and when your budget allows.

For Laura Scher, CEO of Working Assets Funding Service (WAFS), hiring independent contractors allows the company to stay close to its entrepreneurial roots—lean. For WAFS's long-distance leg, "we outsource the entire customer service function through a company we actually helped to create and then helped become independent. And it has probably close to one hundred people by now. Our billing is also outsourced through a company that is expert on doing billing." Out of one hundred people employed, over thirty work exclusively for Working Assets.

For Dena Levy, using freelancers has allowed her to build her business without inflating her overhead. "When companies expand, their overhead increases drastically. Then you have to make a higher quota. By not having the higher overhead, I can pick and choose the jobs I want to do. I can really compete in the industry, instead of taking on every job that comes my way."

The great thing about independent contractors is that you don't have to provide bonuses, sick leave, or health insurance. You also don't have to keep up with their taxes. They charge you a fee for the work they'll be doing, and you pay them. Then you get the fruits of their labor and they get to move on to the next client.

The relationship you have with the contractor you hire will depend greatly on how well you've communicated, both contractually and verbally.

Be sure to write in the contract who will own the material that the contractor has created once it is complete. So, for example, if she designs that special software for your specific needs, you need to clarify, in writing, that the software will belong to either your company or to the contractor. If the contractor owns it, she will be able to sell it to another company. If you own it, she will not, but you may have to pay a higher price for that exclusivity. Enlist the help of an attorney, if necessary, to establish the best approach.

Independent contractors can also hold long-standing positions with you even though they are not considered employees and may not work on site. If you are an author, you may hire a freelance publicist to arrange publicity tours for you. You may be her only client during a fixed period of time, and keep her on a hefty retainer to ensure that she gives you 100 percent of her attention. But she would still be considered an independent contractor, responsible for her own taxes, expenses, and overhead.

In this case, be sure to teach your contractor what your quality standards are. For example, you may have regular meetings with the publicist to go over how she pitches you to the media, what the press kit is made up of, and how successful she has been at securing media interviews. You have the right to instruct her on how you want each leg of her work to take shape. She has the right to disagree with you, but ultimately you need to feel that her approach matches the quality standards you hold.

Some contractors may be in closer touch with the public or vendors than you. That's fine as long as they're doing a good job. It's important, however, to make contact with those people just to know for sure that everything is running smoothly with your contractor. It will also make them feel appreciated and maintain your good reputation.

Before women entered the workforce, the traditional military hierarchy was employed to run businesses, big and small. These operations used a pyramid structure with all the power at the top. The managers had complete autonomy—they were the thinkers in the organization, while the workers were merely "worker bees." Their management incorporated a philosophy of war—strong leadership of troops can kill the enemy. Yet the leaders grappled with many of the same issues that today's managers face: low employee morale, inefficient productivity, rising costs, and tough competition. When women entered the workforce, they brought with them compassion, communication skills, open-door policies, and different ways of thinking. Women leaders have learned the value of employees, fought for better treatment of workers, and, as a result, changed the face of management.

Reengineering, the process of restructuring an organization to be more efficient, is sweeping the country and touching businesses— big and small. The military hierarchy, women leaders find, is just not as efficient as flatter, more-power-to-the-people organizations. In a 1994 study of American companies involved in the reengineering process, 69 percent of organizations were implementing some form of reengineering. Critics of reengineering say that it's just a better word for downsizing and laying off employees. Yet many women managers are finding ways to make their companies horizontal, using coaching and teamwork in place of autocratic government. They attempt to create flatter organizations that consider employee needs as well as the bottom line. Entrepreneurial women are also starting their businesses using a structure that empowers their workers.

While there is no quick solution to solving managerial and company problems, women leaders, ultimately, have to decide what system works best for them—military-style hierarchy or horizontal structure or, perhaps, a bit of both. Rather than conforming to existing styles of management, women are creating their own, based on their company goals, employee needs, and product quality.

Getting the Knack of Industry Networking

The art of networking has long been practiced successfully by businessmen, whose moniker "the old boys' club" has served them well. Women have taken this vital tool of doing business, modified it, and tailor-made it to their needs by stimulating traditional networking with new concepts of cooperation and ingenuity.

While networking in the broadest sense refers to cultivating alliances, relationships, bonds, and interplay on some common ground, women have reinvented the wheel, so to speak, by taking the wide range of interactive possibilities and transforming it into a highly specialized network, one that holds a finger on the pulse of the business world. Few tools may be more valuable to the success of an entrepreneurial woman than effective networking.

Networking is more than just meeting people; it involves sharing, communicating, and listening. Whether the goal is to head a public relations agency, conduct orchestras, operate a cattle ranch, or sell homemade preserves from the garage, interactions with others provide the platform between mere completion and grand success. Active participants in networking—through the wide range of women and related organizations—understand that the continuous process of doing business in the 1990s breaks down simply: it's who you know, what you know, and who knows you.

The key is in building many types of relationships, with many diverse types of people. You may already have contacts within your specialty. If you are a graphic artist, your jobs probably include small-business needs such as newsletters and brochures and the frequent business card/letterhead clients. But by aiming to expand your contacts you may serendipitously meet a nonprofit agency director who is looking to create new brochures for the agency's expanding services. Perhaps you will stumble upon the owner of a floral design shop who is looking to create a mail-order catalog. These types of unplanned interactions not only bring in new work, but allow your creativity to grow by enabling you to expand into wider arenas and tackle greater challenges.

Other networks that can be fulfilling are women-only groups, which can be one of the most productive alliances a woman in business (maybe even especially in the media) can access. Women have to face the harsh fact that outside of the traditional women's fields such as teaching and nursing, men dominate the media and overall business world. Women-only groups help you beat the odds by offering insider track information and invaluable tools for getting your talents recognized and coveted. Outside of providing these imperative leads, these groups also appeal to working women by offering support on many of the hurdles women face, especially the ongoing subject of balancing hectic work lives with family.

By effectively embracing this lifestyle of interaction, you can gain new customers, locate newer and less expensive suppliers, find affordable office or studio space, determine a fair market price for your product or service, discover a solution to a persistent problem, or recommend other peers to complete your support system.

The Significance of Networking

Regardless of where you choose to network, rewards are only as great as the investment. With the long hours entrepreneurs often put in, networking is not easy and often requires you to make the first move.

Graphic designer Janet Brandt finds that treating her networking goals like a job strategy is effective for her. "First I make an outline on paper of tasks, objectives, and ideas," she says. "Then I began to bounce some ideas off my friends and acquaintances within my work community."

Because Brandt really doesn't like to network professionally, she's learned that by borrowing positive experiences from other parts of her life, she can "bluff" her way through. "I'm really good at mimicking a successful scenario," she adds. "I may not know how to network very well, but I can certainly act as though I do."

Networking comes easily for very few people. In fact, more than 70 percent of the population report experiencing shyness. But learning how to motivate yourself to be assertive is part of developing a personal network style. Some women—such as Brandt—find it easier by using some sort of reward system. Use whatever motivates you beyond your inhibitions. By setting the tone and style of networking, you can become comfortable with your interactions. It is better to selectively meet a couple of people and have good, productive conversations than to introduce yourself briefly to everyone in the room.

Networking no longer means formal business organizations or preplanned mixers. Networking can occur anywhere—at volunteer gatherings, grocery stores, the gym, or any place people gather. The potential is everywhere. By keeping yourself open to the range of possibilities available, you may find it easier to discuss who you are and what you do with others and invite them to do the same.

When those negative inner voices begin to recite all the fears and insecurities about networking, one thing to remember is that networking *does* bring results—and is a profitable investment of your time. For women who are selling their work, referrals are 80 percent more likely to turn over a sale than the random opportunity presented by a customer who just walks through the door.

Networking Guidelines

There are no inappropriate times for networking, only inappropriate actions. Conversations in a coffeehouse can yield some valuable leads, as can a PTA or Neighborhood Watch meeting. However, constantly presenting yourself in a networking or schmoozing mode can be a quick turnoff during casual meetings. Think of how it feels to be *sold* when you have been enjoying a quiet afternoon barbecue or party. Networking involves the precise skill of balance. Know when to tune it down and be casual and when to fire yourself up for a sales pitch. According to Dr. Yeou-Cheng Ma, executive director and musician for the Children's Orchestra Society, many of her contacts come casually through after-performance parties or conferences. "I meet many interesting people who will just stop by and say, 'I loved the concert,' and then will follow up with a phone call a few days later. Then my head is clear and I'm able to give them my full attention."

The following are several guidelines for networking successfully:

Have Business Cards Accessible at All Times

If you're working independently and don't like the formality of a traditional business card, create something that reflects what you do. Your name and a contact number are the valuable points to include. Get in the habit of giving a card when people ask about what you do. If giving a referral to someone else, jot down the number on the back of your card. At the very least, when the person reads your name, it reinforces who you are in their mind.

Be Interested in What Others Do

It's amazing how much crossover there is in the media world. A producer may be looking for a public relations agent to work on a special documentary she is working on. A writer may be looking for an experienced director to launch a new talk show. Listen for opportunities to share your information and contacts and be willing to provide referrals whenever possible. Sharing is a reciprocal process, and if you share leads with others, others will be more inclined to share with you. Take the advice heeded by many smart businesspeople: If you can't help, steer them to a colleague who can. These individuals will remember your selflessness and will think of you when making a referral.

Learn to Explain What You Do in under Thirty Seconds

Brevity has a definite advantage, and people, unfortunately, have short attention spans. Always carry a pen with you so you can write on the back of your business card, and jot notes on the cards you collect. If someone offers you a lead or referral, make a quick note on the back of her card. That way you can remember who turned you on to a new opportunity.

Follow Through Promptly on All Leads

Remember, time is of the essence. The person offering the reference may have just heard that a colleague is looking for a person with your abilities. If you wait too long, that possibility is lost.

Jot thank-you notes to individuals who have provided a lead—successful or otherwise—and let them know the outcome. Unfortunately, thanking people for their help is a frequently underemphasized issue of etiquette in the current business climate. Don't allow yourself to fall into this trap. Rude is never fashionable. A brief thank-you note takes moments to write and has a greater impact than the easier option of a phone call—although a quick, heartfelt phone call is better than procrastinating a note indefinitely.

Do Not Sit Around Waiting for Someone Else to Introduce Herself

At social events, take that first step and extend your hand. By acting as though you're in control of the situation, others are likely to follow suit and start up a conversation with you.

Be Sure You're Making the Best Possible Impression

Always use good grammar and proper etiquette and practice good grooming. Make sure you have a confident handshake. A limp handshake will outlast any positive impression the person has of you.

Learn to Be a Good Listener

This includes people's names. Ask for names and then use them in conversation. Listen to what the person has to say, and be attentive to body language—including your own. Remember to smile and face the person you are speaking to. If in a group, remember to address each person with your eyes, rather than just looking at one or two individuals.

Practice the Art of Conversation

This is more than simply discussing the weather. Be well rounded in a variety of topics. Being absorbed in the field that interests you shouldn't prevent you from understanding popular culture, politics, and maybe even organic gardening, if that's what you enjoy. Don't force your ideas on your listener, and learn to sense when the conversation is heading toward its natural end.

The art of networking involves feeling good about what you do and using this satisfaction to sell yourself. It is not about making that heavy-handed pitch to land a client or a job. Networking is, however, the perfect time for sharing ideas, information, and concerns. If you are solicited for work while networking, set up an appropriate later time to conduct business.

Networking Guidelines

1. Have business cards accessible at all times.
2. Be interested in what others do.
3. Learn to explain what you do in under thirty seconds.
4. Follow through promptly on all leads.
5. Do not sit around waiting for someone else to introduce herself.
6. Be sure you're making the best possible impression.
7. Learn to be a good listener.
8. Practice the art of conversation.

Facing Fears of Failure and Success

In the process of creating networks, it is imperative to put your best face forward. But working to appear successful and passionate about your work can be taxing and may uncover underlying fears of both success and failure. These fears, while perfectly natural, can undermine your endeavors and sabotage your success.

The fear of failure is most common for women. Women have generally seen themselves as unskilled, since women's work—traditionally caregiving and taking care of the home—is undervalued in our society. Additionally, since the concept of mentoring is relatively new for women, many feel that they don't fully understand their roles in the working world. Naturally these inequities can contribute to a fear of failure, particularly for the entrepreneur.

Yet a lack of understanding in these areas can also be perceived as a benefit for many women entrepreneurs. Because women aren't bound by traditional roles and stagnant concepts of "paying dues," many women feel liberated to carve their own niche and design guidelines that work exclusively for their business.

One obstacle that women face constantly is their inherent role of peacekeeper. Women are conditioned from childhood to please everyone else. In the business world, consensus cannot always be achieved. Therefore new skills should be learned to deal effectively with conflict. Many women find that good communication is the catalyst in resolving conflicts.

Judith Jamison, artistic director of the Alvin Ailey American Dance Theater, recalls many instances when, as a senior member, she had to make vital decisions regarding the troupe. "I found that, rather than saying, 'Because I said so,' the members would respond more positively when I would tell them my decision and, briefly, how I reached that decision." Jamison found that by taking charge of the situation, while treating her colleagues as rational individuals, she not only maintained their respect, but prevented further conflict. "I never saw myself as a leader, nor really particularly wanted to be one. But when my career demanded it, I found a way of dealing with dissent that was comfortable for me, and worked."

Certainly success appears to be a less formidable obstacle. Everyone wants to achieve success, so how can it be dangerous? Success does not come without its own set of stumbling blocks. Societal expectations may dictate your success or guide you into making unwise career or financial choices. Truly successful people choose their own goals, then stay on track. Create a list of short- and long-term objectives, and make sure your needs are met. Once you achieve a certain level of success, remember to keep your ego in check—just because you've made it doesn't mean you should flaunt it, nor does it mean that it's a permanent thing. Remain focused on your goals, and update those goals constantly to ensure that you're moving forward, not running blindly in the same spot.

According to political consultant and commentator Mary Matalin, fear of failure can prevent competent, intelligent women from even trying to pursue their dreams. "Try to learn from failure. The successful men I've worked with see failure as a step sideways, something to be learned from."

If you perceive yourself as a professional, others will begin to see you that way as well. Your image begins deep within yourself and is shared through your words, your interactions, and how you carry yourself. Believe in yourself. Take some time for self-reflection and to acknowledge your accomplishments before you reevaluate your future goals. It is just as important to recognize how far you've come before embarking on the next leg of your journey. By constantly touching base with yourself—or self-networking—you can best champion yourself to greater success.

Finding Advocates: Getting Help from Associates and Professionals

One of most beneficial products of networking is the assemblage of a group of professional advocates. This group can function as an alliance for sharing ideas, concerns, and information among other professionals in media. A simple way to form this group is to invite several professional or up-and-coming friends and acquaintances for dinner. At this informal gathering, suggest that the group get together monthly and allow each person to share one problem or concern. Stress to each woman that for this process to work, every person must get something as well as contribute to the mix. Creative solutions, new contacts, and innovative approaches to tackling problems are the most common benefits of a group. Outside of discussing business concerns, these groups can be therapeutic in scope when a member finds that some of her obstacles have been faced by others in the group and may be surprised to learn that her stumbling blocks are not so overwhelming after all.

The greatest rewards can be gained by viewing your colleagues as an extended support system, not as competition. Although the vein of competition runs through every professional endeavor, when you go into competition, you begin to limit opportunities to grow together. By being willing to share your knowledge and information within your group, your colleagues will reciprocate. If a project or job begins to be too much for you to handle or you can't fit a client's needs into your schedule, consider recommending a colleague you trust. Women who employ this strategy find that the long-term rewards outweigh any of the doubts they may have originally had.

Many women believe that diversity in a women's group will produce the best results. Think of people who have information to share, whether it is leads, professional advice, or marketing concepts. The group can be of any size, but a number between five and ten may offer the best results.

Rotate who organizes the dinner—it may be easier to find a central meeting place such as a café. For many women, this meeting is not only a break from the long hours an entrepreneurial woman puts in, but it can double as a social event. In this safe, controlled environment, women should feel able to share and hear the ideas each person has, without the threat of criticism or censure. Because of the supportive nature of this type of group, a level of confidentiality should be agreed upon so that every member feels secure in discussing her concerns openly and with candor.

Tricks of the Trade

Dolores Robinson of Robinson Entertainment, on cultivating contacts:

1. *Never, ever burn bridges.* The individual who may be dismissive of you one day may find your services very necessary the next.

2. *Always conduct yourself in a manner appropriate to your business.* It may be acceptable to address your colleagues by "Yo!" if you work on music videos, but probably not if they're the executives of a network.

3. *Make your interests known to others.* You may be temping today so you can pursue your dreams tomorrow. It's okay to let people know there's more to you than eighty words a minute—as long as your work doesn't suffer. You never know who will ultimately be a contact.

4. *Always remember assistants.* Often, an assistant today will be a vice president tomorrow.

5. *Don't be snobbish about making contacts*—and never judge someone by appearance or position. Money is equally negotiable, regardless of the source.

✳ ✳ ✳

The Mysterious Political Arena: Where to Begin

The year 1996 marked the seventy-fifth anniversary of women winning the right to vote. Thus, just within this century women have moved from disenfranchisment to becoming the single largest group of voters. Women have won prominent roles serving in elected office and in the back rooms of politics, serving as campaign managers, pollsters, lobbyists, commentators, and activists.

Each of these categories holds within it the spirit of entreprenurialism that typifies women-owned businesses in other fields. Women entrepreneurs in politics exercise independence, tend to have higher earning power, and are well respected in their fields. Kathryn Rees, who started lobbying when she was thirty, found that starting her own lobbying company tripled her income within six months. Another woman in politics, Mary Matalin, knew she would be an entrepreneur from the moment she worked on the assembly line of the steel mill that had employed her other family members their entire lives. Matalin knew that when she "grew up" she didn't want to have to stare at the clock, waiting for the next lunch hour. Linda Cherry, owner of a conservative political telemarketing firm, knew there was value in what she had been doing for free as a Republican volunteer. These women and others changed their destiny the day they started their own business in politics.

Though the women's suffrage movement has typically been linked with activism of women in the abolition movement, historian Barbara Berg identifies the network of women's volunteer groups that sprang up in urban centers between 1800 and 1860 as the real wellspring of what we experience today as the women's movement. These volunteer groups had names like the Moral Reform Society, the Female Benevolent Society, and the Society for the Relief of Poor Widows and often worked to address the deplorable living conditions in urban centers with the influx of immigrants. According to Berg, "The history of the activities, ideas, and lives of the women who joined associations devoted to helping others of their sex is the chronicle of the origins of women's emancipation. It is the story of her attempts to find freedom from the bonds of an imprisoning ethos that thwarted her efforts at self-realization, denied her autonomous nature, and refuted her common humanity."

Today women are the majority of voters in the United States, and though they tend to prefer voting for women, female candidates and entrepreneurs are to be found in virtually every sector of the political spectrum; pro-choice or pro-life, Republican or Democrat, liberal or conservative, women are succeeding with businesses in politics that blend their commitment to making the world a better place and, typically, communicating and evaluating information, strategizing, organizing, and presenting.

For most women already working in this industry, testing the waters was the first step to dedicating their lives to the political arena. Many acknowledge that participating in a campaign or simply becoming aware of certain candidates and propositions first fueled their passion.

Office holders are the ultimate entrepreneurs; they convince their clients to choose them during an arduous presentation process, then serve their clients (the people)—all the while looking to the next time they'll have to represent themselves to their clients for reconsideration. Though they are compensated, they must be able to treat their own image and career just like a growing company. Ideally, just as in a socially sensitive business, as an office holder you will be able to do some good along the way.

If you're more of a behind-the-scenes person, you can start a business specializing in campaign strategies, politics, policies, and the process of helping others getting elected. These companies—many of which are small, or "boutique"—run an astonishing gamut, ranging from specializing in campaign research to designing political videos. They include campaign telemarketing companies, campaigning training services, pollsters, strategists, and political consultants.

Women lobbyists first emerged working for the International Ladies' Garment Worker's Union in 1964. Now women run some of the most influential lobbying companies in the country and are a powerful—albeit divergent—force working in the nation's legislatures. Lobbyists have clients, much like lawyers, whose interests they represent within the scope of their legislative jurisdiction. Some lobbyists will work on Capitol Hill in Washington, D.C., others in state capitals, lobbying the state legislatures. Being able to put expert, influential information in front of lawmakers is a key element of lobbying.

Women sometimes move from being a candidate or a campaign worker to making commentary for news organizations. Despite great political astuteness, commentators who start as journalists rarely move into actively running for office or supporting a candidate. Much like that of a candidate, a commentator's career is entrepreneurial in the attention she must put into her next move. Just like other political entrepreneurs, commentators may have many clients or just one.

Despite (or perhaps because of) a general impression that people are separated from government and politics, activist groups are becoming more and more prevalent. Though you might presume an activist to be at the fringes of the political spectrum, an increasing number of activist organizations are to be found in the center, perhaps in reaction to the effective organization of extremes in the political spectrum.

Be a Volunteer!

Few sectors of American work life have as easy and risk-free a means of exploration and advancement as politics. Volunteering for a candidate is one of the easiest ways to find out if politics is for you and to move up the ranks. No matter which "category" attracts you, volunteering for a campaign enables you to take steps toward your own goal in any of these categories.

Though not all lobbyists started out campaigning, some have gotten their first lobbying jobs as a direct result of campaigning. And while not all activists have necessarily campaigned, those who have volunteered have a definite advantage. For Susan Estrich and Mary Matalin, volunteer work on campaigns led directly to their work as commentators. Mary Matalin describes campaigns as "the most egalitarian place in the world to work."

Tricks of the Trade

Susan Estrich of the University of Southern California Law School, on benefiting from being a campaign volunteer:

1. *Select your candidate.* Find someone you agree with, but know you could be disappointed. Politics is a lot about compromise, and you've got to be able to draw on your own beliefs as well. Begin to keep your ears open before primary season. Don't hesitate to call your local party leader to see whom they might be lining up to run. You may also want to contact another political organization you identify with, to see if they are fielding a candidate in your area. A third means of hooking up with a candidate early on is to call Emily's List, a Washington, D.C., organization that supports Democratic pro-choice women candidates for public office. Who knows, your inquiry could lead to your own recruitment to run!

2. *Don't worry about your age or previous experience.* If you're green, you'll learn a lot campaigning. If you're older, have no fear that campaigns are strictly for the young. You'll be able to bring expertise from wherever else your life has taken you—whether you've been a homemaker or director of sales and marketing. No matter what, you'll be able to help during a campaign.

3. *Go to the big recruitment meetings, but don't sit at home and wait to be called.* Approach the campaign leaders, and go so far as to visit the campaign office on a different day from the big organizational meeting. Make sure to introduce yourself to the campaign manager.

   Talk one-on-one with the campaign manager early on in the season. Let her or him see how serious you are; let them know your special skills. (Don't be shy, tell him or her what

your skills are.) You'll find you'll be assigned special projects that match your skills in no time!

4. *Don't stop yourself from signing up because of the time.*
Even if you are working at another job full-time, you'll be
able to take on a "special project" for the campaign maybe
even a few hours a night, a couple of nights a week.

   To optimize your options in these areas, make sure
you've made contacts in the office. And remember, if you
are looking to change careers, or progress, you'll have to
spend some time putting down the footwork that will be
worth it in the long term—especially if your candidate
wins.

5. *Confidentiality is important to a campaign.* If you are a
rookie volunteer, be particularly careful of this. You might
run into a newspaper reporter. Given your entrepreneurial
spirit, you'll see this as an excellent opportunity to get
some publicity for the campaign. *Don't be tempted.* Clear
anything you talk about to the press with campaign headquarters first. What might seem like a great publicity
opportunity to you could seem like the Inquisition to seasoned campaign veterans—the very people you don't want
to offend.

6. *Do what you say you'll do, and be where you'll say you'll
be.* Enough said. In the volunteer world, you'll stand out
even if this is all you do.

7. *Understand the limitations of a campaign.* If you aren't getting the resources you need to fulfill your personal campaign
mandate, understand, this is a campaign. Often money,
people, time, and resources are at a premium. Keep some
perspective.

   Also, knowing limitations can enable you to brainstorm
workable solutions. You'll be in a better position to impress
people by offering insightful solutions into what is and isn't
available to them.

8. *Keep it fun.* Campaigns are hard whether you win or lose. There is certainly enough grimness to go around when things get tough. Be a volunteer with a sense of humor and some perspective; this will help your sanity in getting through the campaign.

9. *Get to know people.* Use this intense time to get to know people who could help you in your business later on. Take advantage of parties and gatherings. You've put in a lot of time and energy; don't stop short of meeting influential people in the race simply because you're tired. Let the system work for you.

10. *Keep in mind, a lot more people are going to lose than win.* Don't let that stop you; keep in mind, though, the value of the experience. If your candidate loses, don't take that as a sign you shouldn't be in politics. Just know that that is part of the reality of politics you'll be asked to learn how to deal with.

11. *As with any endeavor—but in politics especially—beware of social advances with sexual motives attached.* Don't fall prey to the myth that "putting out" will get you anywhere. Despite whatever guarantees are made, you may just be taken advantage of.

✳ ✳ ✳

Woman on the Way

✳

Mary Matalin
Campaign consultant and political commentator
Business Philosophy: Take risks
Greatest Achievement: Happy marriage; happy kid

Mary Matalin grew up in a working-class steel mill family, where she was bred to be a Democrat. It wasn't until she left home for college that she realized she was a conservative. "You had to be brain dead not to see The Great Society programs weren't working," she says.

In graduate school her interest in history, politics, people, and conservatism led to the beginning of her now legendary political career, when a conservative professor asked her if she'd be interested in working on a campaign with him. She jumped at the chance and rose through the ranks to become a Republican powerhouse.

Matalin has been instrumental in four presidential campaigns. In 1992 she served as deputy campaign manager for the Bush-Quayle campaign and was responsible for the overview and organization of all fifty state operations. As the on-board planner who traveled with the former president, she emerged as a sometimes controversial defender of the president. Following the election, she married her political nemesis, James Carville, who had been the campaign mastermind behind the winning Clinton campaign. The two published a book about their relationship and the campaign, *All's Fair: Love, War and Running for President.*

Currently Matalin is working as a nationally syndicated radio commentator. Of her decision to skip the 1996 presidential circus, Matalin cites family commitments. "I thought long and hard before we had Matty [Matalin Mary Carville, born in 1995]. I knew I couldn't campaign with a baby, but I've been happy with my decision."

Matalin's advice to aspiring female politicos: "Men BS their way through a lot of stuff, and it works for them. Once you learn the art of exuding confidence, you're all set. Success begets success, but don't be afraid to fail."

✳   ✳   ✳

Behind the Scenes: Get in the Running

Again, the first recommendation is to volunteer for a campaign. Depending on what you are doing now, you may be able to garner yourself a top position in the campaign organization—especially if you are willing to demonstrate your expertise and intelligence at no charge. At some point, however, you must value yourself and demand a fee—and that's when your business formally begins.

Some people say being in a campaign is like being in the middle of a hurricane that you know will stop. Long hours and personal sacrifice are required. You will most likely take a part of your existing business or personal skills and adapt them to politics. These skills, along with your past campaigning experiences, will enable you to inspire confidence in your first clients. Depending on where you've come from, you may have a ready pool of potential clients.

Linda DiVall, strategist and pollster, had worked with the National Republican Congressional Committee for five years when she identified a niche for herself as a female Republican pollster. In her opinion, integrity, campaign experience, and the ability to give confident advice carry more weight than a Ph.D. "Your reputation is everything," she says. DiVall has found that taking the time to answer questions from the media—while maintaining client confidentiality—has gone a long way to improving her business. "Your clients like the cachet," she adds. Her recommendation is to start with clients from your past business experience. But soon you'll be selling new clients based on your experience with past clients, and the market niche you have defined for yourself.

DiVall's company, American Viewpoint, fits the classic polling, campaign strategy format and, along with her Republican counterpart, Kelly Ann Fitzpatrick, founder of the polling company, offers services in traditional telephone polling, focus groups, surveys of Congress, strategies, political training, and media design and placement.

Linda Cherry began volunteering for campaigns, working her way up to become deputy director of voter programs for the 1984 Reagan-Bush campaign, where she coordinated the first nationwide presidential campaign telemarketing operation, generating over ten million phone calls. In 1985 she opened Linda Z. Cherry Consulting, and in 1990 she started Cherry Communications. "I'm proud to say, we've made the difference in a lot of races. I'm not saying using Cherry Communications will win the race for you, just that I can see we make a positive difference, especially in really close races," she says.

Despite the fulfilling nature of her company's work, Cherry flat-out states, "If I had had a crystal ball to see where I'd be now when I started, I assure you I'd be doing something else." Cherry's main complaint is that her business is so labor intensive. "With 150 people on the phone making calls, it can get kind of crazy. All of our callers have to be trained and monitored. It's really quite an operation. Because of my commitment to the cause, I really feel every call must be perfect."

Financially, Cherry Communications is successful. "Our billings for the year are doing well beyond our wildest dreams." But such compensation is not without its cost. She recently hit a fork in the road. "I had to make a decision when I moved from being a consultant to starting this company, and now I'm responsible for all these employees. It's been a real strain on my personal life and my marriage. But this my calling." Cherry's advice to others: "Be committed to what you are doing, be extremely honest, and always be willing to go beyond what is necessary for your clients."

A Breed Apart: The Lobbyist

As owner and president of Rees & Associates, Inc., a top lobbying firm working before the California legislature and state government, Kathryn Rees did not start out by campaigning. She answered an ad in the newspaper for a legislative liaison. She was hired first by the California Optometric Association and then by the California Hospital Association to lobby the state legislature. After excelling at lobbying for others, she realized the only way to receive compensation on par with her male peers was to open her own lobbying company in 1983. Within six months of starting her own firm, she saw her income triple. It would seem that lobbying requires partisan commitment, but Kathryn Rees says that being able to stay objective is crucial to serving her clients. "It's all about compromise."

While running a telemarketing firm requires the ability to coordinate large numbers of people quickly, and strategic polling requires the ability to determine the public's perception of a thing and recommend a course of action, lobbying involves much more analyzing—your subject, the path you are advocating, and the lawmakers in a particular legislature.

"We research every angle of an issue, including what our opponents might be up to, then we strategize on how best to represent the issue to each legislator. Lobbyists have gotten a bad rap; I see what we do as fulfilling a constitutional role envisioned by our forefathers."

According to Rees, it takes time to become an effective lobbyist. "It takes two years to have a modicum of functionality. You can become effective after five, and hit your stride after ten, when you've really gotten to know the legislative process." Rees's clients pay by retainer and typically agree on a flat fee for services, which include monitoring the legislature for any laws that might affect her clients. In addition, she will research and recommend whom her clients should support for office. Her advice for aspiring lobbyists: "Friends you will come to work with are those same people you are opposing today, so always allow people their dignity.

"With term limits we experience constant legislative turnover. The benefit to us as lobbyists is that we have become the institutional memory. We are educating the legislators. We really have to prove our worth. Gone are the days when someone can just ask a legislator to vote a certain way for a favor. You have to do your homework, and justify it to the legislator's constituency.

"Unfortunately, every time one of my clients has a personnel change, we have to prove our worth all over again. Fortunately we are the best. In lobbying you really have to learn how to pay attention to your clients. It's not enough to do the work. You have to spend time with your clients. Sometimes it's frustrating for us, because we like to get out there and make things happen for our clients. But we're competing with people who stay on the phone with their clients all day."

What Does It Take? Passion vs. Impartiality

If you are beginning a business in politics, do you need to be particularly partisan, or is it possible to be neutral politically? That really depends on you. Kathryn Rees says it is crucial for her to be able to work with both Republicans and Democrats to do her job effectively. She adds that it is crucial to keep some distance from issues, to be able to negotiate, compromise, and build consensus. "You cannot function effectively for your client if you are too personally involved in your issue," she says.

Still, as a lobbyist, Rees does feel that she makes a difference. She and her workers and colleagues serve a crucial role in the legislative system. "We are the voice of the people, giving legislators information so that they can make good decisions." Along with her role of enabling legislators to make good decisions, Rees's goal is to make everyone a winner. "You can't think about winners and losers in lobbying. You've succeeded when you walk away from a situation with everyone feeling like a winner."

Rees is also able to act on her beliefs by not representing certain clients. "I couldn't in good conscience represent a tobacco concern. Part of that is because I have so many health care clients." Still, temperance and equanimity are the watchwords of the day in the world of lobbying. "A guy you're going against today might turn out to be on your side tomorrow. You have to be professional with everyone."

In contrast, women working in more partisan capacities, such as campaign manager or activist, say strong passionate beliefs in one side or another are crucially sustaining. Mary Matalin, campaign manager for George Bush's bid for reelection, and longtime Republican campaigner, says, "Especially in politics, you really have to believe in your side because there are so few rewards. The pay isn't good and you don't get a lot of recognition. You need some belief to sustain you through the darkest hours. Even if you believe in your candidates—and believe me, I've loved the candidates I've worked for—you still need your own beliefs and commitment to draw on." In fact, Matalin believes that in her experience, women tend to stick to their core beliefs more fiercely than men. "It amazes me to see people, all men, jumping ship when things are getting rough. I can't understand having such a weak commitment to one's philosophical principles."

Linda DiVall believes that pollsters and strategists should be committed to one side or another. Though certainly pollsters and strategists have worked for both parties, clearly to some pollsters that would be a controversial choice. DiVall explains that the main reason she opposes bipartisan strategizing is that the pollster knows the other side's strategy.

Thus you can be a part of the political and legislative process without having to be a diehard Republican or Democrat, Socialist, Libertarian, or Conservative. Alternately, if you do feel strongly about these issues, politics may be your only choice. As Mary Matalin defines her journey into politics, "I had a unstructured compulsion, a people compulsion, and with my other interests, like history (history is yesterday's politics), everything I love just came together for me in politics. It was perfect for me."

Political Commentators and Correspondents

For journalists and writers who have a fascination with politics, sometimes a transition can be made to cover local, regional, state, or national politics. While obviously the premium spots—such as White House correspondent—go to a few seasoned reporters, novice writers can often cut their teeth on school board or city council beats for local or alternative publications.

One successful commentator who rose through the ranks is Cokie Roberts. Currently a senior political analyst with National Public Radio, political correspondent with ABC News, and a regular member of the roundtable discussion on *This Week,* Roberts also serves as a substitute anchor on *Nightline* and writes a weekly syndicated newspaper column.

In 1966 Cokie Roberts gave up her first job as anchor of *Meeting of Minds,* a public affairs program in Washington, D.C., to follow her husband to New York, where he wrote for *The New York Times.* She found that in her search for fulfilling work, men would flat-out tell her that "we couldn't have the jobs, while their hands were on our knees."

Ultimately she landed a reporting job with Cowles Communications in New York. While Roberts raised a family—following her husband around the world—the easiest work for her to do was reporting. "It was by far the easiest thing to do—go out and report a story and come back and write it—because it's portable. That is how my career evolved."

When her family came back to Washington, Roberts took her writing clips and went to National Public Radio where she was greeted by Nina Totenberg and Linda Wertheimer. "When I came in for an interview, Linda and Nina were there, greeting me and encouraging me. And it just made all the difference in the world.

NPR was a place where I wanted to work because they were there."
That's how Roberts began covering the U.S. Congress in 1977.

"I've had a much better balance [between family and career] than
most women are able to achieve. And my message to young women
is: You'll be in the workforce for fifty years—you don't have to do
everything at once. I turned down lots of good jobs along the way
because they were inappropriate for my family at that time."

Opportunities in media and public opinion are as diverse as the
field itself, and while testing the waters has never been easier, understand that it may take some time to find your niche. As Mary
Matalin says, "Have a plan, even if it's a little one. Have a vision.
You don't have to know the details, but let it be a mountain out there
that you can keep heading toward."

7

Nonprofit and Socially Responsible Business

The giving professions such as social work, nursing, and teaching were generally the vocations our foremothers were directed toward—if they were "allowed" to work at all. In spite of this social imprinting, it's not unusual that even today many women look for ways to blend their work lives with inherent traits of kindness and compassion. While women have flexed their muscles in many avenues of business, some have found that their need for social activism is equal to their need for making money.

As popular sentiment decries "profits without conscience," newer, more successful businesses are breaking the mold and becoming models for entrepreneurs who believe that managing profits and the common good should go hand in hand. The seeds for this current trend have taken root with people who sincerely believe that it is possible—indeed preferable—to create or run a profitable company and also care about people at the same time.

The businesses featured in this chapter use myriad formulas to achieve their successes. Some combine for-profit with an altruistic component; others are nonprofit agencies that are funded by separate for-profit businesses; and others reinvest financial rewards into the organization as a bank for the future. Throughout these pages, women who have found success will share how their work in the social arena is both fulfilling and profitable. As the women relay their obstacles and victories, they impart the strong belief that it is indeed possible to change the world, one individual business at a time.

Balancing the Budget and Your Values: Four Steps to Consider Before Pursuing Humanitarian Work

Even in today's modern society, many members of the workforce stumble aimlessly into their profession. While many are able to transform their tenure into a satisfying vocation, other enterprising women take their work experience and "make a job" rather than continuing in the career track they feel ambivalent toward. This is the founding tenet of An Income of Her Own, a nonprofit agency developed by successful entrepreneur and author Joline Godfrey to empower teen women by educating them in the language and skills of business.

An annual business plan competition, Camp $tart-Up—a series of summer camps where teenage girls can learn the basics of business—and conferences and workshops that bring teen women and businesswomen together, are all vehicles for involving girls in their own economic development *and* for delivering a message that they are taken seriously. And while 75 percent of all women work outside the home, 40 percent of those are working below the poverty level, according to Godfrey. Her goal? "To show young women that they have options outside of working for someone else." Godfrey's favorite quote for her young flock comes from Sojourner Truth: "If I can't see it, I can't be it."

Women who choose independence in their work lives look for a work situation that complements their true selves. So many women pursue entrepreneurial endeavors linking social responsibility and profits. The women who make this choice acknowledge daily that work impacts every other aspect of life.

Success is, of course, what all entrepreneurs strive for. Yet success is a term that means something different to everyone. Some define success monetarily, while others may count their successes using the names of valued friends and loved ones. Do you consider yourself a successful person? You undoubtedly are in some regard. Subjecting themselves to the harshest standards at times, women with great potential often say they don't feel successful.

For many, real success is in finding contentment. Celebrated psychologist Abraham Maslow termed success simply as a need for self-actualization. If you are self-actualized, you are better able to realize your life potential. Another way of stating this is that contented people are emotionally healthy. Whether it's termed "good karma," "social consciousness," or "emotional well-being," success on a variety of levels may be achieved through a business that maintains a level of civic involvement.

In his work, Dr. Maslow attributed these seven characteristics to a self-actualized individual:

- an accurate picture of reality

- the ability to remove oneself from daily turmoil

- a personal mission to make a difference in life

- a sense of satisfaction from one's own personal development

- a capacity to experience and greatly appreciate life

- a passion for both the goals pursued and the journey toward those goals

- sufficient opportunities for creativity in one's work

Although many women in many fields participate in a self-actualization process, it seems especially true for women who work in a socially responsible field, because the lines between one's work and personal life are not clearly drawn. Many women who work in the nonprofit sector, for example, often say that what they do and who they are are identifiers they find interchangeable. According to Jean Mason and Joan Black, cofounders of Kids In Danger Surviving (KIDS), "Some of our kids call us 'Mama,' 'cause we're the only mama they know. That can certainly blur the lines between work and home."

Although running a socially responsible business may seem like a "softer" and thus "easier" way of conducting business, every business bears the same basic responsibilities. A successful business—regardless of the field—must be based on solid ethics, smart strategic planning, and the basic tenets of supply and demand. You must determine your values and beliefs and analyze how they will be folded into your business, both before embarking on your journey and during daily operations.

Assess Your Values

We all have values that are important to us, whether they be cultural, religious, or moral. Most people make decisions based on their values. Therefore it is key to be actively aware of your values.

For example, if you're a staunch environmentalist, you probably wouldn't be happy contracting for a clear-cut logging company. If you're concerned about cleaning up the community for your children, you may not accept donations from a company known for dumping toxic waste.

Sharon Meyer was recruited by a high-powered law firm while she was barely in her second year of law school. She was thrilled at the prospect and did excellent work for the firm—topping eighty hours a week and many successes. Even though she enjoyed the work and was offered a partnership track, Meyer found that her schedule didn't allow her time to perform the pro bono hours she'd been promised. Meyer wanted to give her time to help individuals and organizations who couldn't afford her expensive fees.

She opened her own firm, which focused heavily on the needs and rights of recent immigrants. To pay her overhead, Meyer took on a select number of premium retainer clients who could afford to pay her higher fees. By shifting the balance between high- and low-paying clients, Meyer found herself making almost what she had before and calling her own shots.

Break Down Self-Doubt and Listen to Your Soul

The goal-setting process of forming a socially responsible business will stem from a clear assessment of your values. Before you can articulate your goals, you'll want to face any negative thoughts that impact your decision-making process. These are the thoughts that tell you you're not good enough, smart enough, or savvy enough to do this.

Addressing negative thoughts isn't the same as tossing common sense out the window, however. If you don't have, or can't easily acquire, the skills needed to perform your role, you may be in over your head. That's okay, too. It doesn't mean you have to give your plans up entirely, only that you'll need to modify them for maximum impact.

After a thorough self-review, you will be better able to clearly determine what you'd like to do with your life. Be honest—and critical—but don't sabotage yourself from the start. If you've come this far, you can take it all the way.

Annie Kostiner, cofounder of Gallery 312, knew from the start that her philanthropic gallery would secure corporate funding and her ancillary programs would be successful. "I pretty much imagined it from the very beginning and simply made it happen," says Kostiner. "What it is evolving into is really something not beyond that expectation because I had set realistic goals."

Set Realistic Goals

This is where it all comes together and where short- and long-term planning figures in.

You may have an immediate goal of running an ethical business. This is a goal that will remain rewarding over time. One of your next goals may be to get a new project up and running. If the project is successful, the goal may expand into how to carry this project to the next phase.

For Laura Scher of Working Assets, creating a system of "painless giving" was on the top of her list of goals. She and her colleagues realized that people wanted to give money to help certain causes but were also feeling some pain from the economy.

Out of this goal-setting process came Working Assets' hallmark products. "We started by creating products that raised money every time you used them. Every time you made a purchase on our credit card, we put ten cents into a donation pool. And if you used our long distance, we put 1 percent of the phone bill into the same donation pool." And last year Working Assets gave away $2 million to a variety of charitable causes.

Yet Scher's not resting on her laurels. "I'm constantly looking for new obstacles to face, new goals to set. It's the only way to keep a business fresh and my energy alive."

Define Your Mission Statement

Your mission can be made up of one simple fact. For many companies their mission is simply to make money. For others, their mission can head in several directions. Like a business plan, a mission statement can be created for all kinds of businesses and in some form should be part of any type of business. Define what is important to you and which of these elements in your definition you find integral to doing business. This will provide you with a good start for forging your mission statement.

Laura Scher and her colleagues defined a mission that combined sage corporate practices with their deeply rooted social values. They wanted to build a company around the concepts of superior product, consistent service, strong civic responsibility, environmentalism, and good faith. It worked. Working Assets Funding Service has become the template for many other successful, yet conscious, organizations.

In Tom Chappell's book, *The Soul of a Business*, author and cofounder of Tom's of Maine, the United States' leading producer of natural personal health care products, states, "The mission of [any] company shapes the hopes, expectations, and aspirations of this business community in noneconomic terms. . . . [The] mission statement should provide some description of distinction in our purpose. Our point of view that natural ingredients are better for you than synthetic distinguished us in one way. All in all, the mission should evoke our passion for risking resources in a competitive marketplace."

Although your mission statement may not be as evolved as Tom's of Maine's, this entrepreneurial company prides itself on having a well-developed philosophy that impacts every aspect of its business—from staff meetings to product development strategy.

- To serve our customers by providing safe, effective, innovative, natural products of high quality

- To build a relationship with our customers that extends beyond product usage to include full and honest dialogue, responsiveness to feedback, and the exchange of information about products and issues

- To respect, value, and serve not only our customers, but also our co-workers, owners, agents, suppliers, and our community; to be concerned about and contribute to their well-being; and to operate with integrity so as to be deserving of their trust

- To provide meaningful work, fair compensation, and a safe, healthy work environment that encourages openness, creativity, self-discipline, and growth

- To acknowledge the value of each person's contribution to our goals and to foster teamwork in our tasks

- To be distinctive in products and policies which honor and sustain our natural world

- To address community concerns, in Maine and around the globe, by devoting a portion of our time, talents, and resources to the environment, human needs, the arts, and education

- To work together to contribute to the long-term value and sustainability of our company

- To be a profitable and successful company, while acting in a socially and environmentally responsible manner

Today, Tom's of Maine has put their mission to work by contributing 10 percent of their pretax profits to the common good—charities serving the environment, education, the arts, and human needs. Their employees are also encouraged to use 5 percent of their paid work time for volunteer activities. They do not animal test or use animal ingredients, and they only use packaging that respects nature.

For some, this may seem like a lot, and it is. But if your values are a part of your business, then your values dictate how you do your business. Tom's of Maine is not only a highly profitable company, but a company well respected by its investors, its employees, its consumers, and the community at large. They've obviously proven that goodness *can* have a place in the market today.

Balancing the Budget and Your Values

1. Assess your values.
2. Break down self-doubt and listen to your soul.
3. Set realistic goals.
4. Define your mission statement.

Doing Well by Doing Good:
Making a Profit While Making a Difference

Because your business has a greater goal doesn't mean that it has no bottom line. Sales and profits are essential for your business—and your sanity. And while it may sound clever, savvy, or responsible to run a business with heart, your values will impact how your business performs.

Laurie Snyder, owner of Flap Happy, a designer and manufacturer of children's wear, uses only U.S. materials and labor for her garments, so that she can monitor the quality and also the treatment of the workers who assemble her stock. "It would be much cheaper for me to go overseas for my product," she says. "But there are too many unknowns out there." As a result, Flap Happy's hats and clothing reflect the higher prices of American manufacturing. "What I pass on to the consumer is high quality," says Snyder. "My customers understand that and will pay for it."

Judy Wicks, owner of Philadelphia's White Dog Cafe, always saw herself as a social justice activist, and running a capitalist enterprise had never figured into her plans. Believing that if more business owners "saw their connection to the community, they would make decisions for the common good," Wicks makes many decisions that set her apart from other small-business owners: she provides health insurance and paid vacations for longtime waiters, and her company contributes 10 percent of after-tax profits to various nonprofit projects, including those run by Wicks herself. One is her mentoring program, in which her staff trains high school kids interested in careers in the restaurant business. Efforts like these, as well as sponsoring speakers on issues from homelessness to health care, are all about building community.

For Kim Catrel, a caterer in Salt Lake City, Utah, her gift to the community is an extension of what she does best: cooking. While putting together lavish spreads for many state and local government fetes, Catrel knows that most guests will only nibble at the pricey produce and sumptuous seafood dishes she prepares. That's why she has an agreement with several organizations that feed Catrel victuals left after an event to an assortment of homeless individuals and families in domestic shelters. The tip Catrel offers: "Look inside yourself. There's probably something you're already doing that can be turned into a win-win situation."

Woman on the Way

*

Laura Scher
CEO: Working Assets Funding Service, San Francisco, California
Business Philosophy: You can operate a socially conscious business *and* make a profit
Greatest Accomplishment: Generating over $2 million to give social organizations last year

There aren't many CEOs like Laura Scher, who believes that making money *and* a difference are not mutually exclusive goals. After graduating in the top 5 percent of her Harvard Business School class, she jumped, feet first, into her own company. She was the *only* employee—answering the phone, stuffing envelopes, and developing a plan to change the telecommunications industry.

What germinated became the forward-thinking Working Assets, an organization that has built its market base with customers who elect to save the world, a bit at a time, while saving money on their long-distance phone calls.

Scher and her cofounders developed an innovative idea called "painless generosity," a way to facilitate change doing everyday activities: shopping, going out to dinner, or talking on the telephone. In 1985 Working Assets launched the first donation-linked credit card, a strategy that has been copied by scores of nonprofit and for-profit concerns in the years since. The concept is simple: for every credit card purchase, Working Assets donates ten cents to a range of nonprofit groups working for peace, human rights, economic and social justice, and the environment. Then came the long-distance service.

"We wanted to create something painless, so that every time you picked up the phone or bought a book, a donation was generated at no cost to you," explains Scher.

Her investment paid off big. In 1995, just ten years after she cofounded the company, Working Assets Funding Service generated revenues of $80 million. And to date Working Assets has raised more than $7 million for groups from Habitat for Humanity and the Children's Defense Fund to the Mexican Human Rights Commission.

As she continues to look forward, Scher plans to tackle the bureaucracy-heavy electricity industry. Although full deregulation won't take place until 2003, Scher is forecasting that Working Assets will be among the companies launching pilot programs in 1998. "Customers would continue to receive their energy through the same wires they have now, but they'd get a bill from Working Assets, and 1 percent of the payment will go into our donations pool," she says.

What keeps Scher motivated? "I don't want my daughter to grow up in a world where she can't swim in the local river and where there is a huge gap between the haves and the have-nots," she says. "I can't sit by and not try to make a difference. Making a difference is what Working Assets is founded on."

✳   ✳   ✳

Nonprofit Is More Than Pure Altruism: How Savvy Entrepreneurs Are Transforming the Industry

Until recent years, nonprofit and charity were two closely associated words in most people's minds. To the uninformed, nonprofits were supposed to operate without any intent or motive toward making money.

On the other hand, for-profit businesses run by entrepreneurs were on the opposite end of the spectrum, seen as businesses defined solely by financial success.

Those days are long gone. Nonprofit agencies, stricken by the scale-backs of governmental benefactors and having to vie with other agencies for the precious few grants available, are rapidly motivating to operate as competitive businesses.

This newest trend in nonprofit is to move away from the management of a seasoned administrator and replace her with a successful businessperson who can grow the organization, motivate the staff, and see into the future. This is the new wave of nonprofit.

Don't fret, however, if you've been working in nonprofit and are looking to set up your own agency. Executive director partnerships with one administrator and one business arm are increasing in the nonprofit sector. Additionally, the individuals you propose for your board will speak volumes about your administrative bent.

Because your salary is set largely on your funding base, carefully consider not only the services you will provide, but where you will gather your contributions. Be aware, however, that nonprofit salaries generally do not compete with those of corporate America. And there are no end-of-year sales (or service) bonuses.

In many cases you'll barely eke out a living. If your lifestyle overhead is high, consider consulting for nonprofits—if you have marketable experience—or re-tailoring your life for a leaner, more efficient you.

Many state that the rewards of doing the work can compensate for the lack of cash. Over three decades ago in the Watts section of south-central Los Angeles, Alice Harris, then a neighborhood beautician, vowed to help "black and brown get along together as neighbors instead of enemies," by, among other things, motivating young people to stay in school and out of harm's way.

Harris's creation, Parents of Watts, a nonprofit organization originally developed to save at-risk teens, has since grown into a full-service center that has counseled, fed, baby-sat, and trained thousands of community members to become a contributing part of the city. The center occupies the better part of a tree-lined city block and includes a home for the mentally ill, a learning center with a computer lab, a crisis center that houses parolees entered in work rehabilitation, and housing for college students. No one who comes for help, be it counseling, education, housing, or food, is refused. Harris's only criterion is that those seeking help must be willing to cooperate and help themselves.

Her biggest success thus far is a program of after-school tutoring to prevent dropouts. Every afternoon up to one hundred students parade into Parents of Watts for several hours of crunching through the schoolwork assigned that day at their public schools. Either collegiate volunteers or better-prepared peers supply one-on-one attention. And day after day the students stay until the homework is done.

It's a guaranteed formula for success *if* the kids keep showing up, which is why years ago Harris instituted a remarkably effective reward system: any student who hasn't cut an afternoon session for one year earns a trip to Hawaii, courtesy of local groups and supporters. Almost one hundred Watts kids whose persistence earned one of those vacations are in college right now. "These are youngsters who never even thought of finishing high school," says Alton Arnold, the principal of Watts's Jordan Locke High School. It's no wonder that when tragedy strikes in her community, and a youth is involved in a gang-related activity, Harris is often the first called, even before the authorities.

Harris, who until recently worked two jobs in addition to managing the city- and privately funded center, says she is most proud of the many children who now consider the tutoring a privilege. "I had a boy tell me recently, 'All these kids are smart. I want to bring my sister and brother here because they're smart—and they'd be even smarter if they came here.' "

The recipient of the *Ms.* magazine 1988 Woman of the Year Award and former President Bush's "703rd Daily Point of Light" is busy creating new opportunities for community kids to build self-esteem. Currently she is fund-raising to build a home at the foot of the San Gabriel Mountains as a retreat for neighborhood children to "give them a different environment and expand their horizons."

Tricks of the Trade

Alice Harris of Parents of Watts, on success in the nonprofit arena:

1. *Develop long-term goals.* Your goals may not be grand (one might be simply to survive), but creating an actual list is the first step on the path to attaining them.
2. *Create personal and professional networks.* You can't do it all yourself, but there are plenty out there who have the know-how, finances, connections, and motivation to help you along. Use them.
3. *Get the community behind you.* If people in your immediate community believe in what you're trying to do—and see direct benefit to their community—you'll be able to mobilize them when you're in need. The community is also a great source of emotional support and fund-raising.
4. *Explore new options.* What works for others many not work for you. Try new things and don't be afraid to fail.

5. *See yourself successful.* Everyone wants to ally with a winner—including you. If you view your venture as successful, chances are it will be.

6. *Consolidate your gains.* If four high school students in your program of eight are awarded college scholarships, that's a 50 percent success rate!

7. *Be prepared for an unpleasant backlash.* Somebody, somewhere—regardless of how much good you're doing—is going to dislike you. Maybe they're threatened, maybe it's someone running a competitive program. It's going to happen. Make sure you and your business is beyond reproach, and you'll be able to weather the storm.

8. *Hold it together during the bad times.* Remember, you're a role model. If things are going badly, be open and honest about it, but don't "lose it" or act out on your fears. Your behavior during these hard times will be scrutinized by others, who may model your behavior.

9. *Practice what you preach.* If your agency advocates an alcohol-free workplace, you'd be wise to steer away from two-martini lunches. Likewise, if you're helping ex-cons get back on their feet, you may not want to be conducting questionable business practices.

10. *Share the wealth.* What you learn from your business is valuable information. Share it openly and freely with others looking to follow in your footsteps.

✳ ✳ ✳

Seven Simple Steps to Starting Your Own Nonprofit Organization

There is no substitute for the active responsibility one citizen feels toward another. Whether you choose to serve others directly, indirectly, or through a self-help organization, and whether your main source of funding is the government, foundations, or corporations, as a private citizen group you'll need to comply with the requirements of your state and local government while serving the community. If you're already calculating your lack of time and resources, don't be dismayed. Here are some tips to get you started:

Get Your Facts Straight

Once you decide your issue or cause is worth pursuing, the first step is to find out if your perception of the need is correct—by conducting a thorough review of the information available in the community you wish to serve. The information you gather will help you fight opposition, write a convincing mission statement, and persuade the public to support your cause. Visit the library, the Internet, federal information centers, newspaper clippings libraries, other nonprofit associations, community information centers, local churches, and other community groups to ensure that you are not duplicating an existing program.

Meet Other Interested Citizens Who Can Help You

Approach local individuals and community organizations who know the community and may be interested in the problem, be able to evaluate the issues, and be able to seek out their own information within your community. This is your first step in sharing information and building morale; it will allow you to get new ideas and insights, begin to divide up your workload, and make decisions. An excellent resource is *Getting People Together,* published by the Community Development Branch of the Ministry of Community and Social Services, third floor, Hepburn Block, Toronto, Ontario M7A 1E9.

After the first meeting of interested citizens has been held, it's time to solicit wider community involvement. A public forum is a good way of finding out more about the issue your group is interested in, because there is a lot of two-way communication: you explain the problem; people give facts, their experiences, opinions, and advice. Follow-up makes the difference between action and more hot air: be sure to get everyone's name, address, and telephone number and send a report to everyone who attended as well as notices of further meetings. Hint: This is also a great place to pick up volunteers!

Come Up with a Specific Plan or Solution

Explore viable strategies that address your issue by undertaking a community conference, a well-organized survey, person-to-person interviews, a properly designed research study, a demonstration project to test a plan of action, or a citizen task force or coalition. By actively planning and working on your issue while broadening the base of support and impact of your group on the community, your nonprofit is off to a good organizational start.

Define Your Group's Structure

Most citizen groups start spontaneously in reaction to a local situation, and many do not maintain a conventional organization with a board of directors and standing committee. Rather, everyone joins in and shares responsibilities equally, and a "collective" sense prevails. The members of the small citizen group usually set policy and carry out the programs without hiring a full staff. However, totally unstructured groups can be dangerous and can result in the members pursuing different agendas because there is no leadership or moderator. To avoid this, you may want to consider incorporating, where your organizational structure leans toward a "vertical" hierarchy and there is a chain of command from top to bottom, with a predetermined "pecking order."

Incorporating limits your debt liability, allows you to remain in operation for a defined period of years, helps you commit yourself legally to written objectives, helps you obtain funds from the government and foundations who might otherwise decline to fund you, and qualifies you as a tax-exempt organization for federal and state income tax purposes. Note: It is not necessary to incorporate to acquire tax-exempt status, but it may facilitate the application process; before the IRS will grant an exemption, it must be convinced that your group is organized on a solid basis, and incorporation may help your credibility.

The following steps are general guidelines to nonprofit incorporation:

- *Appoint a committee to act as your executive board.* Being on a board involves more than just influencing people and raising money. Not to minimize the importance of these issues, remember it's just as smart to seek out people who will function beyond "figureheads"—those who will not only advocate for your organization, but possess skills necessary for your nonprofit and take an active interest in the actual mechanics of running it.

- *Get a lawyer.* You may find one willing to volunteer his or her services; if not, your local community legal service might be able to provide the help you need at a reasonable price. Better yet, seek out a lawyer who might be willing to sit on your board. A good referral source is another nonprofit organization that can recommend a lawyer with experience in nonprofit law. Legal fees for incorporation can range from $200 to $1,000.

- *Obtain the necessary application forms and a copy of the act governing nonprofit corporations in your state.* In most states you can write to the office of the secretary of state for these. Incorporation in one state does not restrict your activities to that state; you may operate more or less freely anywhere in the country—subject to local laws. State filing fees range from $50 to $200.

- *Draft a constitution and a set of bylaws, which are the rules that govern your organization.* Although most groups are given boilerplate bylaws by their lawyers, these must be checked carefully to make sure they are in accordance with your nonprofit's mission. (You may want to obtain photocopies of similar organizations' incorporation papers.) These bylaws become law only when formally accepted by your organization. A resolution by the board of directors, ratified by the organization's voting members, can change any bylaw. Obviously your bylaws need to be in harmony with state laws regarding nonprofit organizations.

Apply for Tax Exemption

Whether your group incorporates or not, it is necessary to apply to the IRS if you want tax exemption. Incorporation does *not* automatically register your group with the IRS. An organization's eligibility for federal tax exemption depends upon the nature of its activities.

Groups established for "religious, charitable, educational, scientific, or literary purposes, or to prevent cruelty to children or animals" enjoy a double privilege: they are exempt from income taxes, and donors may deduct their contributions to such groups. Another round of these double-exempt organizations includes labor unions, social clubs, and organizations dedicated to "social welfare." This second category covers all groups whose sole or major activity is the promotion of changes in legislation or government policy.

Requirements for exemption from state income taxes generally follow the federal pattern. Contact your state information office or your secretary of state for details.

Your first step toward securing an exemption should be to obtain a copy of IRS publication #557, *How to Apply for Recognition of Exemption for an Organization,* available from all IRS offices.

Form a Board of Directors

A board of directors is simply a formal policy-setting group that can be held liable for your organization, depending upon certain circumstances. Legally, an incorporated organization must have a minimum number of directors who assume certain official positions (such as president, secretary, and treasurer), but this varies from state to state.

Primarily, boards set policies that embody the intentions of the group; in an incorporated organization, the board is legally responsible for upholding the constitution and bylaws. Also, the board decides who is responsible for what duties within the organization and how the organization should conduct itself in the community. In a small group that does not have a formal staff, the policy makers do not have direct responsibilities for operations and programs; instead they approve or reject major suggestions made by staff. Here are some tips for composing your board:

- Get representatives from different social, economic, and cultural groups involved with the issue your group is facing.

- Get a representation of geographic areas, and have a fair balance of men and women.

- Have appropriate client representation if your group is a service organization, or representation by those who are affected in any way by the issues in question if you're a citizens' rights group.

- Recruit professional or expert representation in the problem area, as well as lawyers, accountants, and other professionals.

- Recruit prestigious people, preferably those who are prepared to work! You can also invite them to participate in a less formal capacity—for example, as a consultant on your advisory board.

- If you are a citizen group, make sure lay citizens outnumber professional representation by at least two-thirds.

Plan Your Work Program

In newly established groups, priorities for programs usually involve the reasons the group came together in the first place. In order to determine your community's needs and where your group should place its program emphasis, hold a brainstorming session that tries to answer questions that affect your target group—specifically, what does the target group need and how can you deliver it? The following simple steps should get you started:

- Collect information about the need for the program.

- Decide clearly on the intent and purpose of the program.

- Plan on how to put the program into action.

- Estimate costs—in human, material, and financial terms. Make a budget based on half your original estimated revenue, and increase estimated expenditures by 10 percent.

- Evaluate your proposed plan.

- Prepare your schedule of steps for putting the program into action. Responsibilities, confirmed in writing, should be given to individuals with a complete list displayed so each hand knows what the other is doing.

- Always have a plan B.

- Evaluate your program in action.

Seven Simple Steps to Starting Your Own Nonprofit Organization

1. Get your facts straight.
2. Meet other interested citizens who can help you.
3. Come up with a specific plan or solution.
4. Define your group's structure.
5. Apply for tax exemption.
6. Form a board of directors.
7. Plan your work program.

Woman on the Way

✳

Anne Neri Kostiner
Executive Director: Gallery 312, Chicago
Business Philosophy: Bringing together the arts, business, community, and children's causes
Greatest Accomplishment: Project PEACH (Patience, Education, Arts, Consistency, and Hope), a nonprofit teaching center for children at risk

By taking Annie Properties, a successful real estate development company specializing in luxury lofts, and using its clout to create an art gallery with all cash donations and 85 percent of gallery commissions going to underprivileged children, "Annie" Kostiner created the template for a new generation of careful giving.

Gallery 312 is a unique melding of arts space and philanthropic institution. The gallery exhibits well-known artists, museum shows, and local Chicago artists, while all donations benefit a variety of children's organizations. To cover the expenses of putting up these shows, Kostiner's business, Annie Properties, underwrites exhibit production and gallery operations. Annie looks to local corporate donors to contribute cash donations, which are placed into the Gallery 312 administered fund 501(k)(3) and donated to a carefully chosen local children's service agency, which Kostiner invites to publicize itself through and during the exhibit.

While converting some of Chicago's old, beautiful warehouses and factories into luxury lofts, Kostiner stumbled into her nonprofit venture when an artist looking for a work space came into her loft office and asked if she had a large space to rent for practically nothing. "We happened to have about six thousand square feet of unrenovated space, and thought this would be nice to have him take over and pay the utility bills for a couple of months," she offers. This segued into another building and an even larger space to start up a gallery for Chicago artists as well as other well-known artists.

Kostiner and her husband realized that owning a gallery is very difficult, so they decided to solicit the private sector contacts they had developed from their real estate dealings. "What we started to do was approach children's organizations and get them involved in the production of the show. They would come to opening night and talk a bit about the organization. Meanwhile people would donate money to go to that organization. Private companies, such as Citibank, donated to the fund, so all the donations and gallery commissions went directly into the pockets of the artists and organizations.

"To date, we've raised over forty thousand dollars through cash donations and the sale of art in Gallery 312." For Kostiner, her success has resulted from a combination of her values and a sharp business sense. "I really feel that if you follow your soul, the right decisions are just waiting for you. Life is so short, it's important to make a difference in your life for other people."

* * *

Tricks of the Trade

Laura Lederer of Lederer Consulting, on getting grants:

1. *Identify five to ten foundations to approach first.* You can research which foundations are most likely to fund your organization at one of the many foundation centers in the United States. Call the New York office at (212) 620-4230 to find a branch in your area.
2. *Study each of your foundation prospects* to determine if the foundation is appropriate for your organization.
3. *Send for the foundation's application* by calling its office, and ask for its annual report, grant procedures, and guidelines. Inquire about the general monetary amount of grants given by that particular foundation, and be sure you request a grant in that range if you send a proposal.
4. *Create a file on each foundation,* and include the annual report and other information. Each time you speak to a foundation officer, make notes of your conversation and keep them in the file.
5. *Write the proposal after studying the foundation's applications procedures.* Follow its guidelines and make sure you include all necessary information in your proposal. If you don't know how to write one, consult one of the many excellent books on the subject or contact the Grantsmanship

Center at (213) 482-9860 for information on a grant-writing seminar in your area.

6. *Identify other groups that have successfully applied for funds from the foundation,* and talk with them about their particular strategy.

7. *Write a short letter of inquiry* (no more than two pages) to the director or a particular program officer; be sure to include who, what, when, where, and how much, and ask whether the foundation would be interested in receiving a full proposal. Most foundations receive tons of paper, so don't send extraneous information. Send your proposal only if the foundation responds positively. Hint: Most foundations have funding cycles—timelines you will have to meet in order to have your proposal considered at their board meetings—so call and find out when theirs is and get your proposal in three months in advance.

8. *Make an appointment—if the foundation is interested—to see its representative* to talk about the fit between your work and its funding programs.

9. *Find out about the foundation's "style" before you go and visit.* Is it conservative or casual? This will help you decide how to dress and whether it is necessary to take along a board member from your organization.

10. *Consider using euphemisms* like "reproductive health" for abortion and "community education" for advocacy or organizing. It may not seem fair, but the reality is that you can increase your chances of success this way.

11. *Keep in mind that service groups are more likely to get funding than advocacy and activist organizations.*

12. *Follow up your visit with a thank-you letter.* Be sure to say that you will be back in touch in the next couple of weeks to find out how to proceed. Try to maintain contact by sending the foundation important new information about your organization as it develops.

* * *

The fact is that women's organizations receive smaller grants than equivalent or comparable men's organizations. But don't let that discourage you; with the right approach, there *is* money available. If a foundation rejects your proposal, call within four weeks to find out why. Ask if the foundation would consider a new proposal in its next funding cycle. If you feel their constructive criticism is valid, use the foundation's feedback to tailor your approach when you apply to the next foundation on your list. And above all, don't give up!

Raising Money from the Community

As Alice Harris so sweetly put it, "If people in your immediate community believe in what you're trying to do—and see direct benefit to their community—you'll be able to mobilize them when you're in need."

But forward-thinking venturers will have forged these connections before they are in need. Local franchises, national corporations with ties to your area, and other socially responsible businesses often have programs set up to benefit organizations just like yours.

Do the Research

Before you go out soliciting money, find out where the money lies. Is your area eligible for any governmental aid on a local, state, or federal level? If so, who are the appropriate people to contact? Making sure to cover your bases before you put your hand out is the first step in securing funds.

Seek out People Who've "Made It"

If little Johnny from the next block is now designing Web pages in Silicon Valley, remind him that you're still around and hit him up for a few bucks for his old neighborhood.

Don't Overlook the Corporations

Annie Kostiner had long-standing relationships with many corporate officers through her development company, Annie Properties. When she began her gallery venture, they were the first people she hit up. "Corporations give money away in large volume," she says. "Don't feel that yours doesn't have a chance."

8

Retail

In the recent past, the retailing business has experienced its share of problems. From high employee turnover rates to poor customer service, many small independent retailers have barely managed to survive. At the same time, they've watched the chain stores and mass merchandisers move in, corner, and control the market. Sadly, the trends indicate that the future for the small retailer—as we know it now—isn't much brighter.

As businesses continue to downsize, part-time work replaces full-time work, and technical knowledge supersedes college degrees, women entrepreneurs are finding the only way to win the retail game is to have a competitive edge and a lot of capital. The only way to even be in the game, they believe, is to compete with the chain stores, which usually means being a chain store. Of all small retail businesses, only a small percent are surviving per year. In the next ten years that number could be much smaller. In order to survive and succeed, retailers must be prepared to adapt to the rapidly changing economic and consumer climate.

Statisticians have predicted that as technology continues to replace human labor it will result in a smaller middle class, thus eroding the retail consumer base. The consumer of today is already transitioning into the consumer of tomorrow. In the next decade retailers believe the market will be made up of consumers who work longer hours and, often, for themselves. Small companies will comprise one to five employees. The small-business owner will spend more time working a job, rather than running the company. Employers will pay commissions for short-term or long-term projects, rather than salaries. People will run out of money before they die, as they make less money in their life and Social Security benefits are reduced. As alarming as these predictions may sound, up-and-coming retailers need to understand just whom they will be selling to.

Overworked and underpaid, the consumer of the near future will be buying from the companies that utilize time-saving technology. As many home businesses are growing, consumers don't necessarily have the time to deal with mall traffic and hassle. Many large retailers are now investing in mail-order catalogs, on-line and Web site catalogs, and television shopping in addition to their chain stores. They are also designing delivery services that respond to the customer's needs twenty-four hours a day.

Moreover, they are creating computer software and databases that allow customers to get exactly what they want, when they want it. One London company, for example, offers an interactive cable station tailored to prospective home buyers. The buyer can hit a button on the remote control and view properties for sale. When 30 percent of the population are lower-income consumers, retailers need to offer lower prices and better value for the money. A superstore may not have as much difficulty lowering prices, but it's death for the small retailer, whose typically higher prices reflect better service and a quality product. Now the chain stores, realizing they can afford to offer better service and products through the aid of technology, are driving small-business retailers right out of the market.

Though the consumers of the future may be earning less, they will be demanding more from large chain stores, including good-quality and personalized service. Even now, increasing numbers of consumers say that they will not return to a particular store if they've been unhappy with the service. While chain stores have always gotten by because of their typically large selection of merchandise, they must now revamp their customer service policies in order to retain customers. Someday these chain stores may even rule the service businesses. As the mass merchandisers react to customer needs, the small retailers are losing their edge.

Despite the bleak outlook for independent retailers, keeping an eye on the consumer's needs, offering high-quality service, being innovative with technology, producing a specialized product, and adapting to change before it happens may keep the small retailer in the competition. Nothing is written in stone, and small retailers may still operate a flourishing business—they'll just have to work harder and smarter for it.

Looking beyond the Hourly Wage: Envisioning Employees as Your Business Lifeblood

Though many business owners invest most of their energy in creating better products and customer service, savvy entrepreneurs are seeing the future and realizing that their employees are equally important to the success of their business. As a result, they are training their employees on every aspect of the business, from reading profit and loss statements to handling customer problems. Able to take on more responsibility, the employees of the future will be used to their maximum potential and take pride in their abilities. Yet many women entrepreneurs believe that their employees will have to be rewarded more if they are working harder and smarter. Some women business owners feel that employers should treat their employees like customers, to reduce their turnover rate and improve morale. Since a company's growth depends on its employees, women entrepreneurs are looking to hire individuals who will treat the company as if they were owners. Indeed, many employees of the future will have stock in the company or share a percentage of the profits. These entrepreneurs are finding that the best way to find the employees of tomorrow is to start changing their policies and procedures today.

Rhonda M. Abrams, president of Abrams Business Strategies, a San Francisco–based management/consulting firm, a syndicated columnist, and author of *The Successful Business Plan: Secrets & Strategies,* says that as small-business owners, "everybody is grappling with these issues." For many business owners, Abrams offers, establishing a relationship between "boss" and "employee" is the hardest thing.

"One of my first times as a supervisor, I had a secretary who always left early. It was very difficult to confront her. When I did, she told me off and two weeks later she quit. Next time, I crossed over the line and became too friendly. It backfired when she wanted me to do something inappropriate and I turned her down. It was her friend rather than her boss turning her down," says Abrams.

It's important to remember that even people who look very successful have these same issues, according to Abrams. "I think women often feel if they set limits or are too strong, their employees won't like them. You can be sure men don't think that way." The problem, Abrams states, is not in being too lenient or too strict. It's more about setting standards: being fair, listening, communicating.

"It's very important to be genuine. You have to develop a management style that is expressive of your values and who you really are. Often this requires a higher degree of self-introspection than many people have," adds Abrams.

Abrams also believes it is essential to be able to translate your vision to the people who work with you. Many times the entrepreneur has a vision but can't pass it on to her employees. "Remember, being a good boss takes time, and it's important to take that time as an investment in your future."

Gertrude Boyle, Columbia Sportswear's chairwoman of the board, believes that Columbia's employees are largely responsible for the company's rapid growth. "We live by the open-door policy—we're always here for everyone." Boyle strongly believes in "walking the shop"—that is, getting out and talking to each and every employee on a regular basis. "It's impossible to make arbitrary decisions about your employees when you know the score of their child's soccer game," says Boyle.

Barbara Bissett, owner of Bissett Steel, agrees. "We have no communication barriers in the company. Everyone knows what's going on, every day. Each person in this organization can communicate openly with any other, and that means that we all work toward the same goal, with the same expectations." She adds, "By giving away a bit of your power and bringing your employees into the heart of the business, you earn their trust. Everyone talks about trusting their employees, but it's reciprocal. And you have to earn that trust."

Interviewing and Hiring Employees

Practically every employee gone wrong can be traced to the hiring process. Employers have been quick to cast the blame on employees for their inability to perform or get along. Yet women entrepreneurs are sharing the responsibility and questioning their hiring procedures. Did they miss a large character flaw in the interview? Did they not check references? Were they so desperate to fill the position that they acted in haste?

Whatever the situation, women entrepreneurs believe the only way to cut down on firing is to hire more effectively. These women are making the hiring process as essential to their businesses as putting out the product. Hiring the wrong people can cost the company in productivity, efficiency, and bottom line, not to mention the effects on employee morale.

According to Rosalind Paaswell, former president of the American Woman's Economic Development (AWED) Corporation, "One of the most momentous—and most hazardous—times for an entrepreneur is the transition between being self-employed and having employees." She suggests two things: study employment law and to understand your rights and your potential employees' rights, and learn how to manage people.

Barbara Bissett believes that the worst mistake an employer can make is to feel desperate to hire someone—anyone—to fill a position. "I will only hire someone I truly want to work with. Many people hire out of need. It took me a year to hire a sales manager. I went through the process a couple of times, and no one had the level of energy and intellect that I needed. I work very closely with people, and they have to be someone I can communicate with and respect. If I hire someone who doesn't work out, we both lose." Bissett recommends that you do your homework and be thorough in your hiring processes.

Though different companies have different specific needs, certain general qualities are always crucial: integrity, humility, and flexibility. Some candidates may have all the required degrees and years of experience, but if they lack one of those basic traits, business owners should be wary. Technology can be taught, equipment can be learned, and knowledge can be acquired, but employers can't change the candidate's basic foundation. All businesses need trustworthy people who can adapt to change and get along well with their associates. Also look for intelligence, confidence, and optimism, which may be more crucial than college degrees or experience. Then look at experience, training, work history, education, and references. Rather than hiring the person who could be productive immediately, though, try to determine who will be successful in the long term, even if they require more initial training.

Lorraine Miller, owner of Cactus and Tropicals in Salt Lake City, Utah, offers, "I'm in an industry that prides itself on minimum wage and then complains about the high turnover." Miller's solution was to hire people actively pursuing careers in horticulture and pay them a bit more hourly. "This way, I bring in employees who are excited about the business, and they get a flexible, supportive working environment and a paycheck they can actually live off of.

"I wanted to be in business for freedom and create a working environment where employees can be free also. I've learned over the years that not everyone wants that. I want employees who have personal creativity, freedom, and accountability. I now look for those people over the 'tell me what you want to do and I'll do it' type."

According to Marcia Radosevich, CEO of HPR Inc., a company

that creates software programs for health insurers, look for a value fit before a skill fit. "No matter how skilled a person is, if their values don't fit, they won't be happy, you won't be happy, and it won't last."

Business owners usually know what they want in an employee but have a difficult time determining if the employee really has what it takes. Many times entrepreneurs think they've found the ideal candidate, only to discover a month later that the employee just happened to mouth the right phrases in the interview. To avoid being sucked in by a slick talker, spend more time interviewing. Create tough questions based on the person's résumé, rather than sticking to the standard interview questions.

Another problem business owners face is determining the truth of an employee's references. As former employers can be sued for giving a bad reference, many don't offer any information at all on the employee. Others sing the employee's praises, even if it's not true. At the same time, someone with an ax to grind may give a former employee a horrible reference, though that information may not be accurate, either. Try not to base your hiring decisions largely on references, and find more creative ways of testing an employee.

Sometimes business owners try to hire people like themselves, when they really need to hire someone who balances their strengths and weaknesses. Other times they expect too much of the employee. Try to separate yourself from your company's needs in order to hire the right candidate instead of a clone. Marcia Radosevich adds, "I try to hire someone who can do the job better than I can. This frees me up to go out on the road."

All too often business owners make the mistake of asking formulaic, "yes or no" questions. You'll find that you can better gauge a person's merit by asking questions that require long answers, such as "Tell me about yourself" or "How did you handle that difficult situation?" Then try to determine honesty by asking candidates what their biggest mistake was. If the interviewee can't think of a thing, chances are you're not getting the full story.

Other times you may want to ask questions to reveal personality traits, such as creativity and originality. You could ask what potential hires find exciting, how would they run the business, and what would they change first if they were the U.S. president. These questions may seem silly, but they reflect the individual's beliefs and attitude. It's also pretty revealing if the individual scoffs at the questions.

As 25 percent of résumés are hyped up, and use impressive words to define mediocre tasks, try to cut through the haze with in-depth questions. Ask questions to determine whether the candidate has an honest résumé. How did you implement that idea? What tools did you utilize? What was the end result? What problems did you encounter? How did you solve them?

What not to ask may be as important as what to ask. The government provides guidelines for inappropriate questions, and if employers cross them, they may find themselves slapped with a lawsuit based on discrimination. Asking questions (or having them on an application form) about a candidate's age, health or disability, plans to start a family, national origin, and criminal record (except for a felony conviction) are against the law. Find out the law in your state, as there are some variances.

Motivating Employees without Promotions or Extra Pay

Companies large and small may be low on capital these days yet still want to reward their employees for a job well done. Employee morale will disintegrate if you don't offer bonuses of some type. Many entrepreneurs have found that praise and recognition is effective in motivating employees.

Whether you give out an award every month or simply thank and praise your employees frequently, entrepreneurs will find that valued employees become valuable. Some owners of large companies suggest employers feature star employees in the company newsletter, which increases the employee's feeling of self-worth while encouraging other employees to strive harder.

In place of cold hard cash, many owners are offering profit-sharing plans and stock options to their employees. When the employees have a stake in the company's profits, they work harder to achieve results. Even a small share can motivate employees to work toward the company's success. If no stock is available and profit sharing is impossible, many companies motivate employees with reward games. For example, whoever makes the most sales in a specific time period receives a gift certificate or luxury item. (Some companies use barter organizations to trade for employee bonuses without having to pay cash.) Usually, though, the bonus doesn't have to be too expensive, as the game itself makes the employees' jobs more fun.

At the Sisterhood Bookstore in West Los Angeles, owners Adele Wallace and Simone Wallace find themselves guarding the budget fiercely, particularly after a Borders superstore opened right across the street from their small women's bookstore. Because they can't pay their employees what they'd like to, they support their employees by allowing creative freedom. "One of our workers decided that she was very interested in the idea of a newsletter. It's a way for her to express her creativity and her writing ability, so she's going to take initiative and start that," says Simone Wallace. "Another is very interested in displays and front windows, and she gets to express that."

Some women business owners have also made it a point to recognize employees' birthdays, graduations, and other such events. A gift doesn't have to be expensive, just thoughtful. The employee will feel genuinely cared about and be motivated to work harder. As often as possible, companies should also recognize their employees' personal talents. Sponsoring the office athlete or dancer, for example, could make a difference in the employee's motivation and subsequent achievement, as that employee's personal goals are being met.

While small businesses may not be financially able to offer some of the perks of larger companies, women-owned businesses are increasingly supportive of employees who wish to take parental leave or work split schedules. "We always try to work with an employee," says Adele Wallace. "In most cases, the employee comes to us with a solution before they've even told us about their problem. If we can find a way to work it out, we do."

Tricks of the Trade

Lorraine Miller of Cactus and Tropicals, on how to stock the shelves:

1. *Anticipate needs.* If you're selling resort wear in a warm tourist climate, think rain. Some days it will be colder than others, and travelers don't always come prepared. Offer inexpensive items to "save the day." This is only an example, but it serves to show how understanding your market and clientele is the key to profitable retailing.
2. *Insure your inventory.* This may seem like common sense, but things happen. Don't be stuck with $30,000 worth of bills on stolen or damaged stock.
3. *Figure out worst-case scenarios.* Okay, so you bought several dozen overpriced O. J. Simpson autographed footballs just a day before the infamous Bronco freeway chase. What would you do? Think creatively: an albatross can be turned into a cash cow with a little bit of brainpower.
4. *Be doubly cautious if your merchandise is perishable.* Perishable merchandise has a limited shelf life.
5. *Have an outlet for overstocks.* If you can find an outlet to take your overstocks, great. If not, try donating to a women's shelter or other tax-deductible cause.
6. *Consider consignment.* Many successful retailers take consignment stock—that is, merchandise that is placed at no cost to you in your store. The catch? You take a smaller profit margin on the sale.

✳ ✳ ✳

Make It Yourself or Buy It: The Retailer's Guide to Stocking the Shelves

Once you've come up with a winning product idea or concept, you must consider carefully how you're going to put it on the shelves. Before deciding whether to become a manufacturer or a buyer, first do your homework.

Define and Research the Product

One of the most crucial steps in product development is knowing exactly what the product is or does. A company that specializes in homemade food products, for example, obviously won't buy their cakes from a mass manufacturer. On the other hand, an auto parts store wouldn't waste time and energy producing parts for every car ever made. They'll buy from many different dealers.

Also consider whom the product is for. Is the product designed for consumers who want high quality above all else? A clothing store catering to upper-class clientele, for example, may make custom-made suits, while a clothing store for teenagers may buy from manufacturers offering lower-quality garments at a lower price or in more trendy styles.

Once you have defined your product, check out the competition. Is the competition making their merchandise or buying it from a manufacturer? Are some products more successful than others? Are they offering their store brand products in addition to other manufacturers' items? Grocery stores are infamous for buying goods from different companies and selling their own brand for a lower price. Some entrepreneurs find that buying and making their products offers the consumer more choices, gives the store more credibility, and increases profits.

Trade shows may also help you decide what options there are. You may find the perfect product match for your store's identity, or you may not, but know that it's important to see what's on the market, who's selling, and who's buying.

Product Development

Whether you specialize in creating soaps or making computers, the developing and manufacturing processes are certainly more difficult than buying an existing product. When developing a product, you will need to have a laboratory or warehouse, experts or scientists on staff, production equipment, and suppliers to provide ingredients or parts. As product development may be labor and time intensive with no guarantees, first-time entrepreneurs may want to get their feet wet with an existing product, and plan to expand later. But, depending on the business, if you want to be competitive and offer the best products, manufacturing may be the only way. To make product development and manufacturing a positive venture, look toward building expert support teams. Meet with consultants, designers, patent attorneys, and market researchers to help avoid potential problems. (See the "Labor and Manufacturing" chapter for more information on how to produce your product.)

Once a product is developed, you will have to spend more time and money testing the merchandise, trial selling, and getting feedback from customers. The product will also have to pass state and federal inspections or rating classifications. Before venturing ahead with mass manufacturing, ascertain the technical and financial risks and the level of difficulty in producing the product. What may have been easy to develop may be impractical to mass-produce.

According to Gertrude Boyle, Columbia Sportswear develops its products differently. "Our sales department reports on what's out there. For example, if they find a need for a jacket in the $75–$100 market, we create something and we take it to our customers for feedback." Boyle considers this a foolproof method. "It gives you incredible feedback, because you're interacting with the target audience, who also ends up buying what they've helped to develop."

Buying from Dealers

Far less complex than developing and manufacturing products, buying from dealers or manufacturers still requires thought and planning. First, question the needs of your store. Are you selling a high-demand product? Will you need warehouse space in addition to the store? What are you ordering from dealers, how much are you ordering, and when are you ordering it?

After selecting the products consumers wish to buy, you should carefully research the dealers. How much time does it take to put through a purchase order? Do they guarantee quality? What are their standards? Will they immediately replace damaged goods, or will you have to wait until the next shipment? Do they deliver the product, or do you have to hire a third party? How much lead time does the distributor need in order to send the merchandise?

The Precarious World of Packaging and Pricing

The best products in the world will sit on the shelves if they're not packaged suitably. Pretty packaging, however, isn't enough by itself, either. Savvy entrepreneurs should desire several qualities in their package designs. Does it fit well with the store's identity? Does it fit the customer's identity? Does it include key information on the product, such as ingredients or features? Is it different from the competition's package? Does it protect the product well? This last question is especially important with edible, perishable, or breakable items. Is the product visible through the packaging? Does it need to be? Aromatherapy candles, for example, aren't going to sell if the buyer can't smell the scent.

People or offices may also be considered "packages," especially in the service sector. In these cases you may want to dress to convey a particular image and decorate your offices in a particular style. Corporate lawyers aren't going to get many clients dressed in jeans and a T-shirt (unless they work in the entertainment industry). Likewise, antique refinishers won't inspire confidence if their offices are decked out with postmodern furniture. Your image is just as important as honing your craft or product.

The key to business survival and profit is in effective pricing, as overpricing and underpricing can quickly send a company into the red. There is no surefire mathematical formula for pricing, but to achieve a return on an investment, make a profit, and increase sales, successful entrepreneurs use several pricing methods.

Cost-Plus Pricing

Used by many manufacturers and retailers, cost-plus pricing involves adding up all business costs—including salaries, rent, manufacturing, distribution, and so on—and then figuring in a profit percentage to arrive at a selling price.

In theory, cost-plus pricing certainly seems to make sense, but experts caution against using this method alone. Usually this approach considers only the numbers and forgets the intangibles, such as the customer's needs or the product demand. Also note that cost-plus pricing is usually effective when selling one product or service. Yet most companies sell many different products, and determining the costs per item may be difficult.

Market-Oriented Pricing

Service businesses tend to rely on the market-oriented approach to pricing, as they are selling intangibles. But you will find this method practical for selling products as well. Market-oriented pricing takes into account several factors: the current economy, competitors' prices and services, the type of product, customers' needs, and costs. Some entrepreneurs actually try to reduce their overhead in order to have more control over their pricing.

Promotional Pricing

Most businesses employ several promotional pricing tactics, from flexible pricing to rebates to trade-ins. Use these methods for a set period of time only in order to attract more or new customers. Garage sales, flea markets, and antique stores tend to use flexible pricing, aka haggling, in order to sell goods, while larger companies may offer mail-in rebates to entice customers. Used-car dealers may mark down the price of a car if a buyer trades in a car. All of these methods can generate more customers and more sales.

Discounts

Like promotional pricing, discount pricing is used to bring in more business. Employee discounts, early-bird discounts, quantity discounts, and seasonal discounts can generate more money even if the prices are lowered. Women entrepreneurs find that customers may purchase more items if they believe they are getting a bargain and, as a result, profit increases.

Pricing Strategies

1. Cost-plus pricing.
2. Market-oriented pricing.
3. Promotional pricing.
4. Discounts.

Woman on the Way

*

Gertrude Boyle
Chairwoman: Columbia Sportswear, Portland, Oregon
Business Philosophy: Quality, above all, in products, service, and relationships
Greatest Accomplishment: Enjoying my work

As the spirited matriarch and chairwoman of the board of family-owned Columbia Sportswear, Gertrude Boyle has been building her sportswear company's unique image, philosophy, and sales.

Boyle's parents started the company in 1938 when they fled Nazi Germany and settled in Portland, Oregon. In the last twenty-seven years Boyle and her son, Tim, have been running the company and have taken it from near bankruptcy to its current position as the world's largest outerwear manufacturer.

A much emulated entrepreneur, Gertrude Boyle is also the center of Columbia's hilarious, award-winning advertising campaign. She portrays cantankerous "Mother Gert," the overbearing taskmistress who enforces Columbia's demanding quality standards.

"People are very interested in technology. Style, for our consumers, isn't as important as performance." Not that Columbia's outerwear isn't stylish. Quite the contrary. There has been such a demand for "Gert-wear" that their line of skiwear, rugged outerwear, sportswear, and footwear are expanding. "A company that doesn't go with the flow misses out on a whole bunch," says Boyle. "You can't say, 'I'm going to make gray slacks and a blue blazer,' if people aren't going to buy it."

Unlike many other manufacturers who are trying to create the trends, Columbia relies heavily on customer input. "Sometimes we don't stay ahead of the pack," she says, "because successful retailing doesn't always involve being a trendsetter—sometimes it means providing a consistent, quality-made, affordable product that your customers can depend on."

✳　✳　✳

The Aggressive Merchandising Market

The miracles of technology have provided women entrepreneurs with some alternatives to the overabundance of stale marketing techniques. Classic marketing schemes, such as advertising in phone books, magazines, and newspapers, are falling on the priority list as women entrepreneurs are setting up Web sites, sending out catalogs, and making infomercials. They're finding that through these methods, they are better able to determine their client base, what their customers want, and how to serve them better and faster. Eventually, as technology becomes more accessible, competitive businesses will utilize many or all of the marketing strategies at once. Until then, entrepreneurs consider the options, based on their customer needs, product needs, and company budget.

Direct-Mail Marketing

For years many companies have been using the direct-mail marketing technique. Rather than send mass mailings to anybody and everybody, these entrepreneurs are using their databases to focus on the existing customer. This system capitalizes on two marketing theories: acquiring new customers costs five times as much as retaining existing customers, and the existing customer will bring in new customers through word of mouth.

In an attempt to satisfy the customer and generate profits, you can use direct-mail marketing in several ways. Some business owners will send out postcards to remind the customer of an important sale date, or they will mail brochures of new services and price changes. Others keep their customers informed by producing a monthly newsletter, which may feature coupons, smart shopping tips for the customer, and updates of company policy. Some entrepreneurs reward their preferred customers by mailing them an added discount or a free gift. You may also use direct mail as an interactive form of entertainment. A travel agency may send customers scratch tickets, with several types of prizes, ranging from the all-expenses-paid vacation to 20 percent off a rental car. Others use raffle tickets and sweepstakes to involve and entice the consumer.

While direct-mail marketing is certainly a proven method of boosting sales, operating a direct-mail campaign can be expensive and time-consuming. As paper costs and postage prices escalate, many companies are spending a pretty penny sending out their mailers. Another problem for business owners is that many aren't sure even how to begin such a campaign. There are, however, new companies that will do all the work for you at a reasonable price.

Catalogs and Mail-Order

Selling merchandise through catalogs can be an extremely profitable business as well as a marketing technique. In 1994 alone, the mail-order business reached a startling $129.74 billion. The catalog business has been so successful because they typically offer specialty products and customer convenience, while decreasing overhead on store space and staff. Many times they don't compete with existing stores because they provide products not currently in the market or near the consumer. And in this fast-paced world, catalog customers don't have to brave the weather, traffic, or mall hassle in search of something they may not find. From a business perspective, catalog owners have an advantage over store owners. Catalog orders require much more information about the buying customer, so catalog owners are better able to target and hit their market again and again. Yet many business owners are supplementing their stores with catalogs in order to satisfy the customer on both levels.

The catalog business is not without its flaws, however. Like direct-mail marketing, it faces higher costs. Most of the problems for catalog companies, though, lie with the consumer. Catalogs provide limited product information, which may be a consumer turnoff. The customer may also see buying from the catalog as a risky venture. They can't see the quality or touch the merchandise. They may have problems visualizing the product on their bodies or in their homes. Furthermore, many catalogs offer unfamiliar brands, so customers feel they really don't know what they're getting.

TV Shopping and Infomercials

No mailing and printing hassles makes TV shopping and infomercials a winner for women entrepreneurs. Besides, these methods provide massive market penetration instantly. They're also the future. Like catalogs, TV shopping provides the customer with a hassle-free environment while selling merchandise that may be difficult to obtain in stores. Unlike catalogs, they offer customers a large amount of product information by showing demonstrations and results. Some savvy entrepreneurs are using television shopping as a marketing strategy for their already existing store or chain, while others are using it to promote independent products.

In order to sell successfully on TV, business owners must first overcome the drawbacks. Though it's proven to be a moneymaker, consumers complain about the quality of the merchandise being sold. As of yet, home shopping hasn't consistently offered name brands, which is driving away consumers who could benefit most from the convenience. Consumers also dislike that fact that they can't instantly find the items they are interested in buying but must wait while the shopping channel goes from selling kitchen wares to jewelry to computers. As a result, consumers would rather go to the store than sit around wondering if the purchase of their dreams will ever appear on cable. However, technology will inevitably improve these problems dramatically.

On-Line Marketing and Selling

Although on-line selling has not yet proven profitable, many believe it's simply a matter of time. This technology is even further reaching than TV, and business owners may eventually find clients in all corners of the globe. Now business owners are starting up Web sites to sell their products and increase their hours of business, without staffing a store or requiring much space. They are mainly using the Internet as a marketing tool, providing product information to consumers as well as helpful hints on subjects related to the merchandise. Through e-mail, business owners can keep close contact with customers who have questions. Business owners may also track their clients' browsing habits on the Net and learn how to better accommodate them.

Not yet an exact science, on-line marketing and selling has hit a few glitches. Not all consumers have the technology available to them or the know-how to use it. Those who do have the means may not be buying for security reasons. Many consumers are fearful of giving out their credit card numbers on the Internet, and rightly so. Though theoretically it is no more dangerous than doing it over the phone, the potential for fraud seems much higher on the Internet. Since the technology is growing so rapidly, the security systems being designed are not invincible and may be outdated quickly by a smart hacker. As consumers become accustomed to this form of shopping and technology changes, business owners will not be able to survive without the Internet.

Women on the Way

✳

Adele Wallace and Simone Wallace
Owners and Partners: Sisterhood Bookstore, Los Angeles
Business Philosophy: Welcome change
Greatest Accomplishment: Being around after twenty-five years

Adele Wallace and Simone Wallace opened Sisterhood Bookstore in fall of 1972. In 1997 they celebrated their twenty-fifth anniversary. What's the secret behind their success?

"We didn't start the business with the intention of having it twenty-five years later," says Simone Wallace.

Adds Adele Wallace, "We really did start it because we had been active in the women's movement and it seemed like a fun, exciting thing to do. I didn't think it would actually support me, much less continue for this many years." As Sisterhood grew, Adele and Simone learned how to run a business.

"The business ran us for a while," admits Simone.

"It was a good time historically, with a lot of women's bookstores popping up. People were driving from fifty miles away to come to our store." They admit that it would be much more difficult to start their store today.

"In the 1970s, we were mostly involved in ordering books and making sure that the space of our store was really the way we wanted it to be and reflected who we were. That was enough for people to be very interested and for people to come to the store. By the late eighties and early nineties it became clear that we had to do something very different. It wasn't enough to have a store filled with the same kinds of materials and things that reflected women's strength and empowerment and all of the areas that were important to women. We had to do way more outreach."

Ten years ago the whole phenomenon of discount bookstores began to emerge, and Sisterhood noted the change but felt that they were protected from it. But the superstore phenomenon is having a profound effect on their business. "Today we really have to find ways to get publicity and keep ourselves on people's minds," says Adele.

Over this quarter century their work relationship has greatly evolved. Simone is obviously the dreamer, while Adele keeps her hand on the bottom line. "We've had to learn to have our business meetings every week, and what we have understood over time is that there is a pretty definitive division of labor," adds Simone. "These days, we really concentrate on different things."

After twenty-five years Adele and Simone have no intention of slowing down or giving up. Rather, they are trying to impart the idea that Sisterhood Bookstore is not only a business that sells books, but also a women's community resource and referral center. "Obviously we sell books. But we've always been a place where you could go when you wanted to find a certain kind of politics and community. We would like the community to support us just as they support any community institution," says Adele Wallace.

✳   ✳   ✳

How to Woo Customers and Keep Them

While many business owners are doing everything they can to stay ahead of the game in terms of pricing, products, and service, the competition is still tough. As a result, forming lasting relationships with customers is the only way to succeed.

Today's customers must deal with mounting demands on their time from work, family, and friends. Yet they are inundated by competing businesses vying for more of their time, energy, and money. They receive flyers on their car windshields, on their doormats, and in their mailboxes. Their calls are interrupted by telemarketers; their voice mails are filled up with a new company's patter; and their doorbells ring at eight A.M. Sunday morning because somebody's selling something. They can't listen to the radio, watch TV, or read the newspaper without avoiding advertisements.

While many corporations have subscribed to the theory that people are replaceable, it's the consumer's turn to view businesses in that manner. A successful retailer will know that customer satisfaction is the difference between a business's survival or death.

In order to determine where they stand in the consumers' eyes, women entrepreneurs are dividing their client bases into three categories—new, loyal, and dissatisfied. The trick is to turn new customers into loyal customers and dissatisfied customers into new customers.

New customers are those who have stumbled onto the store by accident or referral. They may have come in once or twice but are usually sporadic in their spending. If they don't like the service or product, these customers may never come back. Other entrepreneurs have found the best way to deal with the new customer is to establish rapport. Why did they come into the store? What were they looking for? Did they find it? If they didn't, can you help them get it some other way? Are they just browsing? What are their tastes? Would they like to be on your mailing list?

While you want to retain the customer and make a sale, don't be too aggressive or insincere. Many stores have policies on what their salespeople say or do when customers enter the store. As a result, salespeople start sounding like talking dolls after they've greeted the customer the same way for the five hundredth time. Consumers in general find this method to be a turnoff, as they instantly feel like a number. Likewise, if customers feel too much pressure to spend, they are liable not to return to the store.

Loyal customers are naturally the most lucrative, and the smart business owner is rewarding these clients for their time and money spent. They frequently patronize the company and offer lots of referrals. On average, they provide 80 percent of the company's business, though they may make up only 20 percent of the total number of customers. The best way to handle a loyal customer is to offer loyalty in return. Bend over backward to ensure customer satisfaction, and think about offering surveys to find out what your customers are thinking, missing, and wanting. Use the marketing databases you've been compiling to key into the loyal customer's heart, perhaps sending a birthday card or small gift. Know your regulars by sight and name, know what their preferences are, and inform them of new merchandise and discount products. Ask, listen, and react to your customers' suggestions and complaints, and be open even to modifying your store policy if it will keep your loyal customers happy. Without these individuals you'd have no business.

Turning a dissatisfied customer into a new customer (someone who patronizes the store, if infrequently) is a difficult task and sometimes not worth the effort—depending on the customer. Though entrepreneurs struggle to please all their customers, this is virtually impossible. When a problem appears, try to salvage the relationship, regardless of whether the customer is new or loyal. Talking at length with the dissatisfied customer may be the beginning of fixing the situation. What is the source of the customer's complaint? Was it service or product related? Was there a miscommunication between the salesperson and customer? How would the customer like to see the problem handled? Always be gracious in these situations, whether the customer behaves badly or not. When the smoke clears, the unhappy customer may wish to return to the store but won't if harsh words have been spoken.

Sometimes you'll find that keeping a dissatisfied customer may not be worth the trouble. If a customer is being truly unreasonable and cruel to employees, reconsider the relationship. The customer is not "always right," and expecting employees to be abused for the sake of a sale will result in unhappy employees and, chances are, unhappy customers, if the employees' frustration at being treated poorly carries over to affect loyal customers. When faced with such a situation, do some soul-searching. Where will I draw the line? Has this customer ever exhibited such behavior before? If the relationship has been consistently good, you may choose to create a two-strikes policy and forgive the behavior once. Otherwise you can sever the tie completely.

All businesses should have a customer satisfaction policy that states what the company is liable for and what the consumer is liable for. But recognize that rules are occasionally meant to be broken, as customers, situations, and employees change. The policy should serve as a guideline for effective service, but common sense should rule. The Nordstrom department store chain, which has been lauded for their superior service, considers the statement "Use your own best judgment at all times" the entirety of its employee policy manual.

Train your employees to use common sense when dealing with customers, as one policy can't possibly solve every situation. By treating your customers well, maintaining a good relationship with them, and using common sense, you can get a leg up on beating out the competition while working in a healthy environment.

9

Science and Technology

It's not all that surprising that women make up only 16 percent of all working scientists. After all, it wasn't too many centuries ago that the science industry was reserved for celibate monks and women were burned at the stake for practicing the herbal arts. Today's gender discrimination certainly isn't as overt, but women in science and technology are still faced with a silent war, one that may be harder to fight for its subtle attacks.

From elementary school to graduate school and into the marketplace, women pursuing careers in science, math, or technology careers are discouraged at almost every turn. Educational software for children is usually designed for boys; male (and female) science teachers unintentionally cater to their male students; and men scientists and mathematicians receive more grant money, publish more articles, and receive better feedback than their female colleagues of equal stature.

Though extremely successful women scientists, technicians, and mathematicians exist, they may wonder where their female classmates are. For as a woman rises through the education system, the numbers of her women colleagues start to decrease. After high school, only 16 percent of qualified women choose a science major in college. After earning undergraduate degrees in the sciences, many women enter graduate school but never finish.

Studies attribute these low admission and high dropout rates and lack of women in science and technology careers to four principal factors: discrimination in the classroom, lack of mentors, low self-esteem, and difficulty balancing family and career. By making women aware of the problems they may face, entrepreneurs believe they have a much better chance of overcoming these obstacles and becoming successful.

Teachers have been socialized to believe science and technology is no place for women. Even those who know differently, men and women alike, may discriminate unintentionally. Even at the elementary school age, boys tend to be called on more in class and receive more praise and criticism. A report called "How Schools Short-change Girls" shows that even tests are designed for boys. By graduate school, the situation isn't much better. Women often feel invisible, regardless of the merit of their work. They receive less advice, are excluded from important networking functions, and are given less responsibility than their male peers. The good news is that academic institutions are becoming increasingly aware of these problems and many are working to remedy them in time.

According to Dr. G. Charmaine Gilbreath, head of the Electro-Optics Technology section at the U.S. Naval Research Laboratory in Washington, D.C., girls are going into undergraduate school but aren't coming out engineers. "We think it's peer group pressure. There's still the folklore that science and engineering aren't feminine—you can't have a family and a normal life." To combat this, Gilbreath tries to mentor young women. "I talk to high school girls about twice a year about going into engineering. In high school physics, the girls often get left behind, while the boys get much of the attention. It's a subtle yet pervasive thing."

Up-and-coming scientists rely on mentors to help get their careers off the ground. Mentors teach young scientists how to obtain grants, structure their careers, and publish articles. Though their role is informal, mentors are critical to a young scientist's success. Yet women entering science careers have difficulty finding mentors or being taken seriously by them. Rather than offer criticism and challenge the female scientist, many mentors provide only polite indifference. As women make their way up the ranks, though, the opportunities for positive role models and mentors will increase.

As women encounter gender discrimination throughout their lives, it's no wonder their self-esteem suffers. Many women have found that fighting to keep their self-esteem may indeed be the hardest battle of all. In a survey of high school students, women had only slightly lower self-esteem than men. Yet by sophomore year in college, these same female students had significantly lower self-esteem than their male peers, even though their grade-point averages were higher. Women with low self-esteem may take less risks in their career for fear of failure. They also tend to rely on others' opinions of them. Learning to fight their inner battles, entrepreneurs believe, will help women be more confident and stand up for themselves. Charmaine Gilbreath offers her own story. "I'm kind of atypical in that I'm part of the transition generation. I never paid attention to what society said was right. I was never socialized to go into science. I was going to go into law, but for fun, I was doing geometry and physics. When I was twenty-six, I retrained in physics, and I've never regretted it."

Charmaine Gilbreath's work involves shooting laser beams at rocket plumes to learn how particles in rocket fuel react with the atmosphere. It's no small feat to hit a high-speed rocket plume with a laser beam, but Gilbreath's group succeeds, she says, "as a direct result of a collaboration among three well-placed women." Three well-placed women rocket scientists, to be exact.

The science industry rarely offers nine-to-five hours. In most cases scientists work days, nights, and sometimes weekends, depending on their specialties and projects. Many women, especially women with children, have a difficult time balancing personal and job commitments. Some do find time for both, but usually at the expense of promotions and career advancement. It doesn't help that a woman's biological clock starts ticking at the same time she's trying to establish tenure credentials in her scientific field. Luckily the science community is becoming aware of these issues and is working to create an industry that women will want to be a part of.

Tricks of the Trade

G. Charmaine Gilbreath of the U.S. Naval Research Laboratory, on maintaining autonomy in the difficult world of science:

1. *Find mentors.* If someone will help guide your career and steer you clear of the pitfalls, you're already ahead of the pack. A woman is great, but don't overlook a male mentor.
2. *Don't expect special treatment, and don't accept treatment that is less than professional.* By putting yourself up to high standards and expecting nothing less from your colleagues, you'll find respect within your reach.
3. *Look toward agencies and organizations that have supported other women and have a good track record for showcasing women's talents.*
4. *Put yourself in a position of managing funds.* "Whoever controls the money has ultimate control."
5. *Be prepared to leave and find a better match if your current one doesn't work.* "Women often become invested in situations that aren't working—often out of a sense of loyalty." Be selfish. It'll pay off.

＊ ＊ ＊

Science Needs Women: Where We're Headed

As environmentalists and other activist groups have taken center stage in the 1990s, science and scientists are getting a bad rap. The diminishing ozone layer, extinct species, animal cruelty, pollution, and other similar problems have contributed to antiscience attitudes. Even popular culture depicts science as evil. Movies such as *Twelve Monkeys* and *Jurassic Park* portray scientists who have used technology to play God—with disastrous results. The country has also become more fascinated with the metaphysical and religion. In the new age, aliens, the journey of the soul, and God take precedence over what has been proven scientifically. As a result, many people would rather fund their televangelist or psychic than spend money on space exploration or cures for diseases.

In spite of this, consumers are demanding newer and better technology. Even while the technology business is booming, the American paradox is that we've become more concerned about our water, air, and bodies. Many have even begun searching for alternatives to conventional medicine, such as homeopathic remedies, mental healing, and macrobiotic diets. Moreover, as science is more in the public eye, ethical scandals decrease the field's credibility.

Yet women's contribution to science and technology may improve these problems. Studies have proven that women scientists tend to revere quality over quantity, resulting in thorough or more comprehensive work. They also have a tendency to focus on problems that their male colleagues do not. Women's health care, for example, was a virtually untapped subject, and as a result, many women suffered from traditional treatments designed for men. In the last few years, though, women scientists have made great strides in this area.

From an ethical standpoint, women scientists are seeking new ways to save the environment and people from dangerous situations. Rather than asking, "How much of this chemical will hurt people?" women scientists are asking, "How can we solve this problem safely?" They are also challenging the concept of objectivity. For centuries scientists have removed themselves from the public in order to remain objective. As a result, their considerations have been for scientific procedure, not public values. Women scientists are trying to provide society with better information by speaking publicly, rather than merely presenting their findings to the government or industry scientists. These women scientists believe that if society is presented with information, they may be part of the solution. Traditional methods rely on the government to make decisions for the public, rather than with them. In addition to providing excellent research and a different perspective, women scientists are putting the soul back in their field.

Building the Interactive Future

In just twenty years the computer industry has produced some dizzying achievements. From the innovation of 3-D interactive games and Pentium processors to notebooks and talking computers, technology has advanced and surpassed many expectations. Yet the rate of advancement is so accelerated that the average computer user may find it impossible to keep up. For just as the consumer figures out the difference between a 386 and a 486 and an IBM and a Macintosh, another company comes along with a faster, slicker model. Add hundreds of new software programs to the market every year, and buying a computer with all the trappings becomes an intimidating process. Then there's the language. Bits and bytes and chips and RAM and ROM—it's enough to drive even a forward-thinking woman nuts.

After spending around $4,000 on just one decent computer package, you can then look forward to replacing the entire system a few years later. To stay competitive, business owners often have no choice, for today's computers may not even be compatible with those of tomorrow—despite what the salesperson says. Rather than becoming victims of a hyped-up, fast-paced market, though, learn the secrets to buying the right technology for your needs.

Woman on the Way

✳

Dorothy Terrell
President: SunExpress
Corporate Executive Officer: Sun Microsystems, Inc.
**Business Philosophy: Give the customers *more* than they
ask for**
**Greatest Accomplishment: Successfully building a global
enterprise**

Dorothy Terrell found her niche catering to the service aspect of technology. Her company, SunExpress, serves computer clients' after-market needs by ensuring that their customers have easy, convenient access to the information, products, and services required to enhance and expand their network computing environments.

"We heard early on that customers were having trouble getting additional cables or memory, or even questions answered after they made their initial major enterprise purchases." Terrell's research revealed that the entire computer industry was faulted for the lack of continued customer satisfaction over the life of the product. "We wanted to provide not only continued customer satisfaction, but customer delight—which leads to our ultimate goal of customer retention."

Through an independent third-party survey, SunExpress's customers consistently reward them with high ratings. "We like to find out what we're doing right so we can do more of that," Terrell says. She attributes a large piece of their success to avoiding the philosophy of quick sales and low-cost delivery. "We focus on how we can assure that customers will be continually satisfied with their products and all interactions with SunExpress. Sun is the only manufacturer that has an operating company totally dedicated to ease of access and ease of doing business after the sale," she says.

Terrell's foresight has turned SunExpress into a company that has not only cornered the market domestically, but has become a force internationally as well. "Our strategy in Europe was to be located in one place, the Netherlands, and be perceived by our customers in other countries as if we were there also. For example, if a customer calls from Germany, we identify that they are German and respond in their language. We deliver directly within three to five days, bill in their currency, and collect locally." SunExpress now operates in eleven countries on three continents.

SunExpress has also entered the Internet commerce arena, and now offers customers the additional option of purchasing products using the Web. "With services over the Internet, we are now facing new challenges, but we like to offer our customers choice. As a company that utilizes direct-marketing techniques, the Internet is a natural extension of the way we do business. It's very exciting."

✳ ✳ ✳

What to Buy Now and What Can Wait for Later

With the high growth rate of the computer industry, it's often difficult to tell what computer brands and software are fads soon to be obsolete. Rather than run out and buy the fastest and newest machines and programs, buy what best fits your company's requirements. While some women want the packages that best serve their business, others are willing to change their company policy if the software offers a more efficient means to an end. Sometimes you can even buy an existing system that can be customized to your business. This method, however, may be costly, time-consuming, and hard to upgrade. Many entrepreneurs suggest that you talk with computer experts or consultants to find the best systems. In large companies, a vendor is often used to supply their computer needs.

Hiring a software vendor can save the day—as long as they're evaluated carefully beforehand. Software vending is an unstable business, and many companies disappear as fast as they appear. At the same time, a vendor can help provide entrepreneurs with the best equipment and service for a reasonable price. After you've researched your needs, interview selected software vendors (get referred to a vendor from a trusted business associate). Find out how long the vendor has been in business, who their clients are, what products and prices they offer, if they use the software themselves, and if they will provide a full demonstration. After narrowing down the candidates to four or five and expressing your computer needs thoroughly, ask the companies to submit proposals within a limited time frame.

This process will weed out the bad from the good, as you can determine who considers you an important client. At the same time, you can also determine who has the best price and product. Getting and checking references is the next crucial step. Are the other clients happy? Are their needs similar to yours? Have they had any major problems? Before making a decision on a software vendor, you can consider whom you communicate with best.

Evaluating Service Support

Many business owners have lamented their software choices after waiting on hold with the technical hot line. Ten minutes go by, then another ten, then another, and after all that waiting, there's no guarantee the person on the other end of the line will be able to solve the problem. Often individuals call the help line only to be referred to someone else in the company or another company entirely. And that's if it's a normal day.

On a bad day—back in November 1994 with the Pentium chip crisis—consumers waited for hours for information, while the company tried desperately to handle the thousands of consumer phone calls. Though the bug in the computer was minor—it theoretically would fail to do long division once every twenty-seven thousand years—the company had to spend $475 million to not only fix the problem, but appease the consumer. Though accidents happen, look for quality service and support when buying software or computers. What is the company's policy for defects in the system? How long would it take to replace? Do they have service dealers in your area? Do they stand by their products? How helpful is their hot line? Do they answer your questions accurately and quickly? The product is only as good as its maker's support and service.

To Upgrade or Not to Upgrade

Some software companies offer upgrade packages every year. The problem is, many of the upgrades require more computer power than previous versions. After loading an upgrade of a software program, you may find your computer is as slow as molasses. Sometimes the computer freezes and must be rebooted continually or an error message appears when loading the software. In any of these cases, you'll be faced with upgrading the software *and* the hard drive. Then it becomes a question of upgrading the system or buying a whole new computer.

Upgrading the computer can be a good idea if it needs just a few added components. There are programs that upgrade just about everything from memory to hard drive, and talking to a computer expert may save you money—at least for a little while. The problem with computer upgrades is that they may cost substantial money, even though it's not necessarily guaranteed to work and the improvements may be insubstantial. When it's time to upgrade the entire computer, it's time for a new one.

Before upgrading software, ask several questions. Is the new version compatible with your system, or will you have to upgrade your computer as well? How long does it take to learn the new software? Will it convert old files? Are the advantages of the new software worth the ordeal of upgrading?

The decision to upgrade or not is a tricky one. Some programs and computers upgrade better than others. While many technicians and software companies may offer insight, the decision is ultimately between the computer owner and her checkbook.

Web Sites

Putting up a Web site is becoming as important as advertising with newspapers, television stations, and billboards. Reaching a worldwide audience, Web sites offer mass-market saturation and are considerably less expensive than a worldwide media campaign. Someday they'll even be a great place to sell products. For now, though, it's a great way to spread the company's name and communicate with customers.

Setting up a Web site can be relatively easy or ridiculously complex. Large companies often employ an entire department in order to maintain a colorful Web site with good information and splashy pictures or graphics. If they're unable to employ a full Web staff, businesses can get software that enables them to create their own site, though putting one together may be technically challenging.

Some entrepreneurs, however, are going a simpler route and using their on-line network to set up a Web site. Companies such as America Online offer free Web sites to their customers. For the small-business owner, it's a great way to get free advertising.

After putting up the Web page, its important to promote the site. One way to achieve this goal is to place the Web address on business cards, on office stationery, in newspaper or television ads, and in the store or office itself. Some entrepreneurs are getting their sites into search engines, which basically serve as a Web directory. The sooner you become familiar with the Web and its potential, the more of a business edge you'll have.

Taking Your Business to the Next Level: Going Public

Like a roller coaster, an initial public offering (IPO) is a fast track of unpredictable ups and downs. The IPOs, however, crash more. In the first half of 1996 executives were counting their blessings as seventy new IPOs sprang up a month, raising $26 billion—only $1.7 billion less than 1995's yearly total. But then the trader of most IPO stocks, NASDAQ, dropped 11 percent, and even the most high-powered companies began to feel the market strain. As a result, the new and profit-challenged IPOs dreaming of sky-high share prices had to settle for less-than-mediocre earnings. As the market will continue to rise and fall, entrepreneurs who take their companies public had better be prepared for a wild ride.

While some business owners can hardly wait to go public, others prefer to keep their businesses to themselves. Depending on your personal and company needs and goals, the advantages of going public may outweigh the disadvantages, or vice versa. The process is costly, time-consuming, and complex, and you should not venture forward if you have any major doubts. Short of selling a business, going public is the most crucial decision a company owner can make.

The Benefits of Going Public

Increased Money for Expansion

Private companies that go public can make large amounts of money from selling their stock. The U.S. Satellite Broadcasting Company, for example, raised $220 million when it went public in 1995. Going public can also help business owners expand quickly without increasing their debt. Unlike private companies that may need loans to survive, public companies receive a large influx of cash, which they do not have to repay or pay interest on.

More Financing Options

Typically, loans are restrictive, limiting the private business's ability to grow while requiring personal collateral from owners. Yet companies that go public may not need loans or may pay off their existing loans through the sale of stock. Moreover, the public company owner may use stock as collateral on a loan and may not have to sell off their controlling interest to pay off debt.

Prestige

After going public, the entrepreneur and the business are perceived differently. They tend to command more respect from customers, vendors, and suppliers. A public company may find it easier to hire talented employees by offering name recognition and stock incentives. In addition to servicing bigger clients, the public company is also visible in the media, which may attract new customers, while promoting the company's name.

Increased Chances for Future Capital

A public company may raise capital effectively in a second offering because it has a known name in the investment world. Moreover, a public company is easier to sell since the resale value is generally ascertainable, despite market variations.

The Risks of Going Public

Losing Control

If public company owners sell off more than 50 percent of their shares, they will lose controlling interest in the company. Many entrepreneurs structure their IPOs to avoid this problem.

Losing Confidentiality

All the secrets business owners have been trying to hide from their competition and customers come out in an IPO. Since the Securities and Exchange Commission (SEC) tries to protect investors, companies that go public are required to give out detailed financial, personal, and product information, even though it may hurt their business.

Public Scrutiny

Not only must IPOs air their dirty laundry, they must do it quarterly. Any mistakes, problems, and profit decreases must be reported to the SEC and public.

Pressure from the Outside

The public company is ruled by the investor. As a result, companies must perform to increase short-term profits, though that may hurt long-term goals. Shareholders may be fickle and jump ship after one bad quarter, or they may demand dividends. Also, the public company must answer to a board of directors, which may disrupt quick decision making or problem solving.

Tax Nightmares

Public companies must maximize profit and pay higher taxes, rather than minimize income through creative accounting. And a public company owner may have higher estate taxes than a private company owner, since the value of shares is normally higher and easier to determine.

The Benefits of Going Public

1. Increased money for expansion.
2. More financing options.
3. Prestige.
4. Increased chances for future capital.

The Risks of Going Public

1. Losing Control.
2. Losing confidentiality.
3. Public scrutiny.
4. Pressure from the outside.
5. Tax nightmares.

Learning the Process

Turning a private company into an organization owned by many (stockholders), the IPO process usually takes from six months to a year to complete. The smoother the transition, the more profitable the IPO may be.

To aid the process, entrepreneurs typically assemble a high-quality (and usually expensive) team. First try to hire accountants who are members of the SEC practice division of the American Institute of Certified Public Accountants (AICPA). They are the most qualified to handle IPOs. Likewise, it's wise to hire lawyers who are experienced in dealing with the SEC. Investment bankers or underwriters should also be chosen carefully. Try to determine who will work the hardest for your company. Large firms with big clients, for example, may not be the best choice for a small IPO, which may end up at the bottom of the priority list. As the underwriter or investment bank is responsible for buying the stock from the IPO and selling it, you should thoroughly research these team members before making a decision. An incompetent underwriter can sink an IPO deal. Sometimes entrepreneurs don't put their money with just one firm, but hire several with different skills.

Once the team is assembled, you'll have to determine the amount of the issue and then file a preliminary prospectus and a registration statement to the SEC, which regulates public offerings. This information is required by law to protect potential investors from deceptive companies. The registration statement consists of a description of the company's business; the key officers' names, addresses, salaries, five-year business histories, and percentage of ownership; the business's capitalization and how it plans to spend the proceeds; and all legal proceedings the company is going through. The company may also have to provide years' worth of audited financial statements. The SEC, however, does not investigate the statements for accuracy.

When the SEC has cleared the registration statement, the company must file a final prospectus, which includes the preliminary prospectus, amendments, and price of the issue. When this information is finalized, you must then put the show on the road and inform potential buyers of the upcoming sale. Usually the stock is offered to favored clients or companies, especially if the offering is small.

This may cause problems sometimes, however. In the worst cases, small-time investors get scammed when the stock price is jacked up by insiders, who then pull out and drive down its value. It's a long process before the IPO hits NASDAQ or the New York Stock Exchange (NYSE), but that's just the beginning. Though half of IPOs never make it, the ones that do enjoy increased capital, company prestige, and a chance to become a leading industry competitor.

Using the Law to Protect Your Work

While many small-business owners are unwilling to go through the sometimes arduous process of obtaining copyrights, trademarks, and patents, they may live to regret it. Successful entrepreneurs have found that protecting their work legally has saved them considerable aggravation later. Even protected works can be copied or stolen. In that case, the only retribution is in pursuing (and, hopefully, receiving) a large settlement from a lawsuit. Those unprotected, however, can lose everything, especially if their competitor has more money and resources.

Often entrepreneurs use a combination of laws to secure their company name, invention, or artistic work. A company that manufactures toys, for example, would want to register a trademark for the name of the toys as well as a patent for the invention of the toys. As each law covers only specific areas, it is important to know exactly which part of the work is protected and which part is not. Copyright law, for instance, protects a musician's songs, but not the musician's band name or logo. Understanding the law and its intricacies will not only protect your interests, it will help your businesses grow.

Woman on the Way

✳

San Garza
CEO: Counter Technology, Inc.
Business Philosophy: Find your niche and stay focused
Greatest Accomplishment: Winning security management and engineering contracts at fourteen major U.S. airports, including John F. Kennedy, LaGuardia, and Newark airports

From its humble beginnings with four employees in 1987 to almost four hundred today, San Garza has taken America's need for security quite seriously. A former police officer, Garza saw a need to provide security consulting and, with the help of the Small Business Administration's 8(a) program for minority-owned businesses, found herself in the midst of extremely rapid growth.

The program, which allowed her to bid—on equal footing with other, larger companies—for government contracts, enabled Garza to pick up business she normally wouldn't have had access to. And while working on federal contracts had its cache, "it's a low-profit arena," she says.

What Garza did do was take her modest profits and

reinvest them on marketing herself in the commercial sector, where the real money was. "Technology is changing rapidly, and most companies know that whatever security they have in place today could be obsolete tomorrow. We let them know that we were there. And they came looking for us.

"There are lots of people who will tell you how to run your business," says Garza, "but you have to keep a sense of what works for you. Don't spend money on consultants you don't need. And don't be afraid to hire someone who knows more than you do."

In fact, Garza attributes her success to letting go of some of the trappings that come with power. "The smarter the people I surround myself with, the smarter my business is." Garza believes that women are uniquely equipped to ask for help when it's needed and are therefore more likely to reap the rewards of others' expertise.

✳ ✳ ✳

Copyright Law

As stated in the United States Code, Title 17, Chapter 1, copyright protects "original works of authorship fixed in any tangible medium of expression, now known or later developed, from which they can be perceived, reproduced, or otherwise communicated, either directly with the aid of a machine or device."

Literature, music and accompanying words, dramas and accompanying music, pantomimes, pictures, graphics, sculptures, movies, sound recordings, and architecture all fall under and are protected by copyright law. Ideas, inventions, logos, colors, lists of ingredients, phrases, unrecorded choreography, works in intangible form, and works comprising common property alone (such as calendars) are not covered under copyright law.

Though the originator of the work is protected from the moment the work appears in a fixed form—unpublished or not—you should register a copyright immediately as an added protection. Some consider registration as a formality, but if an author files a lawsuit against an infringer, he or she is required to register the work, regardless of when the infringement took place. Not only does registering a work serve as a public record in an infringement lawsuit, it can also save you money. In infringement cases, an author who has registered a copyright three months after the work is published and before the infringement is entitled to statutory damages and attorney fees in addition to awarded damages and profits. Moreover, the owner of a copyright-registered work can notify the U.S. Customs Department, which will ensure that no copies are exported.

Entrepreneurs who wish to register a work should send a completed application form, a nonrefundable filing fee of $20, and two nonreturnable copies (unless otherwise specified) of the work together in the same envelope to the Register of Copyrights, Copyright Office, Library of Congress, Washington, D.C. 20559. You can register an unpublished collection for one filing fee if the works are organized, under a single title, and created by the copyright owner.

The owner of a copyright isn't always the creator of a work, however. In a work-for-hire situation, employers (rather than the authors) own the copyright. This is true only if the employees' work is within the boundaries of their jobs or the employer commissions the work through a written agreement. Writers, for example, who are salaried employees hired to write articles for a magazine, would not own the rights to their work; their employers would. In the case of coauthors, the copyright belongs to each jointly, unless they have an agreement in writing stating otherwise. Authors may also transfer their copyrights exclusively or nonexclusively. In either case, the written agreements should be signed by both parties, though it is not necessarily required when transferring nonexclusive copyrights.

Regardless of who owns the copyright or whether it is officially registered, women entrepreneurs should visually display the copyright symbol somewhere on their product, so competitors can't argue that an infringement was unintentional. With literary works, an author must display on the copy the traditional symbol of the encircled c, as well as the year of first publication and the name of the copyright owner. It would appear as "copyright ©, Jane Doe, 1996." For a sound recording, the owner would use the symbol of the encircled p (instead of the encircled c) somewhere on the tape, CD, or record. In the event of an unpublished work, entrepreneurs use the same format, except it would appear as "unpublished: Jane Doe, 1996."

As copyright law was revamped, the length of copyright protection has changed. For works created on or after January 1, 1978, the copyright begins from the day the work was created to fifty years after the author's death. In a coauthor situation, the copyright would be extended to fifty years after the last author dies. For works that are unpublished or unregistered before January 1, 1978, the copyright will not be terminated before December 31, 2002, but if the work is published before or on December 31, 2002, the copyright will not be terminated before December 31, 2027. For published works before January 1, 1978, the author may reapply for copyright, extending the original twenty-eight-year term to seventy-five years.

For more information, contact the Library of Congress at (202) 707-3000.

Trademarks

Where copyright leaves off, trademarks pick up. The U.S. Patent and Trademark Office defines a trademark as "a word, phrase, symbol or design, or combination of words, phrases, symbols or designs, which identifies and distinguishes the source of the goods or services of one party from those of others." Whether a company is small or large, business owners should register their product names, slogans, and logos, for a competitor may easily swoop in and capitalize on the company's success. Registering a trademark is more difficult and expensive than copyright registration, but the protection is worth the effort.

Before applying for a trademark, business owners must conduct a search to see if the trademark or a confusingly similar version is already being used. Some hire trademark attorneys or companies, while others try to save money by doing the research themselves. This may be rather time-consuming, as the search must be done on a statewide level. A federal trademark (for products sold in more than one state) requires a national search. If no likenesses are found, the business owner may proceed with the trademark application.

To apply for a trademark, business owners have to do one of three things: use the trademark, prove a bona fide intention to use the trademark, or use the trademark they have already registered in another country. Trademarks may be used for ten-year terms with the right to renew. As long as the company proves the trademark is being used, it may continue to be used indefinitely.

When applying for a trademark, business owners submit a written application form, a drawing of the trademark on a separate piece of paper, and the required filing fee ($245 for each class of services or goods). If the trademark has already been used by the applicant, he or she must submit three examples of how the trademark has been used. Completed applications should be sent to the Assistant Commissioner for Trademarks, 2900 Crystal Dr., Arlington, Va., 22202-3513.

After the application is examined for similarities with registered trademarks and none are found, the Patent and Trademark Office publishes the trademark in their weekly *Official Gazette*. If the mark is considered damaging to someone else's business, the contestor has thirty days to file an opposition, which the trademark applicant must fight in front of the Trademark Trial and Appeal Board. If no one contests the mark, the trademark applicant will receive a registration certificate. If the trademark applicant hasn't used the mark yet, he or she has six months from the certificate date to use the mark or apply for a six-month extension.

Patents

While a copyright protects an author's words, a patent protects ideas expressed in the form of an invention, machine, process, or manufactured item. Obtaining a patent may take several years and cost several thousand dollars, but the patent owner is protected for a term of twenty years from date of application. The owner may exclusively make, sell, manufacture, and commercially exploit an invention. If anyone else tries to make or sell the invention without permission during the twenty years, the patent owner may sue for damages.

Not every invention will receive a patent, however. The U.S. Patent and Trademark Office has strict conditions for patentability. If the patent applicant abandons the invention, for example, he or she loses the right to the patent. For detailed information regarding patent conditions, read United States Code, Title 35, Part II, Chapter 10, or call the U.S. Patent and Trademark Office in Washington, D.C. (703-557-3071). As the law concerning patents is complex, many entrepreneurs hire patent attorneys with a specialty in the field of the invention to advise them on applications.

The application itself consists of three elements: a filing fee, a drawing of the invention, and a document that includes descriptions of the invention and an oath or declaration. The United States Code, Title 35, Part II, Chapter 11, dictates that "[the] applicant shall make oath that he believes himself to be the original and first inventor of the process, machine, manufacture, or composition of matter, or improvement, thereof, for which he solicits a patent, and shall state of what country he is a citizen." If any of the application elements are missing, the inventor shall be given the opportunity to correct the errors. If refused, the application and filing fee will be returned, though the inventor may be required to pay a handling fee.

10

Service

Employing over thirty million people in 1996, the service industries continue to grow rapidly and create more jobs than many other industries. At the same time, consumers who once considered using service businesses a luxury are now beginning to view them as necessities. Women entrepreneurs are certainly cashing in on this trend, as 55 percent of women-owned businesses are service oriented, and their numbers are climbing.

Women look to careers in the service industry for a variety of reasons. Some are qualified in a particular field and would rather work for themselves, perhaps serving as a consultant or freelancer. Other women find that a service business can be started from a home office and often requires less start-up capital than other types of ventures. Because women use the service industries more heavily than men, they may also find themselves well equipped to create a marketable niche for themselves. To top this off, entrepreneurs also express that owning a service business allows them to live a more flexible lifestyle while achieving their career goals. According to chef and author Alice Waters of Chez Panisse in Berkeley, California, while running a restaurant is much more than full-time work, it gives her the flexibility to do the things she loves—such as gardening and travel—as part of the job.

Overall, entrepreneurs have found the most profitable service industries in the country include health (medical and "wellness" practices), business services (advertising and employment agencies, and the like), and personal services (house cleaning, dog walking, house painting, and so on). If these don't suit your style, though, there are many more service businesses to choose from: automotive services, legal and social services, recreation services, accounting services, and educational services.

According to Faye Becker, owner of Bubbles and Bleach, people who live today's busy lifestyle simply don't have time for the minutiae of daily life. "People don't mind paying for a good service, if it makes their days a bit easier," she says.

Finding the Service Gap: Creating a Business around an Unmet Need

As so many types of service businesses exist, women entrepreneurs are looking to create their own niche by starting companies that focus on the consumers' unmet—or yet unknown—needs. It's certainly no wonder the service industry is expanding so quickly, for these women are constantly redefining business as we know it and are coming up with new and creative ways to make money using their unique talents.

For Faye Becker, the concept for her venture stemmed from a need to do laundry—lots of it. Shortly after her daughter had her first child, Becker and her husband visited the new family. "There was a ton of laundry that just hadn't been dealt with . . . we thought this would be a good way to help out." Piling baskets of clothes into the car, the couple went in search of a Laundromat.

"I was appalled by what I saw," said she. "Poor lighting, machines that didn't work, dirty floors, and high prices." So she took it upon herself to reinvent the Laundromat as it was known. "I'm redefining the industry and turning it around," she says. "And other facilities are either upgrading or closing down." Becker is expanding, too. By the year 2000 she expects to have over one hundred Bubbles and Bleach stores across the East Coast.

If the service industries appeal to you, but you're not quite sure where you'd like to put your energy, you may want to follow these steps for creating a blueprint for your own specialized service business:

- *Before anything else, write down on a piece of paper your strengths, weaknesses, and favorite activities.* Rather than trying to fit into an existing business mold, many entrepreneurs believe that great success comes from being involved in businesses that fit their abilities and passions. Once your list is made, review each item carefully, then write down what services you have wanted or needed at some time—but have never been able to find. Even write down ideas that may seem childish or outlandish.

- *Next, write down the age range and types of people you want to deal with on a daily basis.* Do you want to work with children, corporate executives, or parents? It's crucial for service business owners to like the people they are serving, or they won't be very successful—regardless of whether the service is needed or not. After determining the types of people (your target market) you'd like to work with, research that group. What is their income? Can they afford to pay for your service? What are these people looking for and can't find? What are their needs, goals, or dreams? What are their problems? Are they overworked, underresourced, or undereducated? After answering these questions, check your business ideas against these answers. Does anything click?

- *Research the community to see if any of your business ideas are already being done.* If so, who's doing it? Are their customers satisfied? Do they have any competition? (If there's no competition, consider becoming the competition.) Is the area so specialized that there's no room for competition? Could your business offer services that the competition doesn't? Does it seem profitable?

- *If the business doesn't exist, do more research.* Surveys of the target market might be helpful, as would talking to friends or family in that target market. If the service proves to be a good idea, consider operational needs before moving ahead. The hardest part, many entrepreneurs believe, is creating the winning idea—the rest is simply follow-through.

Woman on the Way

*

Faye Becker
Owner: Bubbles and Bleach, Milwaukee, Wisconsin
Business Philosophy: Give the customers the very best: best service, best products, best quality
Greatest Accomplishment: Creating a high-class Laundromat that people *want* to visit

Dissatisfied with the low service, grimy conditions, and high prices of coin-operated laundry facilities, Faye Becker set out to redefine the industry. And in doing so, she's giving people many more reasons to come to Bubbles and Bleach than simply for a fluff and fold.

Aside from the laundry and dry-cleaning facilities, Bubbles and Bleach offers amenities such as a children's center, exercise equipment, a tanning bed, a cappuccino and juice bar, an ATM machine, a giant-screen TV, VCRs, and an "office away from the office" with fax, copy, and telephone facilities. It's a one-stop place. She's also organized a singles night with refreshments and has promised to pay for the wedding of the first couple who meets at singles night, provided the wedding takes place at Bubbles and Bleach.

Bubbles and Bleach started in mid-1994, after Becker conducted a comprehensive study of existing Laundromat stores. She found that despite poor-quality machines and nonexistent service, people were still visiting these facilities in droves. "People were paying for this abuse," she exclaims.

So Becker opened her first facility, and she hasn't looked back. "Over 72 percent of our customers have a washer and dryer at home and find they can do their laundry quicker here," she states. "It's a very high-class, detail-oriented experience. We have state-of-the art machines and the largest washer in the Midwest, which is capable of handling twelve to fourteen normal loads at one time."

To further cater to her clientele, uniformed attendants are present to help customers carry their laundry to and from the car. If a customer needs to leave, the attendant hands the person a pager so he or she will know when to return. "If the customer doesn't return in time, we empty the dryer and keep their laundry behind the counter. It's all very secure." To ensure that the attendants are equipped to handle any customer request or problem, Becker spent a lot of money and time in training and grooming them.

Combating the Laundromat stereotype of dimly lit facilities and parking lots, Bubbles and Bleach stores maintain security guards on duty from opening through closing, and the parking lots are lit like an outdoor stadium. "Our customers appreciate being treated as though they matter. That's where our success lies," says Becker. And good service is why customers come back. "I don't do coupons, I don't discount. I don't do anything that's the norm in the industry. Lifestyles have changed, and people will pay more to get value for their dollar."

Becker truly has transformed in the industry. "To date, we put twenty-seven dry cleaners and Laundromat units out of business," she says. "They weren't providing the service, and when customers had an option, they took their business elsewhere. That's what it's all about."

✳ ✳ ✳

Buying an Existing Business: The Pros and Cons

While starting a business from the ground up has its merits, many women entrepreneurs choose to take over an existing business. If the market is already flooded with a particular product or service, you might decide that, while there may be room for another player, a start-up would have tough competition. Others may not have an idea for a new product but have a specialized background in an existing product. Mainly women buy existing businesses because it's a lot easier to step in and turn a profit if a company has been around for several years and already has a client base.

Women business owners have found that it is less risky to buy an existing company. The waters have already been tested, so to speak, and the chances of a company's success are greater. In the best case, look for a business that has an effective product or service, location, and staff and already has clients and vendors as well as equipment, permits, and contracts.

Additionally, you may have an easier time securing a loan, because an established company will have assets that can be used for collateral. Creative financing should definitely not be ruled out when it comes to buying an existing business. You may be able to work with the seller on a finance plan. The seller may ask only for a small down payment, financing the rest over a period of years. The interest rate may be a bit higher in these situations, but for an entrepreneur without large amounts of cash, it can be worth it in the long haul.

On the other hand, some buyers are so eager to get into business, they don't care whether it's a buyer's market or a seller's dream. The wise entrepreneur examines the economic climate closely to decide when and what type of company to buy. You may still choose to make the acquisition in a seller's market but should do so only if the company seems to have major potential for long-term growth. Never buy blindly. Try to determine if, in a year, the business is going to be worth half of what you're paying for it or double the purchase price. Local business associations and trade publications help offer insight into the market for potential buyers.

Entrepreneurial women also question the type of business they're buying. Are you catching the tail end of a trend? Is new technology going to push the service right out of the market? Jumping into any business without examining these factors can lead to financial trouble. Do your homework!

How to Evaluate the Viability of a Business

Buying the right business takes some time and can cost some money, but as many have found, paying now is better than paying later. As a prospective buyer, research all aspects of the business, from every financial detail to every product detail. Understand that buying a business is quite an undertaking, and consider the following suggestions that may make the process easier and more efficient.

Know Why the Seller Is Selling

The seller may be painting a bright picture, and the business could be in severe trouble. Even if the seller seems to be legitimate, keep looking for the business's big flaw. You may never find one, but know that it's crucial to uncover all the dark corners. Does the seller really want to retire, or is the business in such dire straits that he has no choice? Asking questions like these has saved myriad buyers from unknowingly purchasing a lemon.

Hire an Accountant, Appraiser, Lawyer, and Negotiator

This dream team will be able to root out problems with the books, determine the actual value of the business, write up the contracts, and negotiate the final deal. They save buyers from making big mistakes by noticing all the details. Successful business buyers don't leave home without them.

Review the Books

With your accountant, look at all the business's paperwork. The accountant will search several years back to ensure the seller has maintained a decent track record. He or she will also help you become familiar the company's cash flow, profit-and-loss statements, existing contracts, salary and wages, inventory, hidden debts, credit rating, and value and liability of the assets. Are the tangible assets (desks, equipment, and so on) worth the price? What about the intangibles (relationships with customers, clients, and the like)? No nook is left uncovered if you want to protect yourself.

Know the Competition

Visit the competing businesses and get to know their product or service. Then compare stores. What is the competition doing better? What aren't they providing their customers with? Can you beat them with a better product and higher-quality service? Does the competition advertise? Entrepreneurs have found that observing the competition gives them creative solutions to problems, as well as determining the value of the business they are potentially buying.

Know the Business's Reputation

Buying a business with a bad rep can be entrepreneurial suicide. Changing a company's image may be difficult, depending on the situation. While some entrepreneurs delight in the challenge of turning around a bad business, you may not. Either way, talking to people in the same market can help you discover what the business's reputation truly is. Is the business taken seriously? By whom? Are customers and vendors satisfied with the way the seller does business? What do they like or dislike about the current operation?

Check out the Location

Many businesses fail to be successful because of where they are located. Search the area and find out if competition is moving in nearby. Have your lawyer(s) look carefully at the lease to make sure it is renewable and will not increase drastically in the next few years. You may also want to know if you have the possibility of expansion.

Evaluate the Employees

This is key. Determine who is responsible for the success of the business. Is it the owner or the key managers? Observe the employees, talk to management, and find out the working habits of each individual. Are the employees well trained and gracious? Are they an asset or a liability?

Evaluate the Growth Potential

Assess the business carefully and ask key questions. Has the business gone as far as it can go? Or is it barely living up to its potential? Is there room for new products and services?

How to Evaluate the Viability of a Business

1. Know why the seller is selling.
2. Hire an accountant, appraiser, lawyer, and negotiator.
3. Review the books.
4. Know the competition.
5. Know the business's reputation.
6. Check out the location.
7. Evaluate the employees.
8. Evaluate the growth potential.

After all the research is in, be prepared to walk away if the business isn't up to snuff. This may be a difficult thing to do, especially when you've spent considerable time and money on research. "Before we purchased this business, we were in negotiations with three other diners," offers Nada Stell of Nada's Diner. "In each instance, the restaurant looked great up front, and then something sticky was discovered when we did our research." While none of the cover-ups were illegal, or even grossly negligent, the circumstances revealed would have put Nada's eatery at an initial disadvantage.

It's also natural to become emotionally attached to the product or service and easier to make bad decisions as a result. Before the deal is closed, prospective buyers need to reevaluate their reasons for buying and make sure they're purchasing the right business for the right reason.

The Franchise: Capitalizing on a Proven Thing

While the franchising industry expands to all corners of the globe, from Mexico and Canada to Bolivia and Zimbabwe, many women entrepreneurs are cashing in on this fast-growing trend in the United States—in 1992 a new franchise opened every seventeen minutes.

An extension of a larger company, a franchise is a business that is part of a chain but owned privately. The franchisor, also called the "mother" or "parent" company, offers the buyer its name, product, and training in return for a percentage of the franchise's profits. The franchise owner, however, is responsible for putting up the money to start a store in a new location, as well as for making it profitable.

For the first-time business buyer, purchasing a franchise can be a golden opportunity, as the risks may be fewer than starting a business from scratch or buying an existing business. This does not mean, however, that a franchise is without risk. According to Carol Safford, who purchased a Padgett Business Services franchise after two decades as a corporate comptroller, "I was unusually well

equipped to evaluate this franchise because I had lived with the terminology of the business for so long. Many people aren't so fortunate." Before deciding whether buying a franchise is the right move
for you, carefully weigh the pros and cons.

Depending on what company you buy from, many women have
found that franchises are a prosperous concept—many fast-food
restaurant, motel, and barber salon owners have made a bundle off
the franchise game, and some owners have been able to earn six-
figure salaries after just a few years.

As opposed to buying an existing business, franchise buyers
receive training, merchandise, and products from the mother company. Since they have a stake in the profits, many franchisors will
provide excellent support. For the franchisees, it's a great way to
learn the ins and outs of running a company while growing a healthy
business. Moreover, many franchisees have found that buying a successful name helps their business get off the ground faster than if
they had created a start-up.

Purchasing a franchise can be a lower-cost and lower-risk alternative to your own start-up or purchasing an existing business. Obviously nothing is guaranteed, but often the franchisors will have laid
the groundwork and created the product/service identity necessary
for success. Franchises are not always less expensive, though. A
high-profile, high-support franchise such as a McDonald's, for
example, can be quite costly to invest in. For many entrepreneurs,
the investment is worth the rewards.

Women entrepreneurs sometimes dislike franchises because they
are forced to follow the mother company's specific rules even if they
disagree with them. To some degree, franchisees don't have control
over the way they run the business or the product they put out. In this
case, entrepreneurs who love to run the company their own way may
do better to create a new company or buy a business they can totally
control.

A common myth about franchising is that it is a risk-free venture,
but there are no guarantees that a franchise will be any more profitable than an independent company. The chances of success may be

greater, depending on the franchisor, but buyers need to be aware that a franchise, just because it is a franchise of a successful company, does not of itself guarantee success. Another problem with franchises is that the legal contracts tend to benefit the mother company instead of the franchise owner. Hiring a lawyer knowledgeable in contract law is your best negotiating tool in working out a fair agreement with the franchisor.

While there are many legitimate franchisor-franchisee relationships, watch out for scams. Some parent companies have been known to embellish the amount of revenue a franchise can bring in, while others have taken the franchisee's start-up money and invested it poorly, rather than in the new business. In other cases, the mother company has dealt with its own increasing debt by jacking up the prices of the products the franchisees purchase. They have forced the franchisee out of business in hopes of reselling it and creating new cash flow.

Now that the state and federal government regulate franchising, entrepreneurs have more protection against these problems, but women franchisees suggest that buyers investigate thoroughly before taking the plunge.

Tricks of the Trade

Carol Safford of Padgett Business Services, on questions to ask when researching a franchise:

1. *How much is the initial investment?* Since there are a number of franchisors in the same business, potential buyers should do some pricing. If one travel agency is asking $30,000 in start-up fees and another is asking $50,000, the buyer must find out what she is getting for her money. Does one offer more training or keep a larger percentage of profits?

2. *What support is the parent company providing?* Potential buyers find this question to be extremely important, especially if they're inexperienced owners. Will you receive full training? What products will the parent company provide? Do they help with advertising and marketing? Will they be there if you need them?

3. *Are the other franchisees happy?* Meeting with several of the franchisees in a particular chain may help potential buyers to determine whether the company is a safe bet. How many years have they owned the franchise? What are the benefits and drawbacks? Do they have any regrets? How has the parent company treated them? Are they turning a profit? What is their market like compared with the one you're entering?

4. *Visit headquarters.* Meeting the officers in charge of the parent company is a great way to determine the legitimacy of the business. Is headquarters a professional operation? Are the owners professional? Are you compatible? Do they deflect hard questions, or do they seem open and honest with their answers? Are they willing to back up their words in a contract?

5. *Has the parent company done a market survey in your area?* Franchisees find that the location of the franchise is critical, even more so than with an independent company. Is the parent company selling another franchise around the corner from yours and possibly hurting your profits? Has the parent company researched the area and found a need for the franchise? Or are they testing an untried market at your expense? Many franchisees make sure they are protected in their contracts from problems like these.

6. *What are the financing and profit potentials?* Buyers who don't have a lot of cash need to find out if the parent company offers any financing. If they don't, a buyer might be better off finding a franchisor who does. How much money can you anticipate making over a period of time? And at

what point can you plan on paying off your initial investment?

*   *   *

Are You Really Prepared to Buy?

After carefully researching a business for sale, women buyers may have decided they've found a gold mine. The business may be a great moneymaker with room for growth, but buyers realize they must now scrutinize themselves. They ask themselves whether they know the product or service well enough to run the business. They assess their strengths and weaknesses. Are they great with numbers and bad with people? Do they have the wherewithal to run a business? Do they need to hire an experienced manager to run the day-to-day? Or do they plan to be involved in that aspect themselves? Are they really ready for this level of commitment, personally and financially?

Money is certainly the biggest factor in the decision to buy a business. Buyers reexamine their financial situation before signing on the dotted line. Is an all-cash deal, spending their life savings, the right way to go? Do they have a backup plan, in case things go wrong? Will they be personally financially ruined if the business goes under? What other options do they have? By rethinking their financial situation, many entrepreneurs have found more creative ways of buying businesses.

Benefiting from Partnerships

Many entrepreneurs lacking in finances or product expertise seek out partners to complement their weaknesses. Whether buyers go into business with friends, family, or strangers, they must consider the relationship carefully and set down boundaries on a contract. They must research the person to determine whether he or she would make an effective partner in terms of finances, management skills, compatibility, commitment, and product/service knowledge.

The buyer's best friend may not be the buyer's best partner, and the friendship could be ruined by business turmoil. Industry lawyers and accountants may be great contacts in searching for a potential partner.

The Most Valuable Network:
Forging Alliances with Vendors and Clients

Most women business owners can partly attribute their business's success to their relationships with vendors and clients. By communicating effectively with their dealers, suppliers, and customers, these women have minimized problems and maximized solutions.

Whether they are dealing with a consumer or a vendor, women entrepreneurs consider the bond a partnership, in which one business cannot exist without the other. By treating them as equals, they have found that they work together to solve problems. In a vendor relationship, for example, women business owners clearly explain the needs of the company to the vendor. The vendor then offers options to the business owner, and together they discuss what the most efficient solution will be, what the drawbacks are, and what the various costs will be. Instead of relying on the vendor to work miracles, women entrepreneurs work with them to find the best equipment for the best price.

According to Bubbles and Bleach's Faye Becker, the relationships you form with your vendors early on will demonstrate the type of service you can expect later. "I researched the industry and went to the biggest vendors right away. Some weren't interested in working with us, because we weren't established. The vendors who recognized our potential have grown with us. Now everyone wants to do business with me."

Many women business owners use this method with their own clients as well. Listen to your customers' needs and find several ways to accommodate them, taking into account time, money, and the desired end result. Working in this manner, entrepreneurs have

found that not only will their businesses be more productive and cost-effective, but the strong relationship will give them an edge over their competitors and keep their customers coming back for more.

The Benefits of Using Vendors

While it may seem easier to order supplies such as copy machines and computers from a superstore, many entrepreneurs have come to rely on the expertise of vendors. The superstore may offer a greater selection of goods, but the vendor will offer expertise and problem-solving advice. Many vendors will also be on call in the midst of an equipment crisis, while a superstore's commitment ends with the purchase and a warranty from the dealer (which may be hundreds of miles away and unable to provide immediate service).

Women entrepreneurs note, however, that it is important to find the right vendor. First, they recommend that business owners assess their needs and their future needs. They will be better equipped to find the right vendor if they know where they are and where they're going. Then, business owners will need to question several vendors before making a decision. Do they have the equipment you need at an affordable price? Do they offer round-the-clock service? Will they loan equipment if yours is malfunctioning? What exactly is included in the cost—parts, service, drive time? Do they offer a warranty? What is their history? Are they a solid operation?

The ultimate result of this reciprocal match is to the benefit of the customer. "The vendors who helped me out when I started are the ones I work with today," says Jan Baxter of Chicago's Landmark building. "I expect high service from all my vendors, and in turn, I'm very loyal to them and they're loyal to me."

Tricks of the Trade

Jan Baxter of The Landmark, on promoting your business and yourself effectively:

1. *Get your name in print.* Expensive advertising isn't as effective or as credible as an editorial or article about you or your company. One story about the special laundry service you deliver to your customer's door will attract immediate business and has immeasurable residual value when reprinted and mailed to business prospects.

2. *Get on the broadcast media.* Get interviewed. TV or radio talk shows, even if they're only local or regional, can have a large impact. One evening news report on how your service saved the day can lift you from small time to a major contender.

3. *Be an expert.* Make yourself available—and knowledgeable—to speak not only about your business, but about the service industries in general. If you have lively, insightful commentary, reporters are sure to call you when in need of an observation or quick quote.

4. *Speak in public.* Use business and civic groups to get your message out—and make sure you have one. If you are a powerful presenter, your audience will assume you have a powerful business.

5. *Network with the right people.* Be seen and get known by those who can have an impact on or can be customers of your business. Directed networking is the fulcrum of entrepreneurial marketing. And it's inexpensive, great one-on-one exposure, productive, time effective, and fun.

6. *Join the Chamber of Commerce.* It's the single most powerful business organization in your community, so get involved. Meet with the leaders, attend every networking

event you can, exhibit at its business fair, and make a five-year plan to join their board of directors.

7. *Join the trade associations* of the businesses you most want to establish or maintain relationships with. You will be an associate member with a chance to affect your customer—and others like him or her. Attend meetings regularly, get involved, and speak to or lead a group. Magnify your impact by developing a reputation for helping others get business (by providing them with leads and referrals).

* * *

Sound difficult? Putting these ideas into practice is the first step, but executing them creatively is the key to getting results. Do everything with a creative flair, which makes the time and effort you contribute unique and worth remembering: get the best business card and letterhead money can buy, with your own logo; give away an advertising item that's novel; and combine your outreaches, like making a donation of your service in honor of a significant event in a customer's life.

Woman on the Way

*

Alice Waters
Proprietor: Chez Panisse, Berkeley, California
Business Philosophy: Reach out to the community and they will reach back
Greatest Accomplishment: The Garden Project, a job-training program for prisoners to help reinvest them in their community

Alice Waters opened Chez Panisse in 1971, with the simple goal of serving a five-course, fixed-price menu that changed daily. To this day, this menu format remains at the heart of Waters's philosophy of serving the highest-quality products according to the season. Over the past two decades she has discovered and encouraged a network of farmers and ranchers who now enjoy a reciprocal relationship with Chez Panisse.

Waters is fascinated with the emotional connection we have with good food and dining. Her cooking and her philosophies have been shared in print several times with her Chez Panisse cookbooks, and she has been instrumental in redeveloping menus for children's lunch programs in the San Francisco Bay Area. Additionally, Waters has spawned a movement for neighborhood gardens that are cultivated by communities and feed all.

Currently Waters is involved with developing an edible garden at Berkeley's Martin Luther King Junior High School. This project seeks to involve the children directly in planting, gardening, harvesting, cooking, and eating, with the goal of illuminating the vital relationship of food to their lives while teaching them respect for each other and for the planet as a whole. It is intended to be a significant part of the school's curriculum and to help resuscitate its lunch program. The King Junior High Edible Schoolyard is being conceived as a pilot project to serve as a model for schools across the country.

Waters also has ongoing extensive involvement with the Horticulture Project at the San Francisco County Jail and its related program, The Garden Project, a job-training organization and organic garden. These programs teach organic gardening to prisoners and parolees in order to renew their self-esteem and instill community responsibility.

For Waters, food is a method of communication on

the most basic level. It is needed for sustenance, used for barter, exchanged as a gift, and extended as an offering. And while her business extends far beyond the mere serving of food, it is the reciprocity of the relationship that is most appealing. "Food puts us all on equal footing," says Waters. "Rich, poor, young, or old, we all have to eat." And find some common ground.

* * *

The Business of Barter

The oldest form of doing business has come back into vogue, and many women entrepreneurs find bartering an efficient means to a more productive end. Exchanging goods for goods or services for services has enabled small- and big-time companies to free up their cash while fulfilling their business needs.

Some women entrepreneurs trade directly with another business in an informal way. A small-time restaurant owner, for example, may want to add some decorative flair to the dining room but may not have the cash to spend on paintings or antique lamps. The owner may approach an art dealer or an antique store and offer free meals equaling the price of the desired items. In addition to the exchange, the art dealer gets free advertising by having the work appear in another establishment, while the restaurant owner builds a bigger client base, especially if the art dealer brings in a range of business associates.

For photographer Lissa Sample, barter is one way to cover her high-end business expenses. One obstacle with this type of transaction is that the government still deems trade as taxable income, and business owners must make sure to account for their exchanges.

Be wary of doing too much trade, as women entrepreneurs have found that over time it does reduce cash flow. They also advise that barter be used for business, not personal, needs. Business owners should also check prices at nonbartering companies. Are you paying more in trade than you would pay in cash?

Many small-business owners join barter organizations (check with your local Chamber of Commerce or SBA office), which act as a third party in a trade transaction. Instead of bartering with one particular company, women have found that such an organization offers a variety of services and products. After paying a small entry fee to the barter organization, a business owner could build up credit in barter dollars—equivalent to the U.S. dollar—and then use those dollars on any other product or service in the company. Many barter organizations use a magnetic strip card that can be used like a credit card at a number of locations. The barter credits will be deducted automatically from the account.

Trading in organizations is also taxable, but usually the barter company will inform business owners of the amount of tax they need to pay at the end of the business quarter. It is important to keep track of the tax amount, or on tax day business owners may find themselves owing a large sum of cash they don't have.

Because they are listed and advertised in the barter organization's brochure, business owners will instantly reach a larger market and bring in consumers they may never have had otherwise. Also, if a company has slow-moving or excessive inventory, they may exchange it for maximum barter credits, which cuts down on company waste or decrease in profit due to selling merchandise at discount rates. Furthermore, bartering can reduce the need for credit card use and certainly doesn't charge interest.

Before joining a barter organization, make sure to investigate it thoroughly. Ask the following questions: Who are the members? Do they have the services or products you need at the quality you require? How many businesses are members? Will you be able to get a variety of needs fulfilled or not? Do they need your business as well? How long have they been in business? Do they have a decent track record?

The best way of finding out about a barter organization is to speak directly with the members. Ask whether the members are satisfied and if they've encountered any problems. Then check what perks the organization offers. Some trade businesses, for example, will give free frequent flyer miles for every barter dollar spent.

Many women entrepreneurs have found that bartering in moderation can be an asset to any business—it's just a matter of finding the right organization, maintaining control of your spending, and trading only for what you really need.

To Sell or Not to Sell: An Important Question

As your business becomes successful, you'll want to keep it in tight running order. Faye Becker says, "Business owners should always be prepared to sell, even though they may never want to or have to. Everyone has a price."

Regardless of whether your business is booming, plodding along steadily, or struggling to survive, the future can be uncertain. An economic depression, stock market crash, or a change in trends may weaken even the strongest of businesses, while growing too rapidly can hurt small companies. In the best cases, entrepreneurs may decide to sell because they wish to retire or change career goals. Being open to offers from buyers may increase entrepreneurs' chances of getting the best deal for themselves and their company.

"My career is in building businesses and making them profitable. A big conglomerate lets the others think up the ideas, work out the bugs, and build up a company to a major level, and then they step in and buy it out," says Faye Becker.

Selling is never easy, emotionally or financially, many women have stated, but if you receive a call from an interested buyer, offer to call them back after you've done some thinking. Asking some basic questions may help business owners to evaluate the company's success, their future goals, and whether or not they would consider selling, before talking to a potential buyer.

Look over your future projections and current profit and loss statements. Are you a business that's been around for twenty-five years and has profit increases regularly? Is your business on an upward or downward slope? Are your competitors squeezing you out of the market? Are you paying the bills?

Many business owners experience severe burnout after years of hard work and find themselves too exhausted to continue. Has ownership become more stressful than exciting? Are you ready to retire? Are you bored with running this particular business? Do you need more excitement and risk?

While it is possible that the right buyer comes around only once, this is a rarity. Business owners must check the facts. What on the surface might seem to be a sweet deal could turn out to be sour grapes.

Some entrepreneurs find that selling is the only way to recoup losses. Have you looked for other options for financial growth and come up empty? Is your business at such a crisis point that you will be financially ruined if you do not sell?

Deciding to Sell: Is It the Right Time?

Many business owners believe that selling a business means signing a few papers and collecting a check. Successful women entrepreneurs know that far more is involved. The selling process may be long and arduous, taking several months to several years, and business owners need to protect themselves against hidden obstacles. Entrepreneurs strongly advise those seriously thinking about selling to follow some basic rules.

Always Be Prepared to Sell

From the start-up of your company to the sale, entrepreneurs suggest that business owners keep the books clean. Not only will your business have integrity, but you'll be able to sell it at a better price. If your books include some shady practices, such as tax problems or legal disputes, women entrepreneurs believe that it is critical to tidy them up, as prospective buyers will disappear fast and word of your illicit transactions will get out in the business community to other potential buyers. Don't worry about a few minor problems, though, because that is normal in every business. Most buyers will want to peruse several years of financial statements. Entrepreneurs believe it is important to have everything in order as much as possible, because the right offer may come unexpectedly.

Check out the Market

Know the current climate of the industry. Is business going to continue to improve in the next several years? This is the best time to sell, as the business is more attractive to buyers. In addition to giving business owners bargaining power, it also gives them the ability to walk away from an undesirable deal.

If you are made an offer by a prospective buyer, search around for others. Your intention is not necessarily to start a bidding war, but to find the best buyer for the company. Lie low while looking for a buyer, as employees, clients, and vendors may panic if they think the company is being sold. To many, a business for sale means a business in trouble, and they may take their services to another company if they find out, regardless of the business's growth or productivity. How do you let people know your business is for sale without informing the world? Talk to industry lawyers, accountants, and bankers to find leads and ensure confidentiality. Some even offer a finder's fee to the individual who brings in the right buyer.

Consider Signing Nondisclosure Agreements

Many sellers and buyers choose to sign nondisclosure agreements, which force the buyer to keep confidential all financial and company secrets, as well as knowledge of the impending negotiations, until the deal is finalized. While it makes sense for buyers and sellers to protect themselves against possible interference from competition, employees, and clients, a nondisclosure agreement can create a difficult situation. Basically, they must lie to their employees and clients if asked any questions regarding a sale. Also, by not informing employees of an impending sale, the employees may be unprepared for the possibility of losing their jobs. Can you, in good conscience, hurt your faithful employees of ten years by signing a nondisclosure agreement? There's no easy answer, but effective entrepreneurs strive to protect themselves and their employees when making a deal.

Hire Experts

Lawyers, appraisers, negotiators, and accountants are necessities when planning to sell a business. Attempting to sell without hiring any of these professionals can result in deal disaster. Lawyers will ensure a seller's contract is solid; appraisers will accurately measure the company's assets and full value; accountants can prepare the necessary financial paperwork, while finding and solving problems the seller overlooked; and expert negotiators will arbitrate the deal in the best interest of the seller. Negotiators are especially important because they deal in fact, not emotion, and many owners are emotional when it comes to selling their company.

Prepare for the IRS

Before women entrepreneurs commit to negotiations with a buyer, they discuss with their accountant "how" to sell the business and invest their money legally to avoid excessive taxes. Accountants and financial planners have ingenious solutions and will help business owners best plan their futures, based on whether they have children, family, or partners or plan to retire.

Investigating Potential Buyers

While many sellers jump to the highest bidder or biggest name, women entrepreneurs believe that much more is at stake. Price is certainly a factor, but so is having some say in what actually happens to the business and employees. Just because someone has a reputation for buying existing businesses and improving them doesn't mean they're not going to liquidate or destroy your company. How do you know you're selling to the right buyer? Here are some suggestions from successful women entrepreneurs.

Smart women entrepreneurs intensely research their potential buyers, to make sure the buyer is legitimate and has both integrity and capital. Is this buyer a small-timer who loves the business and is looking for a great opportunity, or is it a corporate chain that wants to mold your business into its own style and brand, erasing all traces of your influence? Is it a competitor whose owners plan on closing down the business to increase their own sales? What is their history? Have they bought other businesses? How did they handle the acquisition? Do they have good credit? If the potential buyer is an employee, friend, or family member, women entrepreneurs ask other questions. Does this person know the industry well enough? Can he or she afford it? A difficult question may be, Am I selling a sinking ship to someone I care about? By answering all of these questions at length, business owners will be in a better bartering position and will feel that the decision to sell will be an informed one.

Consider how the new owner might handle the business. Many entrepreneurs feel that after sweating through many years on a labor of love, they don't want to sell to just anybody. To make sure your goals for your company's future are carried out—especially if you plan to remain on as an employee—you'll want certainty that some things will remain the same. Some questions you may want to ask potential buyers: Will my product or service meet the same standards under new ownership? This is especially important if your company name is attached—if the business goes sour, it will reflect on your name, regardless of your involvement. Does the buyer plan on carrying new services or products that mesh well with the ones I've created? Are they merging with another company to form a stronger business? Do they have the same philosophies on management, service, and product design? If the buyer is in danger of wrecking your credible company but offering a good price, consider carefully before selling.

Don't forget the people who made the business successful; find out what impact the sale will have on your employees. Ask potential buyers if they plan to keep the staff, and in what capacity. Find out if the buyer plans on downsizing or replacing key personnel with his or her own people. Negotiate to make sure salaries remain the same or are improved. If all else fails and you must sell, at the very least ensure your employees receive notice, job-placement services, and decent severance packages. Employees are typically considered an asset by the buyer, but you must never assume that the new buyer will treat your employees fairly—make sure.

In many small businesses, the owner is responsible for the company's success. A buyer unfamiliar with the service or product may want the owner to continue on as company president. Alternatively, the seller may be tired of the pressures of running a business but still wants to maintain some control. Entrepreneurs sometimes find that it's tough to give up total control but can adjust if the job and price is right. If, as the seller, you want to remain on, work with your lawyer and accountant to make sure the buyer's employment contract is reasonable in terms of length and price. Sometimes you can even negotiate to buy back the business after a couple of years if the new owners aren't successful.

After You Make the Decision, Then What?

After doing your research and deciding to sell to a particular buyer, strive for the best deal possible financially and for the company. You can rely heavily on the advice of lawyers, accountants, and negotiators, but sell only if you believe it's the right choice.

Setting the Price

Many women entrepreneurs have found that pricing too high will scare off informed buyers and pricing too low will hurt their profit. Price aggressively in the high end of the company's determined value (by an appraiser), to leave room for negotiations. Be sure to estimate what price you expect to sell for and what price is unacceptable. By tacking on 11 percent to the expected sale price, you can leave yourself enough bartering room to get what you want, while making the buyers feel that they got a deal.

Hold Firm Down to the Wire

After months of investigation on both sides, even the stoutest of heart are feeling the pressure of negotiations. Both sides may be given to outbursts as they attempt to work their will. That's why savvy women entrepreneurs hire experienced negotiators who are objective. These professionals don't weaken when it comes to the make-or-break moment of the deal, because they understand the buyer's motives and know the buyer's breaking point. Hold firm and reevaluate the deal. If you don't wish to concede certain points, then don't. You may lose the buyer, but you may find a better one. This is after months of dealing with one party, but if the offer is right, you'll sell. If not, find a better one. In extreme cases, however, you may have no choice but to sell if the business is in severe trouble.

Close Quickly

When the deal has been hashed out, seek to close quickly. You do not want buyers to rethink their position and change their minds. Realize that anything can happen, such as a fire at the store or a stock market crash, that will immediately drive down their price and wreck the deal.

Steps to Selling Your Business

1. Always be prepared to sell.
2. Check out the market.
3. Consider signing nondisclosure agreements.
4. Hire experts.
5. Prepare for the IRS.
6. Investigate potential buyers.
7. Set the price.
8. Hold firm down to the wire.
9. Close quickly.

Appendix

RESOURCES

This list of resources is meant as a general one, with some excellent trade associations to join and participate in and some other ideas and leads on how to find useful information.

One of the first places to start any research into your business, whether you are just thinking about starting one or need advice in growing it, is a library or bookstore with a good business section. Just browsing through the many titles is bound to inform and inspire you. A huge variety of business-related books and magazines is now available to help you.

The Internet is also an excellent research tool. Two World Wide Web sites to check out are Women's Wire and BizWomen. There will be links to other sites that will be of interest there. The large Internet providers, such as America Online, CompuServe, and Prodigy will also have small-business-related sites and information and will sponsor newsgroups. The Internet is a great source for up-to-the-minute financial information as well.

Women's Wire
435 Grand Ave., Suite D
South San Francisco, CA 94080
(415) 378-6500
http://www.women.com

BizWomen
http://www.bizwomen.com

MCI Small Business Center
http://mci.com/smallbiz

Netmarquee
http://www.nmq.com

A wide variety of business software is also available. Some will help you to write a business plan, and others will help you run your business or maintain control of your inventory. Consult your local software store, catalog, or computer magazine for specifics and reviews.

Local resources are a good place to start in any search for information or help. Check your telephone directory for local listings. Offices to contact include

- City and/or country development agencies

    Many local governments have programs for small businesses. Information may be available through the mayor's office.

- Local Chambers of Commerce

    Often offering seminars and classes, and usually excellent for networking, local Chambers of Commerce can offer valuable information specific to your region, such as business licenses, permits, and demographics.

• Local colleges

Nearby colleges may offer small-business programs or workshops and may also have programs for finding or training employees.

• Local financial institutions

• Local libraries

• Local planning departments

Specific information on zoning and other local requirements will be available through your local planning department.

State agencies to contact include

• Small Business Development Centers (SBDCs)

Each state has a network of SBDCs to provide technical and management assistance and training to small companies. For the SBDC near you, call (402) 595-2387.

• State Chambers of Commerce

State chambers of commerce usually offer start-up kits to small businesses, as well as other publications. They will have information as to state legislation affecting small business.

• State departments of commerce

State departments of commerce usually have small-business offices to help answer questions concerning licenses, regulations, and so on and may also have other education programs or specialized offices directed toward the small business.

• State economic development agencies

Most states have an economic development office that helps to promote business opportunities through assistance programs. These agencies also help with information and advice on procurement of state government contracts through small-business programs. In addition, most states will have an office specifically for the advocacy and support of women's business issues.

• Governor's office

The governor's office may be able to help you sift through the various state agencies that might help you with whatever assistance you require.

• Tax agency

Refer to your state's tax office for general tax information pertaining to your state and your business.

Business Book Publishers (General)

Amacom Books
135 West 50th St.
New York, NY 10020
(800) 262-9699
Fax (518) 891-3653
Amacom is the book publishing division of the American Management Association. In addition to a wide variety of general and specific business books, they publish get-ahead guides targeted for women, including how-to books on advancing from administrative positions to the top and great guides for building your own profitable business. Amacom also offers self-study courses for women who want to sharpen their professional skills.

Nolo Books
950 Parker St.
Berkeley, CA 94710
General information (510) 549-1976
Orders (800) 992-6656
Fax (800) 645-0895
http://www.nolo.com
Nolo provides comprehensive self-help law and small-business books and software. You'll find everything from how to copyright and patent materials yourself, to legal and tax issues for the small business, to software for writing your own partnership agreement. Nolo also sponsors a Self-Help Law Center on America Online.

Reference books can also be particularly helpful. Ask at your local library or call the publishers listed to find out about ordering your own copy:

The Business Women's Network Directory
The Business Women's Network
1146 19th St. NW, 3rd fl.

Washington, DC 20036
(202) 466-8209
A directory containing detailed profiles and information on the top four hundred business, trade, and professional organizations for women.

Encyclopedia of Associations
Published by the American Society of Association Executives
(202) 626-7223

The Information Please Business Almanac & Sourcebook
Edited by Seth Goodin
Houghton Mifflin Company
215 Park Ave. S.
New York, NY 10003
This handy resource book offers more than four thousand associations, organizations, and government agencies that you may be interested in accessing. Updated yearly, this volume also offers great business statistics such as how many women-owned businesses started up the previous year.

Small Business Sourcebook
Edited by Charity Anne Dorgon
Gale Research Inc.
Book Tower
Detroit, MI 48226
A source guide for the entrepreneur who wants to know where to go for information and help on specific types of businesses.

The Women's Business Resource Guide
P.O. Box 25505
Eugene, OR 97402
(503) 683-5330
A national directory of more than six hundred programs, resources, and organizations to help women start or expand a busi-

ness. Contents include training and technical assistance; information sources; selling to the government; membership organizations; and resource, program, and agency listings.

Winning in Small Business
(800) 585-1300
A study course offered by the nonprofit American Success Institute, which includes a textbook, videotape, and other materials for the upstart entrepreneur.

General Business Associations

American Business Women's Association (ABWA)
National Headquarters
9100 Ward Pkwy.
P.O. Box 8728
Kansas City, MO 64114-0728
(816) 361-6621
Fax (816) 361-4991
ABWA's mission is to bring together a variety of women in business (both professionals and entrepreneurs) in order to help them grow, both personally and professionally. They provide education, networking support, and recognition through over two thousand local chapters and the national organization. This established and highly regarded businesswomen's membership organization publishes *Women in Business* magazine. They honor outstanding members, sponsor scholarships, hold training seminars, and promote women in business throughout the country. Membership benefits include insurance. Membership.

American Woman's Economic Development (AWED)
    Corporation
60 East 42nd St., Suite 405
New York, NY 10165

(212) 692-9100
America's leading nonprofit organization providing women with a wide range of management training and business counseling. Membership.

National Association of Women Business Owners (NAWBO)
600 S. Federal St., Suite 400
Chicago IL 60605
(312) 922-0465
(800) 55-NAWBO
This very active membership organization consisting of women entrepreneurs works to broaden opportunities for women and, in partnership with major corporations, to increase contracting opportunities for women business owners. Services include workshops, seminars, and conferences. There are regional groups to serve various areas of the country. NAWBO has established the Women's Business Ownership Corporation (WBOC) as an information clearinghouse for certification for government and corporate procurement information and issues. Membership.

National Education Center for Women in Business (NECWB)
Seton Hill College
Seton Hill Dr.
Greensburg, PA 15601-1599
(800) 632-9248
Fax (412) 834-7131
A nonprofit organization devoted to promoting women and business ownership by conducting collaborative research, providing education programs and curriculum development, and serving as an information clearinghouse for women entrepreneurs. They offer workshops, conferences, and seminars and sponsor a youth entrepreneurship program, Camp Entrepreneur. NECWB sponsors research into such subjects as managerial style and women's access to credit. They offer a catalog of publications and products promoting women business ownership.

Association of Small Business Development Centers (SBDC)
1050 17th St. NW, Suite 810
Washington, DC 20036
(202) 887-5599
You can find local Small Business Development Centers in all fifty states, Puerto Rico, and the Virgin Islands. These centers provide training and free counseling for small-business owners and potential entrepreneurs. Their programs include international trade, research and development funding, procurement, rural development, and business law. They are particularly interested in helping women develop businesses.

Federation of Organizations for Professional Women (FOPW)
2001 S St. NW, Suite 540
Washington, DC 20009
(202) 328-1415
FOPW, founded in 1972, is devoted to equal opportunities of women. The bimonthly newsletter, *Alert,* publishes legislative issues that affect women and businesses. It is also a networking group and hosts awards ceremonies honoring women of achievement in the arts, sciences, media, and other professions. Membership.

Women Incorporated
1401 21st St., Suite 310
Sacramento, CA 95814
(800) 930-3993
Women Inc. is dedicated to improving the business environment for women by aggregating the economic power of women entrepreneurs, by developing a new approach to providing access to capital for women business owners, and by strengthening the national voice of women business owners. They publish a series of "Busy Woman's" guides (booklets addressing such topics as business plans). Membership.

294 * THE ENTERPRISING WOMAN

An Income of Her Own (AIOHO)
1804 W. Burbank Blvd.
Burbank, CA 91506
(800) 350-2978
AIOHO provides entrepreneurial education for adolescent girls
and teen women. It trains educators and parents on entrepreneurship
education, sponsors conferences, and hosts the National Teen Business Plan Competition. Its Camp $tart-Up is held each summer,
offering training and development for teens to explore the basics of
creating and running a business.

Women's Business Development Center (WBDC)
230 N. Michigan Ave., Suite 1800
Chicago, IL 60601
(312) 853-3477
WBDC offers comprehensive assistance programs for empowering women through business ownership. It is a nonprofit organization, offering training in marketing, management, accounting, and
business plan formulation. Its counseling services are free.

National Association for Home-Based Business
10451 Mill Run Circle, Suite 400
Owings Mills, MD 21117
(410) 363-3698
This organization provides support, services, and publications
pertinent to those running a home-based business. Membership.

American Management Association (AMA)
1601 Broadway
New York, NY 10019-7420
The American Management Association also offers a self-study
series in many aspects of business, such as management, business
writing, and strategic planning.

National Organization for Women (NOW)
National Headquarters
1000 16th St. NW, Suite 700
Washington, DC 20005-5705
(202) 331-0066
The foremost organization for defining and tracking major issues
of concern to women. Membership.

The National Federation of Business and Professional
    Women/USA (BPW)
2012 Massachusetts Ave. NW
Washington, DC 20036
(202) 293-1100
Fax (202) 861-0298
E-mail BPWMRRC@capcon.net
Marguerite Rawalt Resource Center (202) 293-1200
BPW is a national organization of the full spectrum of career-
minded women, from office workers to managers to nontraditional
jobs. BPW sponsors scholarships, financial services, and a research
library dedicated to working women, with the goal of helping to
achieve equity for all women in the workplace. It has over two thousand local groups in addition to the national organization. It publishes a quarterly magazine and maintains a legislative hot line to
keep members up-to-date on legal issues affecting working women.
The Marguerite Rawalt Resource Center (MRRC) maintains a comprehensive reference and referral service on issues of particular
interest to women, specializing in information on women starting
businesses and women's access to credit. Membership.

Women's World Banking (WWB)
8 W. 40th St., 10th fl.
New York, NY 10018
(212) 768-8513
A nonprofit group dedicated to promoting entrepreneurship for
women, especially those without access to formal financial institu-

tions. WWB's goal is to establish an international network of women's financial resources and to encourage women's confidence as businesspersons. WWB makes some loans to women owning a majority share in their business.

National Small Business United (NSBU)
1155 15th St. NW, Suite 710
Washington, DC 20005
(202) 293-8830
NSBU is the oldest trade association in America, whose main objective is to advocate for an economic environment that allows small businesses to operate at a profit. This national watchdog organization reports on issues affecting small business and serves as a go-between for business owners and legislators. They offer publications and small-business counseling. Membership.

National Association for the Self-Employed (NASE)
(800) 232-NASE
Largely a lobbying organization, the NASE also offers a variety of publications including *Self-Employed America.* They staff a hot line called "Shop Talk" to answer questions pertaining to the business concerns of the self-employed. Membership.

Institute for Women's Policy Research (IWPR)
1400 20th St. NW, Suite 104
Washington, DC 20036
(202) 785-5100
This nonprofit agency advocates, researches, and acts as a liaison with policy makers concerning women's issues. IWPR publishes periodicals for women on employment equity issues, child care, health, and family concerns. They specifically promote policies to help low-income women achieve self-sufficiency. They offer a catalog of publications covering a wide variety of topics, involving the status of women. Membership.

U.S. Government Programs for Small Business

Small Business Administration (SBA)
and
SBA Office of Women's Business Ownership (OWBO)
1441 L St. NW, Suite 414
Washington, D.C. 20416
(202) 653-8000
Small Business Answer Desk: (800) 827-5722 (9 A.M. to 5 P.M.
    EST)
SBA On-Line: http://www.sbaonline.sba.gov.
SCORE: (800) 634-0245
SBA Office of Women's Business Ownership provides information especially for women entrepreneurs. They have a mentoring program, the Women's Network for Entrepreneurial Training. They sponsor the Answer Desk, (800) 368-5855, to provide information on start-ups, financing, SBA services, and business data. They also sponsor small-business loans through banks. Through OWBO, the Women's Network for Ownership Entrepreneurial Training (WNOET) matches women starting out or expanding their business with mentors, in one-year programs.

Local offices of the SBA provide one-on-one counseling (through SCORE, Service Corps of Retired Executives). Regional offices of the SBA and the Women's Business Ownership program can be found in your local area telephone book. The SBA also publishes books and brochures of interest to the entrepreneur, available through the U.S. Government Printing Office, or SBA Publications at P.O. Box 30, Denver, CO 80201-0030; (202) 205-6666.

The SBA also is a valuable resource for international trade information.

SBA Office of Financial Assistance
409 Third St. SW
Washington, DC 20416
(202) 205-6490

This office can provide advice on the various types of loans available to small businesses through federal programs. They can also help with advice on supplies and facilities acquisition and expansion.

U.S. Business Advisor
http://www.business.gov
This is Uncle Sam's one-stop business resource for the U.S. government's one thousand–plus Internet Web sites. From this easy-to-use home page you can download applications for SBA-backed loans, get tips for developing a marketing plan, or find facts and contact information for other government agencies, including OSHA and the IRS.

Office of Minority Enterprise Development
(202) 205-6410
This U.S. government office provides counseling to help socially and economically disadvantaged people run their own businesses and apply for government contracts. Assistance is available in basic business training such as accounting but can also be more specific such as help in market analyses for your particular type of business.

U.S. Department of Commerce
Minority Business Development Agency (MBDA)
Fourteenth St. and Constitution Ave. NW, Room 6723
Washington, DC 20230
(202) 377-8275
MBDA provides funding for Minority Business Development Centers across America. These centers provide minority entrepreneurs with management and technical assistance services to start, expand, and manage a business. Call the main office for a regional office near you, or consult your local area telephone book.

U.S. Department of Commerce
Business Assistance Service, Office of Business Liaison
Fourteenth St. and Constitution Ave. NW, Room 5062
Washington, DC 20230
(202) 482-3176
This office helps guide small businesses to the correct federal agency to serve their needs. They publish the *Business Services Directory,* which may also help you to find the right services.

Department of Commerce
U.S. Patent and Trademark Office
Washington, DC 20231
(703) 557-3071
They supply information for applying for and receiving a patent or trademark. If you are developing an idea and want to protect your ownership rights before putting the product on the market, request information about the Patent Office's Document Disclosure Program.

Department of Labor
The Women's Bureau
200 Constitution Ave. NW
Washington, DC 20210
(202) 523-6611 (general information)
The Women's Bureau of the U.S. Department of Labor provides programs and technical assistance, policy analysis, and general information on women business owners and minority women business owners.

Federal Trade Commission (FTC)
Room 238
Washington, DC 20580
(202) 326-2000
The FTC has many useful documents and brochures, which may be applicable to your type of business. Write for a listing of free and for sale publications.

House of Representatives Committee on Small Business
Rayburn House Office Building
Room 2361
Washington, DC 20515
(202) 225-5821
http://www.house.gov
Write for House legislation concerning small businesses. Weekly
and monthly bulletins for small businesses.

Venture Capital/Banking

Venture Capital Network, Inc.
P.O. Box 882
Durham, NH 03824-9964
The University of New Hampshire Center for Venture Research
provides people who have venture capital to invest with a convenient, confidential mechanism for examining investment opportunities in entrepreneurial ventures. For entrepreneurs it provides up to
$1 million for early-stage or high-growth private companies.

Neuberger & Berman Socially Responsive Fund
605 Third Ave., 3rd fl.
New York, NY 10158-0180
(800) 877-9700
Janet Prindle, portfolio manager, helps people to grow their
investments while leaving a world where the air is a little cleaner
and where the doors of the executive suite are a little more open. The
fund invests in pioneering companies that meet both financial and
social criteria.

Minority Business Associations

National Association of Minority Women in Business
906 Grand Ave. #200
Kansas City, MO 64106
(816) 492-5546
A membership organization that gives support and guidance.

Black Business Association
3910 W. Martin Luther King Jr. Blvd., Suite 206
Los Angeles, CA 90008
(213) 291-9334
Fax (213) 291-9234
http://www.bbala.com
This advocacy organization for black economic development sponsors contract-procurement meetings, seminars, trade missions, and networking events. Membership.

Black Women in Sisterhood for Action, Inc.
P.O. Box 1592
Washington, DC 20013
(301) 460-1565
Nonprofit corporation develops and promotes education and careers for black women. They provide social assistance for senior black women. The support a mentor program and publish a magazine. Membership.

Financial Women's Association
215 Park Ave. S., Suite 2010
New York, NY 10003
(212) 533-2141
Fax (212) 982-3008

Resources by Industry

Arts and Entertainment

American Craft Council
National Headquarters
40 W. 53rd St.
New York, NY 10019
(212) 869-9422
This nonprofit trade organization offers services for craftspeople working in all media, including listing in their artist registry. They offer various publications and publish *America Craft* magazine, which lists craft fairs and shows all around the country. Membership.

Professional Women Photographers
c/o Photographics Unlimited
17 West 17th St., Suite 17
New York, NY 10011
(212) 726-8292
This group promotes the appreciation of photographic art. They sponsor traveling group exhibitions. Membership well worthwhile.

National Association of Women Artists (NAWA)
41 Union Square West
New York, NY 10003
(212) 675-1616
NAWA membership consists of printers, paper artists, print makers, and sculptors. They sponsor international traveling exhibitions and publish a journal and a newsletter.

Women in Film
6464 Sunset Blvd., Suite 530
Hollywood, CA 90028
(213) 463-6040
Fax (213) 463-0963
Women in film sponsors screening and discussions of issues pertaining to women in the film community. Additionally it conducts workshops featuring lectures and discussions on such areas as direction, producing, contract negotiation, writing, production development, acting, and the technical crafts.

The Whole Arts Directory lists supply houses, alternative spaces, cooperative galleries, and special artists' colonies, retreats, and study centers. Contact them by writing Midmarch Arts Books, P.O. Box 3304, Grand Central Station, New York, N.Y. 10163.

Finance and Consulting

Financial Women International
7910 Woodmont Ave.
Bethesda, MD 20814
(301) 657-8288
An association for women officers in the financial industry. Supports 350 local and 51 state groups. Publishes a monthly magazine, *Financial Women Today.*

National Association of Small Business Investment Companies
1156 15th St. NW, Suite 1101
Washington, DC 20005
(202) 833-8230
A trade association that represents the vast majority of small-business investment companies (SBICs). Their book, *Venture Capital—Where to Find It,* is available for $5 including postage.

Health Care

American Society of Health Professionals
Women's Issues Section
1101 Connecticut Ave. NW, Suite 700
Washington, DC 20036
(202) 857-1150
Concerned with educational and practical issues of health care.

Labor and Manufacturing

Manufacturer's News, Inc.
3 Huron St.
Chicago, IL 60601
Publishes directories of manufacturers in nearly all fifty states.

Nontraditional Employment for Women
243 W. 20th St.
New York, NY 10011
(212) 627-6252
Serves as a clearinghouse and advocacy organization for women in nontraditional industries.

Professional Women in Construction
342 Madison Ave., Room 451
New York, NY 10173
(212) 687-0610
Provides a forum for exchange of ideas and promotion of legal action, education, and job opportunities for women in construction and relationed fields such as architecture and engineering.

Media

International Association of Business Communicators (IABC)
One Hallidie Plaza, Suite 600
San Francisco, CA 94102
(415) 433-3400
http://www.IABC.com

This organization specializes in the world of communications, such as marketing, customer relations, community relations, public affairs, and employee communications. They publish books and the magazine *Communications World*. There are regional groups and conferences and workshops and an annual international conference. The IABC Communication Bank provides publications covering a wide variety of topics, such as corporate identity, and internal publications. They offer research services, targeted networking, and a speakers bureau, as well as career planning and counseling services. Membership.

Women in Management (WIM)
P.O. Box 691
Stamford, CT 06904
(203) 329-0854

WIM includes both corporate managers and entrepreneurs. It provides forums for learning and exchange.

Nonprofit and Socially Responsible Businesses

Catalyst
64 Main St.
Montpelier, VT 05602
(802) 223-7943

This nonprofit organization provides resources and networking for women in business, particularly addressing issues of personal values in business and environmental issues. It sponsors research and offers information on topics of interest to the socially conscious entrepreneur.

The Social Venture Network
1388 Sutter Street, Suite 1010
San Francisco, CA 94109
(415) 771-4308
Fax (415) 771-0535

Good Intentions Aside: A Manager's Guide to Resolving Ethical Problems
Nash, Laura. Boston, MA: Harvard Business School Press, 1990.

The Soul of a Business: Managing for Profit and the Common Good
Chappel, Tom. New York: Bantam Books, 1993.

Politics and Public Opinion

Committee of 200
625 N. Michigan Ave., Suite 500
Chicago, IL 60601-3108
(312) 751-3477
Society of women executives who are leaders in their industries. Provides a forum for the exchange of ideas and enhancement of business opportunities for women.

Retail

National Retail Merchants Association
100 W. 31st St.
New York, NY 10001
(212) 244-8780

Retail in Detail: How to Start and Manage a Small Retail Business
Bond, Ronald L. Grants Pass, Ore.: Oasis Press, 1996.

Science and Technology

International Network of Women in Technology (WITI)
4641 Burnet Ave.
Sherman Oaks, CA 91403
(800) 334-9484
Fax (818) 906-3299
http//www.witi.com
WITI is dedicated to increasing the awareness of the contributions of women in technology, expanding opportunities for women in technical fields, facilitating the representation of women in key positions on boards and committees, and improving the professional and work environments of women in the field. WITI's Internet address contains a list of job postings, among other things.

National Network of Minority Women in Science
c/o American Association for the Advancement of Science
Directorate for Education and Human Resources Programs
1333 H St. NW
Washington, DC 20005
(202) 326-6670
This agency promotes the advancement of minority women in science fields and improvement of the science and mathematics education and career awareness. Offers writing and conference presentations, seminars, and workshops and maintains a speakers bureau in addition to serving as a clearinghouse for identifying women scientists.

Service

Women in Franchising, Inc. (WIF)
53 W. Jackson Blvd., Suite 205
Chicago, IL 60604
(312) 431-1467
Fax (312) 431-1469
http://infonews.com/franchise/wif

A group exclusively for women involved in, or thinking about getting involved in, a franchised business. They offer a franchise interest newsletter with information from franchise companies targeted toward women and minorities as entrepreneurs. They have publications and assistance programs for franchisees. Membership.

International Franchise Association (IFA)
World Headquarters
1350 New York Ave. NW, Suite 900
Washington, DC 20005
(800) 543-1038
Membership phone (202) 628-8000
Fax-on-demand (202) 628-3IFA
Publications order line (800) 543-1038

The world's leading resource for information concerning franchising. IFA publishes a special report for minorities, including women, and offers a comprehensive catalog of publications having to do with franchising.

Start & Run Your Own Profitable Service Business
Burstiner, Irving. Englewood Cliffs, N.J.: Prentice Hall, 1993.

National Black Chamber of Commerce, Inc. (202) 416-1622
National Indian Business Association (505) 256-0589
National Minority Supplier Development Council (212) 944-2430
U.S. Hispanic Chamber of Commerce (202) 842-1212
U.S. Pan-Asian American Chamber of Commerce (202) 296-5221